The Third Century

LATIN AMERICAN SILHOUETTES

Series Editors: William H. Beezley
and Judith Ewell

The Birth of Modern Mexico, 1780–1824, edited by Christon I. Archer

Recollections of Mexico: The Last Ten Months of Maximilian's Empire, by Samuel M. Basch, edited and translated by Fred D. Ullman

Plutarco Elías Calles and the Mexican Revolution, by Jürgen Buchenau

State Governors in the Mexican Revolution, 1910–1952: Portraits in Conflict, Courage, and Corruption, edited by Jürgen Buchenau and William H. Beezley

The U.S.-Mexican Border Today, Third Edition, by Paul Ganster and David E. Lorey

The Third Century: U.S.–Latin American Relations since 1889, Second Edition, by Mark Gilderhus, David C. LaFevor, and Michael J. LaRosa

Revolution in Mexico's Heartland: Politics, War, and State Building in Puebla, 1913–1920, by David G. LaFrance

Simón Bolívar: Venezuelan Rebel, American Revolutionary, by Lester D. Langley

Simón Bolívar: Essays on the Life and Legacy of the Liberator, edited by Lester D. Langley and David Bushnell

Addicted to Failure: U.S. Security Policy in Latin America and the Andean Region, edited by Brian Loveman

The Women's Revolution in Mexico, 1910–1953, edited by Stephanie E. Mitchell and Patience A. Schell

Gringolandia: Mexican Identity and Perceptions of the United States, by Stephen D. Morris

Brazil in the Making: Facets of National Identity, edited by Carmen Nava and Ludwig Lauerhass, Jr.

Artifacts of Revolution: Architecture, Society, and Politics in Mexico City, 1920–1940, by Patrice Elizabeth Olsen

The Divine Charter: Constitutionalism and Liberalism in Nineteenth-Century Mexico, edited by by Jaime E. Rodríguez O.

Francisco Solano López and the Ruination of Paraguay: Honor and Egocentrism, by James Schofield Saeger

Integral Outsiders: The American Colony in Mexico City, 1876–1911, by William Schell Jr.

Hacienda and Market in Eighteenth-Century Mexico: The Rural Economy of the Guadalajara Region, 1675–1820, 25th Anniversary Edition, by Eric Van Young

Vagrants and Citizens: Politics and the Masses in Mexico City from Colony to Republic, by Richard A. Warren

Problems in Modern Latin American History: Sources and Interpretations, Fourth Edition, edited by James A. Wood

Latin America since Independence: Two Centuries of Continuity and Change, by Thomas C. Wright

State Terrorism in Latin America: Chile, Argentina, and International Human Rights, by Thomas C. Wright

For a complete listing of titles, visit https://rowman.com/Action/SERIES/_/LTA.

The Third Century

U.S.–Latin American Relations since 1889

Second Edition

Mark T. Gilderhus, David C. LaFevor,
and Michael J. LaRosa

ROWMAN & LITTLEFIELD
Lanham • Boulder • New York • London

Published by Rowman & Littlefield
A wholly owned subsidiary of The Rowman & Littlefield Publishing Group, Inc.
4501 Forbes Boulevard, Suite 200, Lanham, Maryland 20706
www.rowman.com

Unit A, Whitacre Mews, 26-34 Stannary Street, London SE11 4AB, United Kingdom

British Library Cataloguing in Publication Information Available

Library of Congress Cataloging-in-Publication Data Available

ISBN 978-1-4422-5715-3 (cloth : alk. paper)
ISBN 978-1-4422-5716-0 (pbk. : alk. paper)
ISBN 978-1-4422-5717-7 (electronic)

∞ ™ The paper used in this publication meets the minimum requirements of American National Standard for Information Sciences Permanence of Paper for Printed Library Materials, ANSI/NISO Z39.48-1992.

Printed in the United States of America

To Nancy, for everything,
and to Jackson Cole LaFevor, born November 17, 2015.

Contents

Acknowledgments ix

Preface to the Second Edition xi

Introduction to the First Edition 1

1 Expansion, Empire, and Intervention, 1889–1913 7
2 Revolution, War, and Expansion, 1913–1929 39
3 Depression, War, and the Good Neighbor, 1929–1945 69
4 Cold War, Dependency, and Change, 1945–1959 105
5 Castro, Cuba, and Containment, 1959–1979 149
6 Cuba, the United States, and the World: From Mariel to Obama 195
7 The Limits of Hegemony? 1979–c. 1990 219
8 NAFTA to Now in Three Keys: Commerce, Conflict, and Culture 249

Conclusion 271

Selected Bibliography 277

Index 291

About the Authors 303

Acknowledgments

ACKNOWLEDGMENTS TO THE FIRST EDITION (2000)

While pursuing this project, I accumulated more debts to friends and colleagues than I can possibly acknowledge. I owe special thanks to Richard M. Hopper, vice president and general manager of Scholarly Resources, for his patience and enthusiasm. Also I am grateful for the friendship, good counsel, and hilarity of William H. Beezley of the University of Arizona and Judith Ewell of the College of William and Mary, the series editors. We go back many years. Don Coerver, former History Department chair, and Michael McCracken, dean of the College of Arts and Sciences at my new base, Texas Christian University, allowed me the time and opportunity to complete this book. Most significant, my wife, Nancy, urged me in times of lethargy "to get the damn thing done" and accepted some wrenching but happy changes in our personal lives during the final stages. Of course, I alone have responsibility for errors and misconceptions.

—Mark Gilderhus

ACKNOWLEDGMENTS TO THE SECOND EDITION (2017)

First and foremost we would like to thank Susan McEachern of Rowman & Littlefield Publishers, Inc. She offered us the opportunity to update and revise Professor Gilderhus's 2000 text. Professor Bill Beezley supported the project. At the University of Texas at Arlington, the Center for Mexican American Studies and the History Department provided important research support. At Rhodes College, dean Milton Moreland offered funding for research. Lance Ingwersen, at Vanderbilt, reviewed an early prospectus and offered advice. Mr. Weldon (Tat) Whitley provided technical support at Rhodes College. Timothy Garton worked with us for the duration of the project as researcher and editor; he helped compile the bibliography and wrote the final index. Photographer Bill LaFevor helped with photo selection and cover design. Paul Angelo assisted with research as the project neared completion. We appreciate the comments and excellent advice of the reviewers who supported this project both at the initial prospectus and final manuscript stages.

—David C. LaFevor and Michael J. LaRosa

Preface to the Second Edition

We are pleased to present this updated version of Mark Gilderhus's critically acclaimed work on United States-Latin American relations, which appeared in 2000 under the title *The Second Century*. For nearly two decades, students, scholars, and policy makers have studied Gilderhus's text and commented on its lucid prose, clear organizational structure, and remarkable synthesis of a long, often contentious, and changing relationship.

Like many in the academic community, we were saddened to learn of Professor Gilderhus's death in 2015, but grateful for the opportunity to work on a new edition of a book we're titling *The Third Century*. The work before you, therefore, represents the efforts of three historians, spanning three generations of scholarly engagement. Mark Gilderhus was a diplomatic historian who wrote and worked in collaboration with the great revisionist historians of U.S. foreign policy, including Walter LaFeber, William Appleman Williams, and David Green. His voice joined theirs in critical reflection of the role of the United States in Latin America. The actions, policies, priorities, and economic determinism of the United States in Latin America were subject to intense criticism and "revision" starting in the 1960s. Unlike the foundational generation of diplomatic historians in Latin America, that is, Samuel Flagg Bemis and others, the revisionists refused to accept the prevailing narrative of a benevolent, democracy-bearing United States, acting (almost always) altruistically in Latin America. Bemis's 1943 work, *The Latin-American Policy of the United States* generally supported the actions of the United States in Latin America; Professor Bemis objects to the U.S. intervention at Colombia and the creation of Panama in 1903, but qualifies his criticism by remarking that the canal became "indispensable" to U.S. interests.

For a variety of reasons, diplomatic history fell out of fashion in the second half of the twentieth century. The Asian and Latin American surprises of 1949 and 1959 (China's takeover by Communists and Cuba's takeover by Fidel Castro) caught American policy makers off guard, and Washington insiders, American scholars, journalists, and others called for a much more robust, reflective, and systematic study of foreign places. The diplomatic cables and musings of a few well-intended American diplomats abroad seemed, after 1949, wholly inadequate to explain the totality and complexity of a place like China, or even Cuba, for that matter. Thus, funding, interest, and intentionality turned toward the development of interdisciplinary "area studies" programs shortly after the Second World War, with important growth and a funding push during the 1950s and 1960s. Private foundations, such as Ford and Rockefeller, stepped in to support a more systematic, inter-disciplinary study of "society" abroad, not just policies and politics.

We have been influenced by the "new social history" of the late 1970s and 1980s—particularly Michael LaRosa who earned his doctorate in 1995 at the University of Miami and who studied with extraordinary social historians Robert M. Levine and Steve Stein, as well as diplomatic historian of Latin America, Michael Krenn, in conjunction with Brazilian social historian José Carlos Sebe Bom Meihy. David LaFevor's doctoral work at Vanderbilt University—completed in 2011—was shaped by the emergent cultural history of the past twenty years. He studied with cultural historian of Mexico, Edward Wright-Rios, and others who form a team of superb historians of Latin America in Nashville, including Brazilianist Marshall Eakin and Atlantic World scholar Jane Landers.

Our book—*The Third Century*—brings the story of the relationship between the United States and Latin America up to 2016. Gilderhus's chronology stretches from 1889 into the final days of the twentieth century. In addition to updating and editing throughout the text, we've restructured two of Mark's chapters and added two new chapters; thus, we've expanded the original book by about 20 percent. Chapter 6 is a new study of U.S.-Cuban relations, written in the spirit of détente that developed with the December 17, 2014, announcement of normalization of diplomatic relations between the United States and Cuba. Chapter 8 is a new chapter that studies some of the cultural factors that shape the relationship between the United States and Latin America. That chapter not only focuses on film, food, literature, and sport but also addresses some of the conflict (political and economic) that has defined interactions between the two regions over the past quarter century—since the implementation of NAFTA in 1994. NAFTA, the North American Free Trade Agreement, has dramatically influenced trade patterns, commerce, and wealth distribution in the three signatory nations (Canada, Mexico, and the United States). Chapter 8, additionally, studies the free trade agreement frenzy that emerged in the 1990s at a time when the "Washington Consensus" seemed inevitable and irreproachable.

Much scholarly work has emerged since 2000, since the publication of *The Second Century*. A few titles that have influenced our thinking include Stephen Kinzer's 2013 "dual" biography of the Dulles brothers, titled *The Brothers*. The book demonstrates the immense power of two unelected persons (Allen Dulles, head of the CIA, and John Foster Dulles, Secretary of State) in the period between the Second World War and the early 1960s. Allen's reign at the CIA ended with the Bay of Pigs in 1961—a complete fiasco in the early days of the Kennedy administration driven by faulty intelligence and Washington bumbling (among other factors), leading to a failed invasion of Cuba which embarrassed the nation and emboldened the Castro regime. Kinzer looks "globally" for examples of United States' misunderstandings and maladaptation abroad, with specific focus on six examples: Cuba, Guatemala, Vietnam, Indonesia, Iran, and the Congo. We have studied Greg Grandin's trenchant work from 2006 *Empire's Workshop*, which suggests that Latin America served as a sort of "test case" for some of the unsavory tactics of American imperialism, including support for coups d'état, the training of death squads, paramilitary insurgencies—and torture. None of which makes for pleasant conversation but we live in the post–Abu Ghraib era and, as such, Grandin's book, ten years after publication, seems almost prescient. The 1998 work *Close Encounters of Empire,* edited by Gilbert Joseph, Catherine LeGrand, and Ricardo Salvatore, has helped us to study the cultural significance of U.S. policy and actions in Latin America. Many other works have been consulted and appear in notes and in our revised and updated bibliography.

This book includes a photo essay that appears between chapters 4 and 5. Most of the photos are original works shot by David LaFevor, published here for the first time. The photos, and captions, can be read as a sort of "chapter" of the book, and the images help students visualize the region, the people of Latin America, and the indescribable beauty of the culture and landscape/cityscape. We would like to see students view Latin America as more than a series of diplomatic cables and policy options. As educators, we want to encourage students to study Latin America in its totality—to see and experience the richness and vibrancy of the culture, to travel there, study there, meet the people, and learn the languages of Latin America. "We must try," said the visionary senator from Arkansas, J. William Fulbright, "to expand the boundaries of human wisdom, empathy and perception and there is no way of doing that except through education."

Introduction to the First Edition

The Second Century is about U.S. relations with Latin America during a period bounded by the advent of the New Diplomacy late in the nineteenth century and the end of the Cold War about one hundred years later. The main themes center on the political and economic aspects of the relationship, taking two approaches. The first explores U.S. goals and tactics, that is, the nature of hegemony in the Western Hemisphere. The second examines Latin American responses, often nationalistic reactions to unwanted dependencies upon the "Colossus of the North." To mitigate any tendency toward national self-centeredness, this work looks at reciprocal interactions between the two regions, each with distinctive purposes, outlooks, interests, and cultures. It also suggests the place of U.S.-Latin American relations within the larger context of global politics and economics.

Most historians accept the view that international behavior is determined by shifting combinations of security needs, economic interests, domestic politics, pressure groups, ideological and cultural commitments, bureaucratic configurations, personality structures, and psychological states. Some argue that international relations form a system with incentives and deterrents all its own. Yet scholars disagree upon the points of emphasis and the overall effects. The ambiguities of historical evidence are often subject to multiple interpretations, compelling historians to regard their discipline as consisting of ongoing debates over the meaning of human experience.[1]

For an earlier generation, Arthur P. Whitaker's conception of "the Western Hemisphere idea" obtained a large measure of interpretive power. Whitaker described a distinctive community of nations characterized by similar political values and aspirations, all shaped by common experiences. For him, the republican rebellions in the New World against the monarchies of the Old during "the age of democratic revolutions" assumed a special importance.[2]

1

This view, implying that the countries of the Western Hemisphere acted on the basis of certain uniform beliefs and practices, took on particular poignancy during the Second World War when, in a sense, such a community of nations actually existed. In more recent times, notions of hemispheric solidarity have impressed scholars as harder to sustain. Instead, researchers have underscored the significance of an unequal distribution of wealth, power, and influence, sometimes depicted as a consequence of the capitalist proclivities and hegemonic purposes of the United States.

As a point of reference in this debate, Samuel Flagg Bemis's classic work, *The Latin American Policy of the United States*, still holds importance. First published in 1943, it incorporates traditional views from the time of the Second World War and presents the kind of interpretation usually characterized as "nationalist." More often than not, this account endorses the legitimacy and good intentions of U.S. goals and purposes and presumes common interests with other Western Hemisphere countries. For Bemis, such international compatibilities came about when Latin Americans practiced deference by following the U.S. lead in the defense of regional security and republican ideology. Otherwise, Latin American behavior typically impresses him as misguided, perverse, or malevolent. Although he acknowledges the reality of U.S. imperialism around the turn of the twentieth century, Bemis regards it as a mistake, a "great aberration," and downgrades its significance over the long term. He also argues against economic interpretations, claiming that interventionist practices in the Caribbean region served mainly as strategic defenses of Latin America against European threats and functioned as a form of "protective imperialism." He sees Franklin Roosevelt's Good Neighbor policy as having accomplished good purposes by eliminating the Caribbean and Central American protectorates and, in a culminating moment during the Second World War, allowing for the development of high levels of inter-American cooperation against the Axis powers.[3]

Although forceful and erudite, Bemis's work aroused criticism because of its strong opinions and self-congratulatory judgments. In 1974, for example, Gordon Connell-Smith, a British historian, anticipated contemporary historiographical tendencies. In the United States and Latin America he charges that Bemis projected ethnocentric and nationalistic biases into his writings. More specifically, in Connell-Smith's view, Bemis attributed unwarranted benevolence to the United States and presumed the existence of strong political and ideological bonds with Latin America when in actuality few existed. Seeking to set the record straight, Connell-Smith proposes to depict more faithfully the techniques of U.S. domination, control, manipulation, and exploitation.[4]

The issue retains importance. A variety of more recently published syntheses, although distinct in approach and conception, illustrate the point by emphasizing the effects of competition, inequality, and strife. For example,

Lester D. Langley's provocatively personalistic *America and the Americas* employs a version of the idealist/realist distinction, arguing that diplomatic relations in the Western Hemisphere have featured an ongoing contest between the particularistic interests of the United States (America) and the more idealistic concerns within the collectivity (the Americas). Langley hopes for transcendence over national self-centeredness through a triumph of the larger good.[5] Less optimistic in outlook, Robert Freeman Smith's "Latin America, the United States, and the European Powers, 1830–1930" situates regional diplomacy within the context of Great-Power political and economic rivalry. Stressing the clash of divergent aims and purposes, he underscores the unlikelihood that rhetorical devices will ever overcome "basic conflicts of interest" through ritualistic "professions of Pan American harmony."[6] Another recent account, a polemic by Frank Niess, a German Marxist, appears in *A Hemisphere to Itself.* This book develops an unsubtle economic interpretation by highlighting the capitalist insatiabilities of the United States for markets and resources.[7] By contrast, in *Talons of the Eagle*, political scientist Peter H. Smith draws on international relations theory by arguing that "the inter-American relationship" is "a sub-system" within the larger, global system, subject to distinctive "tacit codes of behavior." According to Smith, compatibilities of interest among the nations of Latin America and the United States may or may not come about, depending upon incentives emanating from the global system.[8] Finally, Lars Schoultz, another political scientist, finds no reason for assuming that common endeavors are possible. In *Beneath the United States*, he argues that "a pervasive belief that Latin Americans constitute an inferior branch of the human species" constitutes "the essential core" of U.S. policy toward Latin America and "determines the precise steps" taken by the United States to protect its interests.[9]

This work explores U.S. efforts to manage affairs within the Western Hemisphere, often by seeking to arrange for order and predictability. To such ends, U.S. policy makers have sometimes resorted to Pan American enticements, inviting Latin Americans to take part in a regional system for settling disputes, expanding trade, and rolling back European influences. In this way, according to the governing assumptions, the participants could advance the vital interests common to all of them by obtaining conditions of peace, prosperity, and security. Consequently, my approach describes U.S. initiatives but does not construe Latin American diplomacy as passive or inert. On the contrary, Latin Americans reacted, resisted, and pursued their own aims. Often they perceived a kind of reality different from that assumed by their northern neighbor. Indeed, the skeptics among them typically denounced the Pan American elaborations of the United States as dangerous snares and deceptions, presumably designed as a subtle means of establishing political and economic controls over Latin America.[10]

In my usage the term "Latin America" refers to a group of independent countries south of the Rio Grande in which many of the inhabitants speak languages derived from Latin, that is, Spanish, Portuguese, and French. These countries include the ten republics of South America, the six republics of Central America, and also Mexico, Cuba, Haiti, and the Dominican Republic. In eighteen of the twenty, Spanish is the dominant language; in Brazil, Portuguese; in Haiti, a French-based kreyol (creole). In Mexico, Guatemala, Ecuador, Peru, Bolivia, Paraguay, and Brazil, various native peoples still use their traditional languages. Latin American countries feature Spanish and Portuguese institutional legacies from colonial times, emphasizing hierarchy and authority, and also the economic developmental patterns of the nineteenth century. These patterns stressed the export of raw materials and foodstuffs to the industrializing European countries and to the United States. The consequences have shaped relations with the outside world in significant ways.

I have tried to avoid the use of the term "Americans" as a designation for the inhabitants of the United States. Obviously, all people who dwell in the Americas are Americans. The term "North American" is equally imprecise, since a literal application would have to include Mexicans and Canadians, and the Spanish *estadounidense* allows for no effective translation into English. Although it may be possible to make too much of this issue, I have attempted to deal with it by using terms such as "U.S. citizens."

The rise of the New Diplomacy in the United States late in the nineteenth century and its consequences for the rest of the Western Hemisphere is the focus of chapter 1. The following chapter offers a description of revolution and war during Woodrow Wilson's presidency and its aftermath in the 1920s. Chapter 3 examines the era of the Great Depression and the Second World War, focusing on U.S. efforts to enlist Latin Americans in collaborative undertakings. Next is a look at the onset of the Cold War and the implications for Latin America. The fifth chapter observes the impact of the Cuban Revolution on U.S. policy during the 1960s and 1970s. Finally, chapter 6 [now chapter 7] explores Central American involvements after 1979 and concludes with a brief resume of ramifications when the Cold War ended between 1989 and 1991. On this matter, I follow Peter H. Smith's lead, seeking a suggestive but not a comprehensive account.

NOTES

1. See Michael J. Hogan and Thomas G. Paterson, *Explaining the History of American Foreign Relations* (New York: Cambridge University Press, 1991); Peter H. Smith, *Talons of the Eagle: Dynamics of U.S.-Latin American Relations* (New York: Oxford University Press, 1996); Mark T. Gilderhus, *History and Historians: A Historiographical Introduction*, 3d ed. (Englewood Cliffs, NJ: Prentice-Hall, 1996).

2. Arthur P. Whitaker, *The Western Hemisphere Idea: Its Rise and Decline* (Ithaca, NY: Cornell University Press, 1954).

3. Samuel Flagg Bemis, *The Latin American Policy of the United States: An Historical Interpretation* (1943; reprinted, New York: W. W. Norton, 1967), chaps. 8, 20; Bemis, *A Diplomatic History of the United States*, 5th ed. (New York: Holt, Rinehart and Winston, 1965), chaps. 26, 38, 39; Jerald A. Combs, *American Diplomatic History: Two Centuries of Changing Interpretations* (Berkeley: University of California Press, 1983), 156–62, 248, 272–74, 289–90; Gaddis Smith, "The Two Worlds of Samuel Flagg Bemis," *Diplomatic History* 9 (Fall 1985): 295–302; Mark T. Gilderhus, "Founding Father: Samuel Flagg Bemis and the Study of U.S.-Latin American Relations," *Diplomatic History* 21 (Winter 1997): 1–14.

4. Gordon Connell-Smith, *The United States and Latin America: An Historical Analysis of Inter-American Relations* (New York: John Wiley & Sons, 1974), ix–xviii.

5. Lester D. Langley, *America and the Americas: The United States in the Western Hemisphere* (Athens: University of Georgia Press, 1989).

6. Robert Freeman Smith, "Latin America, the United States, and the European Powers, 1830–1930," in *The Cambridge History of Latin America*, vol. 4, c. 1870–1930, ed. Leslie Bethell (New York: Cambridge University Press, 1986), 91.

7. Frank Niess, *A Hemisphere to Itself: A History of U.S.-Latin American Relations,* trans. Harry Drost (London: Zed Books, 1990).

8. Smith, *Talons of the Eagle,* 5, 7.

9. Lars Schoultz, *Beneath the United States: A History of U.S. Policy toward Latin America* (Cambridge, MA: Harvard University Press, 1998), xv.

10. See Mark T. Gilderhus, *Pan American Visions: Woodrow Wilson in the Western Hemisphere, 1913–1921* (Tucson: University of Arizona Press, 1986).

Chapter One

Expansion, Empire, and Intervention, 1889–1913

The Modern Age in diplomatic relations between the United States and the countries of Latin America began in 1889 at the First International American Conference. During the opening ceremonies on October 2 in Washington, DC, secretary of state James G. Blaine established a central theme by affirming high purposes and common interests. According to his hyperbolic formulation, "no conference of nations" ever before had assembled "to contemplate the possibilities of a future so great and so imposing." Blaine wanted to advance "a close acquaintance" with Latin Americans through peace and trade and to establish what he called "that common confidence on which all international friendship must rest." He also placed his country's wealth and power on display. On the following day most of the seventy-three delegates embarked on a 5,000-mile, 42-day railroad journey through New York, New England, and the industrial heartland into the Midwest, at the conclusion of which the diplomatic work got under way in the nation's capital.[1]

Blaine presented an assortment of proposals. He called for the creation of a formal arbitration system to settle disputes and a customs union to increase trade. He also recommended the adoption of convertible silver currencies and other improvements in customs regulations, steamship travel, copyright laws, and extradition arrangements. Although well intended in his own view, Blaine's initiatives produced controversy because Latin Americans mistrusted his motives and disliked the implications. This wariness was not a reaction to Blaine alone, but was the product of Latin American experiences of U.S. expansionism throughout the nineteenth century. At the expense of their southern neighbors, especially Mexico, the United States had forged its manifest destiny. Washington politicians had long coveted control over Cuba for a variety of geopolitical, economic, and nationalistic motives. Clearly, the

Pan American movement did not start with a blank slate among equals. As a consequence, the larger parts of Blaine's plan never materialized. At the end of the conference on April 19, 1890, only the creation of the International Union of American Republics had obtained approval. Later called the Pan American Union, this body functioned as a promotional agency for the distribution of commercial information to business leaders seeking trade.[2]

Although something of a disappointment for Blaine, this first modern Pan American conference nevertheless anticipated future directions in the U.S. foreign policy by signaling a transition from the "Old" to the "New Diplomacy." Benjamin Harrison's administration from 1889 to 1893 played an important role in this process. Harrison, a modernizer in foreign policy, was "the first president in the post–Civil War era who attempted to coordinate the strategic, diplomatic, and economic factors of United States foreign policy." Beginning in the late 1880s the United States entered "a more aggressive and expansionist phase" and "reached out into the world in an increasingly determined and deliberate fashion." To explain the change, historian Robert L. Beisner invokes Thomas S. Kuhn's conception of a paradigm shift. Defined as a "constellation" of beliefs, values, and perceptions, a paradigm constitutes a way of seeing the world. In this instance the change altered "the manner of thinking about and executing American foreign policy." Among other things, it moved diplomatic practice away from the reactive, improvisational style so characteristic of the immediate post–Civil War era and toward a more systematic, expansive approach.[3]

LEGACIES AND TRADITIONS

During the era of the New Diplomacy, Latin America became more important to the United States than ever before. In previous times the policy makers had taken only a limited, sporadic, and incidental diplomatic interest in the southern regions beyond Mexico, Cuba, and Central America. To be sure, groups of merchants, shippers, and political leaders periodically discerned opportunities for expanding overseas trade, but such ambitions had difficulty overcoming the distances imposed by geography, language, and culture. During colonial times the inhabitants of the two Americas displayed scant knowledge and awareness of each other outside those contentious border zones of Florida and Louisiana and in the sporadic battles over imperial control of the Caribbean.[4]

The gap narrowed for a time during the independence era. As the first people to break free from colonial control, U.S. citizens perceived themselves as a republican vanguard, a model and an inspiration for others; they regarded the Spanish American rebellions against the mother country as emulations of their own example. Such ethnocentric responses somewhat misconstrued complex mixes of motive and purpose. In fact, the Latin American insurrections in 1808 began as defenses of monarchical legitimacy—indeed, as reactions against Napoleon's removal of Ferdinand VII from the Spanish throne and installation of his brother, Joseph Bonaparte. Later, when Latin American rebels broadened their aims to include national independence, patriotic enthusiasts in the United States looked upon the goal as further evidence of shared commitments to the principles of republicanism and free trade. The result, a utopian expectation, anticipated the advent of "an entire hemisphere peopled by republicans, their political systems and moral virtues modeled on the United States, and, like the United States, aloof from Europe."[5]

Conceptions of realpolitik more than ideology guided official U.S. responses during the wars of the French Revolution and later those of Napoleon. Under president James Madison the U.S. government occasionally expressed sympathy for the independence movements but otherwise assumed a neutral stance. Mainly, Madison wanted to avoid provocative displays toward Spain at a time of dangerous European complexities. Relations with France and Great Britain took priority before the War of 1812. Impatient advocates of Latin America, such as congressman Henry Clay of Kentucky, called for diplomatic recognition to win over the new regimes, sustain republican solidarity, and advance commercial opportunity, but U.S. policy makers concentrated on European concerns. After the War of 1812, secretary of state John Quincy Adams successfully resolved outstanding difficulties with Britain and Spain through complicated negotiations over boundaries along the northern and southern frontiers. Meanwhile, triumphant Latin American revolutionaries achieved independence and invited formal diplomatic ties. Insisting upon proper guarantees of order and responsibility, the United States under president James Monroe responded by extending diplomatic recognition to Mexico in 1822, the first country to do so. Recognition followed for Brazil and the Central American Confederation in 1824 and for most of the other countries during the next few years. Haiti, an exception, had to wait until 1862. As an independent nation created through revolution by the descendants of enslaved Africans, Haiti, for reasons of race, experienced isolation in a world dominated by white authority.[6]

Monroe's famous message to Congress on December 2, 1823, proclaimed support for Latin American independence. Known to posterity as the Monroe Doctrine, the terms established sharp distinctions between the policies and practices of the monarchies of the Old World and the republics of the New. Monroe specifically warned against interference by the former in the affairs of the latter. He also placed a prohibition on European expansion beyond "existing colonies or dependencies" and disallowed all the other regions from serving "as subjects for future colonization." In his words, "any attempt" by the Europeans to extend "their system to any portion of this hemisphere" would appear as "an unfriendly disposition," endangering the "peace and safety" of the United States.[7]

Although assuredly a bold statement, the Monroe Doctrine entailed very few risks. As understood by President Monroe, Secretary of State Adams, and other advisers, British interests ran parallel with those of the United States and militated against European interventions for regaining territory. The British also wanted free, trading states in the Western Hemisphere. As John J. Johnson notes, the Monroe Doctrine implied no "binding commitment" to do much of anything except to uphold the basic interests of the country. Similarly, Walter LaFeber argues that the Monroe Doctrine established "the ground rules for the great game of empire . . . in the New World." Essentially, it sought the "containment" of European presences while reserving for the future the extension of U.S. influence in the region.[8]

Except for Mexico, Cuba, and Central America, Latin America subsequently passed out of vogue as a compelling U.S. interest. Geographically distant and culturally remote, South American countries presented neither dangers to nor opportunities for the United States. Meanwhile, Latin American leaders cultivated European ties as balances against their northern neighbor, which was embarking upon the great surge westward. Driven by land hunger, commercial ambition, and a constellation of ideological convictions known as manifest destiny, territorial expansion resulted shortly in the conquest of the continent. Mexico, a principal loser as a consequence of military defeat, suffered some of the effects in 1848 when the Treaty of Guadalupe Hidalgo transferred half of the country's territory to the United States. In the 1850s, Cuba and parts of Central America also took on allure as worthy prizes; for southern slave-owners, Cuba, a slave-owning society until 1886, became a target; for northern commerce, Central American routes became desirable as a means of transit to Asia across the Pacific. In the mid-nineteenth century, a series of American freebooters, or filibusters, such as William Walker, tried to invade various countries in Central America and the Caribbean. Before losing to a combined Central American army, Walker had sought to establish English as the national language of Nicaragua and reestablish slavery there.

The westward march overwhelmed Spanish, Mexican, British, and Native American presences and ultimately exacted a price. Ironically, the acquisitions of the 1840s transformed the territorial status of slavery into an insoluble issue. The consequence of this political breakdown, the American Civil War, cost 620,000 lives and altered the future forever. By abolishing slavery and modifying states' rights, the North's victory sanctioned the use of federal authority and the rise of business and industrial leaders who put faith in the transformative powers of capitalist enterprise. For the rest of the century and beyond, such men controlled U.S. destiny at home and abroad.[9]

THE NEW DIPLOMACY

According to most historians the New Diplomacy originated in larger, more pervasive patterns of change during the second half of the nineteenth century. Usually perceived as the result of shifting economic, strategic, political, and cultural conditions, the advent of overseas expansion requires an explanation of the nature, causes, and consequences of U.S. imperialism. In 1963 the publication of Walter LaFeber's *The New Empire* initiated the debate among modern scholars. Setting forth a nuanced economic analysis, this book generated controversy by arguing a neo-Marxist case. According to LaFeber the Industrial Revolution in the United States and the ensuing quest for markets and resources functioned as fundamental determinants: "It was not accidental that Americans built their new empire at the same time their industrial complex matured."[10] Indeed, the correlation between economics and expansion in both territorial and commercial forms signified a continuity in U.S. history since colonial times.

In response, critics developed discrete commentaries, cautioning against undue reliance upon economic interpretations, historical continuities, and neo-Marxist models. Seeking to capture the different dimensions of a complex, multifaceted reality, they insisted upon the need for balanced, inclusive explanations to account for the effects of domestic and international politics, strategy, culture, psychology, and economics. Without multiple levels of understanding, they warned, historians could run the risk of misrepresenting the past.

For LaFeber, the antecedents of the New Empire came about soon after the Civil War. Although preoccupied with internal affairs such as Reconstruction, the conquest of the West, and the Industrial Revolution, the leaders of the United States retained an interest in the outside world but with a shifting emphasis. Less concerned than previously with territorial acquisitions, they attached more importance to commercial expansion, hoping by this means to moderate the instabilities of the Industrial Age.

This argument stresses the impact of technology on manufacturing and transportation. Through the development of factories and railroads the United States acquired not only immense productive capability but also the capacity to supply far-flung markets. Economically, it assumed the rank of a Great Power. At the same time, cyclical boom-and-bust tendencies brought about unpredictability and wild fluctuations. Beginning with the Panic of 1873 the United States embarked upon twenty-five years of recurrent depression, occasioned in the popular understanding by overproduction and underconsumption. Ironically, high production drove prices down by turning out more goods than consumers could buy. When market glut resulted, the ensuing hard times meant reduced production and high unemployment. Meanwhile, strikes, riots, and other manifestations of class conflict suggested incipient revolution.

In a classic response, national leaders tried to dissipate the adverse effects of depression at home by increasing sales in the markets of Europe, Asia, and Latin America. According to LaFeber, a remarkable continuity of purpose linked the efforts of secretaries of state William Henry Seward in the 1860s, James G. Blaine in the 1880s, and their successors in the following years. For such men, visions of commercial empire and expanding trade formed the core of national aspiration.[11]

LaFeber's critics sometimes conceded an important point, acknowledging that foreign markets counted for something. Yet overall, they characterized the economic approach as too simplistic and misleading to tell the whole story. For example, Robert Beisner advised against exaggerating the effects of continuity. In his view, after the Civil War the practitioners of the Old Diplomacy never possessed the ability "knowingly" and "skillfully" to execute "a farsighted economic diplomacy." Indeed, until the 1890s "most U.S. officials were amateurish and maladroit in their diplomacy, ignorant of other societies and their affairs, and more likely to react to outside events in habitual ways than to come up with fresh policies." During these "awkward years," improvisational responses, operating without much planning and coordination, typified U.S. behavior.

Beisner's study and others sought to expand the focus beyond commercial questions through the inclusion of a more comprehensive range of considerations. As Beisner explains, "Most Americans merged economics into a broader vision" and viewed trade "not just as a source of profits, but also a wellspring of social enlightenment, moral improvement, and international peace." The role of economics in foreign policy was "undeniable," also "subtle and complex."[12] Within the context of the times, it functioned as both an end and a means, intersecting always with cultural and ideological concerns.

In addressing this complicated issue, historians have underscored the impact of fundamental assumptions and inclinations. For example, Michael H. Hunt's *Ideology and U.S. Foreign Policy* points to the existence of three "core ideas," each of which had important effects upon public perceptions of foreign affairs. The first, a conception of mission, defined the American experience as "an active quest for national greatness closely coupled to the promotion of liberty." According to this significant and ethnocentric formulation, the advancement of U.S. ideals and interests simultaneously served the well-being of other peoples by expanding the areas of freedom and enterprise. The second, a manifestation of color consciousness, affirmed attitudes toward other peoples within the context of "a racial hierarchy." In this rating scheme white skin connoted higher forms of human quality and worth—indeed, the whiter, the better. Among white people, attitudes of fear, condescension, and paternalism sometimes suggested a need for imposing civilizing discipline upon persons of color in order to redeem them from their own racial handicaps. The third, a set of conservative political attitudes based on conceptions of constraint and propriety, placed limits on the acceptability of revolutionary change. The people of the United States revered their own revolution but mistrusted others, especially those infused with more radical tendencies: for example, the twentieth-century upheavals in Mexico, Russia, China, and Cuba. In modern times each of those three core ideas shaped stereotypes of Latin Americans, often seen in the United States as politically tyrannized and racially mongrelized but nevertheless capable of violent and fanatical outbursts.[13] And, as more recent historians have convincingly shown, Latin American countries and their inhabitants provided an essential proving ground for the expansion of American political, economic, and cultural power from the late-nineteenth century onward.[14]

The paradigm shift in foreign policy took place when anomalies and inconsistencies debilitated the traditional ways of doing things and rendered them inadequate; the Old Diplomacy could not respond to new realities coherently and effectively. According to Beisner, a series of "sudden and severe shocks" triggered the diplomatic revolution. The first, "a widespread social malaise" during the late 1880s and early 1890s, accentuated "a state of anxiety and gloom" in the United States. The great historian Richard Hofstadter called it "a psychic crisis" whose effects brought into question the viability of American beliefs and institutions. The second, the economic depression of the mid-1890s, intensified bad times and instilled a sense of urgency. The third, intense economic competition manifested by European colonial expansion into Asia and Africa, posed additional threats by closing off foreign markets and restricting exports; its consequences magnified the impact of the other two. In combination, this sequence of "abrupt dislocations" brought about "a reevaluation of diplomatic axioms" and a movement toward the New Diplomacy.[15] Henceforth, U.S. policy makers affirmed their own nation's interests with greater calculation in contests among the Great Powers.

The advocates of the New Diplomacy favored peace and trade without European entanglements but on occasion accepted such risks as unavoidable. They also developed larger aims in Asia and Latin America. In each region the United States preferred informal and indirect means of expansion in contrast with European methods. In India and Africa, for example, the Europeans created formal colonial empires, relying on overt and direct systems of political and economic control. U.S. leaders wanted commercial access but without too many political costs. In Asia the Open Door policy marked an effort by the United States at the turn of the century to prevent the partition of China into spheres of influence. By committing the Great Powers to the principle of "equal commercial opportunity," U.S. leaders hoped to preserve Chinese self-determination and their own prerogative to employ their great economic power "in a fair field with no favor." The United States would rank as the first among equals.[16] Similarly, in Latin America, citizens of the United States intended to compete more actively by establishing new ties of their own.

The extent to which U.S. practices constituted imperialism is an important question. Part of the problem resides in definitions. For Europeans in the nineteenth century, imperialism was colonialism, that is, a formal apparatus of institutional control. In the twentieth century less direct and costly techniques came into vogue and with them new forms of understanding. In the Marxist-Leninist interpretation, imperialism appeared as a stage in the development of capitalism. Though capable of different guises in diverse circumstances, it always served the same set of purposes and interests. According to V. G. Kiernan, imperialism has existed in "protean forms . . . throughout history" but obtained "special new forms" as a consequence of modern capitalism. Regarded as "inherently expansionist," capitalist systems demanded ever greater access to overseas regions for trade and resources and devised new ways of achieving it. The Europeans traditionally founded empires by "annexing and occupying and subjecting peoples to direct rule." The United States, in contrast, became "the chief exponent" of "neo-colonialism," that is, a more subtle approach using informal means to achieve identical ends. In each case the tactics featured "coercion . . . to extort profits above what simple commercial exchange can produce." Expressing a similar view in his famous and influential book *The Tragedy of American Diplomacy,* historian William Appleman Williams described the techniques of "imperial anticolonialism," by which the United States performed as a great imperial power but without the formal instruments of empire.[17] How best to understand this aspect of the U.S. experience remains a vital issue.

THE NEW DIPLOMACY IN ACTION

In the Western Hemisphere the New Diplomacy encouraged repeated affirmations of U.S. power, prestige, and prerogative. In the 1890s such displays produced a series of confrontations, culminating in 1898 with war against Spain. This brief conflict, only four months in duration, had large repercussions. For one thing, it confirmed the standing of the United States among the Great Powers as a presence in the western Pacific and as the hegemon of the Americas. It also bequeathed new problems of management and control of territories within the U.S. sphere of influence; what today is known as "nation building." During the early years of the twentieth century these problems occasioned the use of protectorates and other interventionist practices.

As an intimation of change the Harrison administration's sponsorship of the First International American Conference in 1889 had broad implications.

To an extent, Blaine's plan for peace and trade was sanctioned by past experience. Simón Bolívar, the liberator of South America from Spanish rule, had tried to advance international cooperation by suggesting "an august Congress" of American states in 1815. Though abortive in the first instance, the idea did prompt a series of meetings under Latin American auspices at Panama in 1826, Lima in 1847, Santiago in 1856, and Lima again in 1864.[18] None of them accomplished much. Now, with Blaine in charge, the United States instigated another such endeavor.[19]

Blaine first issued invitations to a Pan American conference during his short stint as secretary of state in 1881, but the assassination of president James A. Garfield ruined the plan. When vice president Chester A. Arthur took over as president, he replaced Blaine with Frederick T. Frelinghuysen, a practitioner of the Old Diplomacy, who wanted no new entanglements and canceled the proposed meeting. The idea nevertheless retained validity among commercial expansionists and other enthusiasts, and so in 1888 the U.S. Congress authorized president Grover Cleveland to try it again. But then, in another twist, Cleveland, a Democrat, lost the presidency that year to Harrison, a Republican, and Blaine returned as secretary of state in time to act as the host.[20] Fundamentally a ceremonial occasion, the First International American Conference in Washington, DC, much like its predecessors, fell short in tangible accomplishment. An assortment of rivalries and cross-purposes created impediments and manifested high levels of mistrust of the United States and its ambitions. The Chileans, for example, objected to Blaine's proposed arbitration treaty out of concern for their stake in Tacna and Arica, the nitrate-rich provinces they had recently taken from Peru in the War of the Pacific. The Argentines, similarly, opposed a customs union on grounds of economic self-interest. As a trading partner they preferred Great Britain, the traditional supplier of capital, markets, and goods, and regarded the United States as a rival whose agricultural and extractive exports competed with their own. Thus, they saw no advantage in closer affiliation, since for them Great Britain served as a counter against the growing power of the United States.[21]

Unable to obtain his more lofty goals, Blaine settled for a recommendation in support of commercial reciprocity. This strategy, though less comprehensive than a customs union, suggested another method for expanding trade. The U.S. Congress in 1890 created incentives by removing import duties on sugar, molasses, coffee, tea, and hides in the hope that other countries would reciprocate with exemptions for U.S. exports. Subsequent agreements, though endorsed by eight nations—Spain, Great Britain, the Dominican Republic, Brazil, Guatemala, Nicaragua, Honduras, and El Salvador—yielded mixed results, showing few actual increases in trade.[22]

Weakened by illness and personal loss—the deaths of a brother, a son, and a daughter—Blaine resigned as secretary of state in 1892 and died the following year. Harrison, assuming the conduct of foreign policy, affirmed strong positions. In Latin America his pugnacity produced a war scare with Chile. Though possibly encouraged by the proximity of the 1892 presidential election, as some historians have argued, Harrison more basically displayed his commitment to the New Diplomacy with readiness to uphold a broad conception of national interest and honor. Moreover, the program of naval arms construction initiated early in the 1880s allowed him to coordinate his actions with credible threats of seagoing force. During the Chilean episode he had seven new naval cruisers at his disposal and several more on the way.

The showdown with Chile that put the New Diplomacy into action developed as a kind of culmination after a period of rising tension created by Chile's victory over Peru and Bolivia in the War of the Pacific, 1879–1882.[23] Seeking to maintain a regional balance of power, Secretary of State Blaine had offended Chilean leaders by appearing to support their military adversaries. He then compounded the problem during the Chilean civil war in 1891, again by seeming to back the loser—in this case, the ousted president, José Manuel Balmaceda.

Consequently, anti-U.S. sentiment was running high when captain Winfield Scott Schley of the USS *Baltimore* permitted his crew to take shore leave in Valparaiso on October 16, 1891. A group of sailors at the True Blue Saloon became embroiled in a violent incident in which two were killed and others were injured and arrested. The Chilean government denied responsibility, blaming the sailors for riotous, drunken behavior. The Harrison administration, however, held the government accountable, demanded an apology and reparations, and forced Chile's capitulation early in 1892 with a threat of war.

Joyce S. Goldberg's careful study places the *Baltimore* affair within the larger international context and explains the process of escalation leading to "extraordinary" effects far out of proportion to the causes. Acute rivalries among the Great Powers at the end of the nineteenth century intensified the impact. Both Chile and the United States "were struggling to develop a dominant position in the Western Hemisphere" and acted according to "their understanding of themselves, the manner in which the rest of the world saw them, and their desire to alter or maintain the images other nations had of them."[24] In other words, perceptions and self-impressions counted for a great deal. Chilean miscalculations in the early stages suggested a dismissive attitude toward the United States and elicited bellicose reactions. In the end the "historical significance" of the episode underscored the extent to which the Harrison administration would assert its presumed prerogatives as a Great Power in the Western Hemisphere.

Another such affirmation took place in 1895, during president Grover Cleveland's second term. On this occasion, secretary of state Richard Olney proclaimed his corollary to the Monroe Doctrine, declaring in unsubtle terms that "today the United States is practically sovereign on this continent, and its fiat is law upon the subjects to which it confines its interposition." Olney affirmed this statement during a controversy with Great Britain over a disputed territory between British Guiana and Venezuela. A problem of long standing, the issue became significant in the 1890s because of the discovery of gold in the region. When, as a consequence, Great Britain and Venezuela broke diplomatic relations, the Cleveland administration claimed the right to invoke its authority, using the Monroe Doctrine as the rationale. To defend the national "safety and welfare" of the United States against a threat of British expansion in South America, the Cleveland administration insisted upon a settlement by means of arbitration.

The British Foreign Office subsequently suggested calculated disdain for the United States, first by withholding a response for five months, and again by denying the applicability of the Monroe Doctrine. Refusing to back down, President Cleveland raised the stakes by publicly supporting Olney in a message to the Congress on December 17, 1895. A compromise settlement then came about. British leaders, distracted by other matters in Asia and Africa, had no wish to force a crisis in the New World if face-saving devices could avoid one at endurable cost. They accepted arbitration, conditioned on the exclusion of territory occupied by the British for more than fifty years. The terms upheld the essential parts of the status quo; Venezuela also retained control of its traditional claims. In the larger context the controversy speeded a change in relations between the United States and Great Britain. This "great rapprochement" manifested a long-term tendency by which the British more readily acknowledged the preeminence of the United States in the Western Hemisphere. Though economic competition persisted, the two countries accepted an arrangement by which the United States assumed the main political responsibility for maintaining the common interest in order and peace.

Historians usually cite a blend of politics, strategy, and economics as the reasons for Cleveland's opposition to Great Britain. Some have described the administration's behavior as a maneuver to build popularity before the election in 1896 or as a bid to strengthen U.S. authority against European rivals. Others have identified commercial incentives, such as a need to prevent British control of the Orinoco River, the main route of access to interior markets. In a balanced synthesis, Richard E. Welch, Jr. also shows the impact of the president's personality upon policy. He argues that Cleveland resented "presumed slights against the national honor" and feared "the expansion of British economic and strategic power in the New World," where he equated "U.S. national security" with "U.S. hemispheric predominance." Yet Welch denies the existence of explicit and aggressive programs of economic expansion. Instead, he depicts U.S. diplomacy under Cleveland as a product of uneven and improvisational attitudes and practices, characterized "by inconsistencies, sporadic personal attention, and an uneasy mixture of anti-imperialism, moralism, and belligerent nationalism."[25]

Similar interpretive difficulties intrude upon studies of the war with Spain. This debate centers on the nature, causes, and consequences of the unfolding imperial policy of the United States. Neo-Marxist historians have affirmed the existence of direct connections between overseas expansion and economic drives for markets and resources; other scholars have insisted upon the multifarious effects of politics, strategy, and cultural motivations. Yet they all recognize the magnitude of change brought about by the dramatic extension of U.S. influence in the Caribbean and Pacific. Whether these developments occurred because of contingency or by design is a central question.

The Cuban revolt against Spanish authority began in 1868 during the Ten Years' War and lasted, off and on, for thirty years. Though initially forced into submission, the insurgents rose again in 1895 in a nationalist rebellion against misgovernment, maladministration, and an assortment of social and economic ills. Ranking high among the latter, the U.S. increase in tariff rates on Cuban sugar in 1894 sharply reduced sales, precipitating hardships for Cubans. In defining their goals the rebels drew directly upon the thinking of José Martí, a revolutionary leader whose nationalistic conception of *Cuba libre* required not only emancipation from Spain but also the avoidance of subsequent dependencies on the United States.[26] In addition, Martí called for the creation of an egalitarian society in Cuba through the elimination of poverty and injustice. Since many poor Cubans had experienced plenty of each, masses of people responded with favor to Martí's calls for a raceless republic.

The anticolonial revolt took on the attributes of racial and class struggle. Among the 1.6 million inhabitants of Cuba, about one-third were descended from African ancestors and slavery had not ended until 1886. Large numbers of free and enslaved Cubans had joined the anticolonial insurgency with unsettling effects upon the privileged elites, who feared a caste war. A guerrilla army of thirty thousand under leaders such as generals Máximo Gómez and Afro-Cuban Antonio Maceo waged a fierce fight, employing the classic hit-and-run, terror, and scorched-earth tactics. By laying waste, the guerrillas hoped to force the Spanish out of Cuba.

The Spanish responded with regular military forces and a pacification program built on the tactic known as *reconcentrado*. As practiced by general Valeriano Weyler y Nicolau, this technique attempted to isolate the rebels by concentrating thousands of Cubans in relocation camps, where they died in the thousands. The brutality shocked observers in the United States and came under scrutiny in such newspapers as William Randolph Hearst's *New York Journal* and Joseph Pulitzer's *New York World*. (Though historians once rated sensational journalism as a cause of the war, scholars today see it as a reflection of public opinion more than as an actual incitement.) Meanwhile,

Cuban factions maneuvered for advantage in the United States. In New York, revolutionary groups sought political support, money, and arms from sympathizers and enthusiasts, while Cuban conservatives asked for intercession by President Cleveland. Unlike José Martí, the conservatives accepted dependency upon the United States as the price for aid in establishing peace and order and in the hope that the rank and file of the rebel army, the *mambises*, would not gain political ascendancy after the war.

The Cuban issue also caused political divisions in the United States. According to one view, the United States possessed both legitimate interests of long standing in Cuba—including investments estimated at $50 million—and also a strategic stake. Only ninety miles away, Cuba commanded Caribbean sea-lanes and presumably could function as a strategic base for hostile powers. Cleveland, worried about European intervention, favored a restoration of Spanish authority, with provision for home rule and other reforms to win over the rebels. Cuban independence, he feared, would result in chaos over differences of color and class. In contrast with Cleveland's position, U.S. advocates of a free Cuba saw ideological affinities with their own War of Independence and thus championed support for the rebels.

Among the Cubans, Cleveland's peace plan had the exceptional effect of offending both sides. Cuban loyalists wanted no dilution of Spanish authority and rejected home rule; the rebels demanded full sovereignty and no compromise. Among Cleveland's deficiencies, "an anti-Cuban bias" suggested "little sympathy for the insurrectionists and little faith in their political intelligence." Indeed, Cleveland's incomprehension of Cuban nationalism became "a major weakness" and a principal source of failure. [27]

His Republican successor, William McKinley, also compiled a controversial record. According to traditional accounts, McKinley displayed weakness and indecision when faced with political pressures at home after his election in 1896. In Theodore Roosevelt's delicious phrase, he showed "no more backbone than a chocolate éclair!" Elaborating upon the same point, a contemporary cartoon showed "Willie" McKinley attired in a dress, holding a broom, seeking ineffectually to drive back huge waves called "Congress" and "The People." The caption read, "Another Old Woman Tries to Sweep Back the Sea." This image depicted the president as "cowardly, bumbling, and politically opportunistic." Unable to establish a steady course, he was supposedly "overwhelmed by public opinion and forced into an unnecessary war." This interpretation established a dominant theme in historical writing until the 1960s, when revisionists mounted a challenge. They regarded McKinley as "more courageous and capable than previously portrayed." Also, they described his decision in favor of war as a logical continuation of his own policies more than as a surrender before public and congressional insistence. The effect has been "a substantial redemption of McKinley's historical reputation." [28]

These historians have depicted McKinley as a shrewd trade expansionist who understood relationships between means and ends. In actuality a strong leader, he hoped to avoid war in his quest for overseas markets, but in the end he desired "what only a war could provide," that is, "the disappearance of the terrible uncertainty in American political and economic life, and a solid basis from which to resume the building of the new American commercial empire." Throughout the preliminaries before the war, McKinley affirmed the standards of the New Diplomacy and implied the possibility of using force finally as a last resort. [29]

Much of the recent writing incorporates revisionist thinking but without the economic emphasis. In fairness to McKinley, according to Lewis L. Gould, historians must acknowledge his capabilities by accurately representing "the complexity of the diplomatic problems" and the extent of his efforts "to discover a way out of the impasse." McKinley's diplomacy was "tenacious," "coherent," "courageous," and "principled." Indeed, "what is significant is not that war came" but that McKinley postponed it "for as long as he did." By so doing, he retained control of "the terms on which the United States commenced hostilities." Indeed, his strong use of the executive power established him as "the first modern president."[30]

Late twentieth-century scholarship describes the unfolding of McKinley's diplomacy through various stages. The president first aspired to a negotiated solution with Spain, seeking a peaceful separation for Cuba and, perhaps, purchase by the United States. The effort failed. McKinley then reluctantly considered war but accepted it only when convinced that Spain would not acquiesce in other alternatives. Affirming his aversion to an endless, inhumane conflict, he announced soon after his inauguration his insistence upon respect for "the military codes of civilization." Spain never accepted this position. Nevertheless, McKinley's expectation of limits on the conduct of war became a tenet of U.S. policy.

As president, McKinley needed to appoint a new minister to the U.S. legation in Madrid. His first choices included such notables as John W. Foster, Henry White, Whitelaw Reid, and Elihu Root, all first-rate, experienced public figures. They turned him down. The president then picked Stewart L. Woodford for this important post. A lawyer, former Civil War general, and New York state politician, Woodford was "loyal" and "conscientious" but uncomfortable with "the subtleties of international diplomacy." As an amateur in the diplomatic arts, he resembled many other practitioners and policy makers in the McKinley administration.

Eager for improved Spanish relations before Congress assembled in December 1897, McKinley hoped for good results from a political change in Spain. Following the assassination of prime minister Antonio Cánovas del Castillo in August 1897, an interim Conservative government failed to make any progress in the Cuban difficulty and relinquished power two months later. A new Liberal government under Práxedes Mateo Sagasta then signaled the possibility of a negotiated settlement by recalling General Weyler and accepting home rule in principle. Designed to rally political moderates in Spain, these concessions also sought U.S. support with shows of reasonability. Meanwhile, Minister Woodford presented his diplomatic credentials in Madrid. In a statement of expectations delivered at the same time, he emphasized that unless peace returned quickly to Cuba, the Spanish government must anticipate some action from the McKinley administration. He also inquired when Spain would "put a stop to this destructive war" by offering "proposals of settlement honorable to herself and just to her Cuban colony and to mankind."

Though McKinley never said so, he probably believed that Spain truly lacked the capacity to suppress the revolt and eventually would have to let Cuba go. At the same time, he understood the futility of an ultimatum. No Spanish government would accept independence outright. For that reason, McKinley maintained the pressure, seeking concessions while moving toward a negotiated outcome. In the fall the Liberal government, in a show of good faith, suspended the policy of *reconcentrado,* bestowed amnesty on political prisoners, and announced an autonomy plan. Though supposedly a step toward Cuban home rule, this approach retained Spanish sovereignty over Cuban military and foreign affairs. McKinley grasped the shortcoming. Probably, he hoped for additional concessions. In his annual message to the Congress on December 6, he commended Spain for the reforms but warned of further action by the United States unless "a righteous peace" ensued in the "near future."

Such determination resulted in part from apprehension over the possibility of European intervention in the Western Hemisphere. As a consequence of imperial competition the Great Powers had partitioned Africa and similarly threatened China. The McKinley administration wanted no such activities in the Caribbean. A supposed German threat, largely illusionary, caused special concern. Definitions of economic interest also functioned as incentives. Business and government leaders perceived the Cuban violence as an obstacle to recovery from the 1890s depression. Some also anticipated the acquisition of new markets and resources through aggressive programs of overseas expansion. Specifically, they wanted dominance in the Caribbean regions and a projection of U.S. influence into the Pacific toward China. Finally, domestic politics also contributed a controlling influence. Ferociously partisan, the struggles between Republicans and Democrats over Cuba reflected deep divisions. Each party hoped to obtain advantage by using the issue against the other. For political reasons, McKinley needed a Cuban settlement on his terms to counter Democrats, many of whom wanted to recognize Cuban independence as "an act of justice to an American nation struggling for liberty against foreign oppression." According to Democrats, the president's autonomy plan was a sham, and the Republican position on Cuba was pro-Spanish.[31]

Significant events early in 1898 created a crisis atmosphere conducive to war. First, Enrique Dupuy de Lôme, the Spanish minister in Washington, precipitated a public furor. In a letter to a friend he unflatteringly described President McKinley as "weak," "a bidder for the admiration of the crowd," and "a would-be politician who tries to leave a door open behind himself while keeping on good terms with the jingoes of his party." Cuban rebels intercepted the missive and forced de Lôme's recall by publishing it in the *New York Journal* on February 9, 1898. The effects damaged Spanish credibility in the United States. A much greater calamity then compounded the difficulty. Late in 1897 the McKinley administration had demonstrated its resolve by sending the battleship USS *Maine* to Havana. During the night of February 15, 1898, an explosion sank the vessel in the harbor and killed 266 sailors. The cause was unknown but in the ensuing investigation a U.S. Naval Court of Inquiry attributed the disaster to an external blast, possibly a torpedo or submarine mine. Such findings fed suspicions of Spanish treachery. More plausibly, modern scholars place the blame on spontaneous combustion in the bituminous coal bins near the powder magazine, though this conclusion remains controversial.[32]

To avert a war, McKinley needed concessions from Spain. Otherwise, he could not satisfy pro-Cuban contingents in the United States. Stepping up the pressure, he set forth terms on March 26, 1898, stipulating an end to *reconcentrado* and also "full self-government, with reasonable indemnity" for Cuba. Further, the United States should play a role as mediator, if necessary, to obtain a settlement between Spain and Cuba. When U.S. Minister Woodford asked for clarification as to whether "full self-government" meant "actual recognition of independence" or "nominal Spanish sovereignty over Cuba," the State Department told him to insist upon "Cuban independence." Woodford's instructions included these specifics: immediate termination of *reconcentrado,* an armistice as a move toward peace, and acceptance of the "friendly offices" of the United States. Otherwise, the McKinley administration would act as "the final arbiter."

Spain tried to buy time. On March 30 the Sagasta ministry abolished *reconcentrado* but yielded nothing else. Spanish leaders, fearing the possibility of a military revolt at home if they accepted either U.S. mediation or Cuban independence, launched other initiatives. On April 10 they suggested a Cuban cease-fire. Though in some ways consistent with U.S. demands for an armistice, the concession fell short because of omissions and loopholes. Notably, it withheld recognition of Cuban independence and allowed for a subsequent resumption of warmaking. Historian John L. Offner regards the proposal as a Spanish ploy, intended to mobilize European support against the United States. The tactic failed. None of the Great Powers wanted to risk much on Spain's behalf. The Cuban crisis then entered the final stage.

Offner's provocative assessment depicts the Spanish-American War as "inevitable" because of "the irreconcilable political positions dividing the Cuban, Spanish, and American people." In his view no grounds existed for a compromise. The Spanish refused to relinquish royal authority; the Cubans demanded independence; and the United States had no means of breaking the deadlock. At last convinced of these realities, McKinley, in a message to the Congress on April 11, 1898, insisted upon two primary goals: "the instant pacification of Cuba" and "the cessation of the misery that afflicts the island." He also called for the use of armed force to attain them. As justifications he explained the necessity of acting "in the name of humanity, in the name of civilization," and, less exaltedly, "in behalf of endangered American interests." Significantly, he advised against diplomatic recognition of the rebels.[33]

In the ensuing debate, the issue of whether to recognize Cuban independence became a central question. Most Democrats and many Republicans initially favored recognition, in opposition to the president, but then came around in McKinley's support. According to some historians, the subsequent denial of diplomatic recognition served to legitimate U.S. aims by leaving open the possibility of political accommodation with Spain, serving notice of Cuban accountability for offenses against U.S. citizens and property, and assuring the independence of U.S. forces from Cuban control. Other historians regard the decision as evidence of imperial design. Among them, Louis A. Pérez, Jr. describes McKinley's policy as the fulfillment of the long-term expansionist ambitions so graphically expressed by John Quincy Adams in 1823. Positing "laws of political as well as physical gravitation," Adams had reasoned metaphorically that just as an apple from a tree "cannot choose but fall to the ground," so also Cuba, "forcibly disjoined from its own unnatural connection with Spain, and incapable of self-support, can gravitate only toward the North American Union." This "same law of nature" required that the United States "cannot cast her off from its bosom." In Pérez's view the Cuban revolt in the 1890s threatened not only "the propriety of colonial rule" but also "the U.S. expectation of colonial succession." U.S. imperialists regarded the acquisition of Cuba "as an act of colonial continuity" by which to take sovereignty "over a territory presumed incapable of separate nationhood." McKinley's intervention, "ostensibly" against Spain but "in fact" against Cuba, had the effect of transforming "a Cuban war of liberation into a U.S. war of conquest."[34]

This indictment rings true or not, depending on interpretations of the Teller amendment to the declaration of war. Introduced by senator Henry M. Teller, a Republican from Colorado, this congressional enactment of April 16, 1898, contained a self-denying pledge against the annexation of Cuba by the United States and is subject to various explanations. The question of intent is critical. Was it an affirmation of good faith, an anticipation of eventual Cuban independence, or, more subtly, a recognition of the need for developing indirect means of control? The initial effects of the Teller amendment served several immediate purposes by rallying support for the Cuban intervention among various groups, including the principled advocates of Cuban independence, the skeptics who doubted McKinley's sincerity of purpose, and the Colorado sugar beet growers who wanted no Cuban competition. Three days later, on April 19, a congressional joint resolution provided authorization for the United States to use force. The president affixed his signature the following day. A U.S. naval blockade took effect on April 22; Spain issued a declaration of war against the United States on April 24; and Congress replied a day later that such a condition already existed. What secretary of state John Hay later called "a splendid little war" was under way.[35]

THE WAR WITH SPAIN AND AFTER

The war with Spain had many consequences. Most important, it consolidated the U.S. position in the New World, projected national interests into Asia, and introduced new problems of management and control. Barred from annexing Cuba by the Teller amendment, the policy makers subsequently experimented with other devices. Cuba, the first among what were called protectorates, became the model, suggesting forms of applicability in other places. For advocates of the New Diplomacy, the war against Spain represented a kind of culmination.

Combat operations began on May 1, 1898, with the destruction of the Spanish Pacific Squadron at Manila Bay in the Philippines. Though conventionally attributed to the bellicose conniving of the Assistant Secretary of the Navy, Theodore Roosevelt, champion of a "Large Policy" in Asia, the undertaking actually had the approval of President McKinley and other war planners. These leaders wanted to inflict injury by attacking Spain at a vulnerable point and to eliminate a potential threat against the Pacific coast. The victory also established "alluring possibilities," such as "expanding America's economic and political influence in Asia" and asserting its role as "a genuine world power."[36]

In the Western Hemisphere the process of military mobilization produced an array of baffling confusions. Indeed, so many foul-ups took place that some historical accounts have depicted the war as partaking of comic opera.[37] For example, the army lacked sufficient summer-weight material for uniforms and sent the soldiers off to Cuba in outfits more suitable for a winter campaign in Montana. The single railroad line leading into Tampa,

Florida, the main embarkation point, produced massive traffic jams; a shortage of transport vessels impeded the movement of troops to their destinations; and an absence of appropriate landing craft meant that animals and men had to leap into the surf to get ashore. Unprepared to conduct large-scale operations anywhere, the War Department had difficulty putting properly trained and equipped ground forces into Cuba, resulting in large-scale congressional investigations after the war. Nevertheless, once landed, regular and volunteer contingents performed creditably in hard fighting around Santiago de Cuba in the south and won additional victories for the United States. The Cuban campaign ended with the eradication of another Spanish naval squadron in the Caribbean, and the loss of Guam and Puerto Rico deprived the Spanish of all hope. An armistice followed, ending the fighting on August 12.

The peace negotiations confirmed Spain's defeat. Under the Treaty of Paris on December 10, 1898, Spain relinquished sovereignty over Cuba and ceded Puerto Rico, Guam, and the Philippines to the United States in return for $20 million. Cuban rebels did not play any role in the negotiation of this peace, even though they had fought for thirty years to oust Spain. The fate of the Philippines especially engendered controversy over the question of expansion into the Pacific. In this instance, no self-denying equivalent of the Teller amendment constricted options, and administration leaders could argue in favor of annexation on the basis of obligation to the inhabitants. Any alternative would supposedly lead to chaos and catastrophe among the Filipinos—often described in racial terms as untutored, un-Christian, and uncivilized—and invite Great-Power intervention. Moreover, trade expansionists regarded the Philippines as an East Asian base from which to move into the fabled, if largely mythical, China market. Critics of annexation, the so-called anti-imperialists, objected for various reasons. Mainly Democrats and free traders who preferred other means, they saw no commercial advantage in possessing formal colonies. They also worried about unwanted effects. What if the United States became involved in dangerous international rivalries? Could the United States maintain the principle of self-determination at home while violating it abroad? What of the incorporation of nonwhite peoples? Such arguments failed to stop annexation during the Senate debate in 1899. The opponents then projected the issue into the presidential campaign of the following year and lost again. McKinley's reelection in 1900 assured the outcome. Meanwhile, the U.S. Army fought a pacification campaign against Filipino guerrillas to make good on the claim.[38] Though precise numbers are difficult to establish, most scholars agree that a conservative estimate is that 200,000–250,000 Filipinos died as a result of this pacification. According to historian Paul A. Kramer, U.S. forces engaged in torture driven by the racist assumption that Filipinos were a lesser human species.[39]

In contrast, in the Caribbean the United States established protectorates instead of colonies. Following the requirements of the Teller amendment, the McKinley administration devised the essential means in Cuba. Later adaptations appeared in Panama, Nicaragua, Haiti, and the Dominican Republic. Under these arrangements the United States allowed for limited self-determination, relying upon the indigenous elites to run the countries but retaining the right of intervention as a form of international police power within their sphere of influence.

At the end of the war with Spain the U.S. military assumed direct control of Cuban governmental functions and placed stringent limits on Cuban participation. According to Louis A. Pérez, Jr., the leading expert on Cuban-U.S. history, the occupation authorities had many reasons, some of them based on racial prejudice, for thinking that Cubans had no capacity for self-government. Perceived as childlike, barbarous, and untrustworthy, the *insurrectos,* especially those of African descent, supposedly lacked the proper requisites. To compensate, U.S. supervisors cultivated the better classes—that is, the members of the old colonial elite—supporting them against the advocates of independence. Nevertheless, some *independentistas* won election to municipal office and to the Constituent Assembly, the body charged with responsibility for writing a Cuban constitution. Once installed in such positions, critics of the U.S. presence called for military withdrawal. Ironically, U.S. officials regarded this outcome as a confirmation of their own misgivings. If irresponsible Cubans rejected pro-U.S. candidates, how could the United States trust them to elect the best government?

A reinterpretation of the Teller amendment provided additional justification for staying in Cuba. A key provision disclaimed "any disposition or intention to exercise sovereignty, jurisdiction, or control over said island except for pacification thereof." But as expediency required, the meaning of the word "pacification" expanded to include "stability" and the capacity to protect life, liberty, and property, that is, the very conditions upon which the United States staked any decision to leave. According to Pérez, "the inability of the old colonial elites to win political control" required the United States "to seek alternative means of hegemony." Though "prepared, even anxious, to end the occupation" by the early part of 1901, the United States would not pull out "without first securing guarantees necessary to U.S. interests."

Secretary of war Elihu Root played a special role in defining the terms, including two provisions. First, the United States must retain "the right of intervention for the preservation of Cuban independence and the maintenance of a stable Government adequately protecting life, property and individual liberty." Second, no Cuban government could enter "into any treaty or engagement with any foreign power" that might "tend to impair or interfere with the independence of Cuba." The term "foreign" in this context meant European. Taken together, these requirements transformed Cuba into a U.S.

protectorate and established the essential parts of the Platt amendment to an army appropriations bill in February 1901. Named for the sponsor, senator Orville H. Platt of Connecticut, this legislation obtained for the United States "an adequate if imperfect substitute for annexation" by diluting Cuban sovereignty through incorporation into the "U.S. national system." It also produced a set of devices suitable for adaptation in other countries.

The explanation of these actions resides in various considerations, many of them well-established among the precepts of the New Diplomacy. First, Cuba always possessed a special attraction for U.S. expansionists. To an extent, the Platt amendment marked the fulfillment of old ambitions to secure control of the island. Moreover, the context of the times created a sense of urgency. U.S. leaders believed in the existence of legitimate strategic and economic interests in Cuba and worried that continued violence and disorder would invite European intrusions, most likely by Germany, whereas a restoration of peace and order under their direction would head off the danger. Finally, Cuba took on additional importance in connection with plans to build a Central American canal. To safeguard the Caribbean approaches, the U.S. Navy acquired a Cuban base at Guantánamo Bay.

When Cubans denounced the Platt amendment as an infringement of state sovereignty, Secretary of War Root gave them an option: either accept those provisions or put up with an ongoing military occupation. The U.S. Army would not go home until the amendment took effect. Without much choice, then, early in June 1901 the Cuban Constituent Assembly endorsed limited sovereignty as the best course available, writing the Platt amendment into the new constitution as an appendix. The occupation forces withdrew about a year later, leaving behind, in Pérez's devastating assessment, a "stunted Cuban republic fashioned by the U.S. proconsuls," the organization and institutions of which had "little relevance to Cuban social reality."[40]

Meanwhile, a significant change had taken place in the United States. On September 6, 1901, an assassin twice shot William McKinley at a reception in Buffalo, New York. McKinley lingered for eight days before dying, and then Theodore Roosevelt became the president. Conservative reformer, nationalist, and exponent of the vigorous life, the former vice president assumed the conduct of foreign relations at a critical time, the aftermath of the war with Spain. As president, he reveled in the responsibilities of his office and brought the New Diplomacy to a kind of fulfillment. Above all, he wanted his country to function as "a force for stability in the world" and saw "no escape from the exercise of American influence." Among his fundamental aims, Roosevelt sought a balance of power in Europe, an Open Door policy in Asia, and U.S. hegemony in the Western Hemisphere. His outspoken views and bellicose rhetoric always produced high levels of controversy. Critics sometimes characterized him as an imperialist and a militarist. As a young man, according to historian Richard Hofstadter, "it had always been his instinct to fight, to shoot things out with someone or something—imaginary lovers of his fiancée, Western Indians, Mexicans, the British navy, Spanish soldiers, American workers, Populists." By the time he became president, however, Roosevelt had acquired self-control and discharged "his penchant for violence . . . on a purely verbal level."[41] The most comprehensive Roosevelt scholarship, Edmund Morris's magisterial biography in three volumes, first appeared in 1979 as *The Rise of Theodore Roosevelt*. The final volume was published in 2010 as *Colonel Roosevelt*. Some Roosevelt scholarship deliberately plays down the Rough Rider's propensity for war. Though typically ready to use force if necessary, according to Lewis L. Gould, he "sent no troops into action, and no Americans died in armed combat while he was in office" except in the Philippines, where the fighting had started before he assumed the presidency.[42]

Roosevelt scholar Richard H. Collin insists that historians have too often misrepresented and misunderstood the president by failing to take into account the appropriate "contexts." Collin particularly dislikes present-minded, neo-Marxist accounts because they are more concerned with "the Cold War or America's role as a superpower than with Kaiser Wilhelm II's Germany." This misplaced emphasis has obscured the principal point that "Roosevelt's main purpose" in the New World was "not the subjugation of Latin America" but "the exclusion of Europe" from the Western Hemisphere. Europe was "central" for Roosevelt. Moreover, his concern about German intrusions was legitimate, "not because Germany could conquer substantial parts of Latin America" but "because the introduction of European national rivalries into the New World, combined with the growing instability of Central America—Latin America's Balkans—would destabilize the entire region." Roosevelt valued order. He also encouraged capitalist enterprise, not so much for purposes of money-grubbing as for tactical reasons: He hoped thereby to promote material progress, peace, and stability.[43]

Roosevelt earned much of his reputation for bravado and bluster in Latin America, where his spheres-of-influence policies in the Caribbean region stirred incessant controversy. Though probably geared in his own thinking to the defense of strategic purposes and the Monroe Doctrine, his actions served the U.S. economic interests as well. Secretary of state Elihu Root acknowledged as much in 1906, when he remarked upon the importance of Latin American markets for the United States.

He also looked upon the region as an outlet for "a surplus of capital beyond the requirements of internal development." During this time the total overseas investments of the United States grew impressively from $0.7 billion in 1897 to $2.5 billion in 1908 to $3.5 billion in 1914. About half went into Latin America.[44]

Roosevelt's actions during the Venezuela crisis in 1902–1903 illustrated his strategic concerns. Germany, already a source of mistrust, posed the problem. The difficulty developed when Cipriano Castro, the Venezuelan president and strongman, defaulted on European loans and disregarded an ultimatum demanding payment from Germany, Italy, and Great Britain. Germany then instituted a naval blockade, sank some Venezuelan ships, landed troops, and shelled the forts along the coastline. Though initially acquiescent, Roosevelt later became alarmed. He would not allow the collection of international debts to serve as a pretext for the establishment of a European base in the Western Hemisphere. Among other things, his plans for a trans-Isthmian canal ruled out European obstructions.

In this instance, Roosevelt's own historical account has generated a controversy. Thirteen years later, when the United States was struggling to maintain neutrality in the First World War, the former chief executive suggested in an interview that he knew better than president Woodrow Wilson how to deal with the Germans. Roosevelt claimed that during the Venezuela crisis he had obtained good effects behind the scenes by employing coercion with threats of force, warning of war unless the Germans accepted arbitration as the means of settlement. In this way, by his own account, Roosevelt applied the adage "speak softly and carry a big stick." For historians the difficulty resides in assessing the credibility of the claim. Since no corroborating evidence exists in the archives of the United States, Great Britain, or Germany, some scholars regard Roosevelt's version as an exaggeration or a fabrication, perhaps the product of fading memory or mounting personal disgust with Woodrow Wilson's efforts to stay out of the war. Other historians credit Roosevelt with truthfulness, citing earlier renditions of the story in his correspondence and even the possibility of a cover-up, that is, the removal of documents from governmental archives to avoid political embarrassment.[45] Whatever the case, German leaders in the end terminated the crisis by consenting to arbitration, thus presumably giving way when faced with Roosevelt's resolve.

Roosevelt's efforts to build a canal in Panama also displayed a robust readiness to act. This complicated and contentious affair raised difficult questions about the propriety of his means in promoting Panamanian independence to secure the route. Panama, a province of the South American country of Colombia, had possessed strategic significance since colonial times as "a crossroads of global trade" and "the keystone of the Great Spanish Empire." For U.S. entrepreneurs the region became particularly important as a consequence of "their quest for continental and commercial empire." As early as 1825, New York interests had laid plans for the construction of a canal to link the Atlantic and Pacific Oceans. The British had similar aims. To head off competition, the United States and Great Britain negotiated the Clayton-Bulwer Treaty of 1850, in which they promised to make any such project a joint venture. The construction of a railroad by New York financiers in 1855 established U.S. influence as dominant.

The French posed a challenge in 1878, when Ferdinand de Lesseps, the builder of the Suez Canal in Egypt, announced plans for the construction of a sea-level waterway across Panama. This project went forward for a decade, despite U.S. opposition, and then failed because of insuperable obstacles, including varieties of poisonous snakes, mud and rock slides, and tropical diseases such as malaria and yellow fever. Unimpressed by the French collapse, U.S. leaders during the economic depression of the 1890s retained a strong interest in reviving the project. Significantly, as McKinley noted in his annual message to the Congress in December 1898, "The prospective expansion of our influence and commerce in the Pacific" provided a strong incentive for building a canal. This commercial justification ran parallel with and reinforced the recommendations of another vocal pressure group, the advocates of sea power in the U.S. Navy and elsewhere, for whom captain Alfred Thayer Mahan of the U.S. Naval War College in Newport, Rhode Island, functioned as a leading publicist and theorist. Mahan argued from the British example that battle fleets always had sustained national power, commerce, and greatness. According to him, the construction of a canal formed an essential part of a grandiose design to advance U.S. interests around the world.[46] For such champions the voyage of the USS *Oregon* during the war with Spain illustrated the obvious point: The 14,000-mile voyage from San Francisco around the southern tip of South America to Cuba took sixty-eight days. A canal would make it much shorter.

One problem was whether to construct the passageway in Nicaragua or Panama. In 1901 the Walker Commission, a group of engineers named by McKinley to study the issue, recommended Nicaragua, mainly because of difficulties with the French-owned New Panama Canal Company over the purchase of equipment and assets. The asking price ran to $109 million, an excess valuation of $69 million, according to the Commission. Panama in other respects displayed advantages, chief among them cheaper construction and maintenance costs and a shorter distance from sea to sea. Roosevelt knew of these benefits, but before choosing Panama he had to deal with other complications.

Lobbyists pressed hard on Panama's behalf. As advocates of the New Panama Canal Company, William Nelson Cromwell, the head of a prestigious New York City law firm, and Philippe Bunau-Varilla, a French engineer formerly employed by de Lesseps, sought to rig a deal by which the United States would designate Panama as the choice and pay for the privilege. Cromwell cultivated support among Republican leaders with arguments and campaign contributions and also reduced the purchase price to $40 million. The Walker Commission responded by issuing a new report in favor of Panama. Meanwhile, Bunau-Varilla pushed for acceptance of a proposal suggested by Republican senator John C. Spooner of Wisconsin. Once adopted into law, the Spooner amendment authorized President Roosevelt to buy the assets of the New Panama Canal Company for $40 million and to employ Panama as the site, provided, of course, that he could obtain the treaty rights.

The diplomatic solution consisted of two parts. First, U.S. leaders wanted to break free from the Clayton-Bulwer Treaty of 1850 in order to exercise exclusive control and fortification rights. Discussions between secretary of state John Hay and British minister Julian Pauncefote produced an agreement in November 1901. Second, the United States devised a treaty with Colombia to obtain a long-term lease on a swath of land six miles wide across Panama. In return, the United States would pay Colombia $10 million and an annual rental fee of $250,000. The stockholders of the New Panama Canal Company also would benefit from the sale of assets to the United States.

John Hay's treaty, worked out with the Colombian diplomat Tomás Herrán, obtained ratification in the United States but was rejected by the Colombian Senate in August 1903. Colombians wanted more money for sacrificing sovereignty in Panama. Only recently their country had emerged from a disastrous civil war. By stalling until 1904, when the charter of the New Panama Canal Company ran out, Colombian leaders conceivably could rake in a $40-million profit, additional resources for their devastated nation. Moreover, president José Marroquín, a provincial and reactionary ideologue, would not support the work of his own government's more cosmopolitan diplomats by endorsing the treaty with the United States. His unyielding stance based on conservative Catholic views "confounded" Roosevelt by ruling out the transfer of land in Panama to a Yankee, Protestant nation. Viewed from another angle, Marroquín possessed "as little understanding of the commercial aspects of Panama canal diplomacy as Theodore Roosevelt had for Colombia's religious politics."[47] Neither Roosevelt nor Marroquín had the disposition or ideology to empathize with the other's position.

Furious, Roosevelt denounced the Colombians for bad faith. He told the secretary of state, "I do not think the Bogotá lot of jack rabbits should be allowed permanently to bar one of the future highways of civilization." Conscious of the consequences "not merely decades, but centuries hence," Roosevelt wanted to take "the right step." A convergence of purposes with Panamanian separatists seeking independence from Colombia provided the solution. Remote and isolated by mountains and jungle, Panama had produced fierce nationalism and a series of revolts in the nineteenth century. New efforts got under way in the fall of 1903, when Philippe Bunau-Varilla assumed the role of intermediary between Panamanian dissidents and U.S. officials. The latter included President Roosevelt, who conveyed a clear impression that he would not permit the failure of a new bid for independence. Coordinating plans with Dr. Manuel Amador Guerrero, the head of a revolutionary junta, Bunau-Varilla brought about an uprising on November 3. The Panamanian rebels swiftly seized control of strategic points, and the arrival of the USS *Nashville* on the following day prevented Colombia from striking back. The revolution cost hardly any bloodshed.

Seeking to salvage something, the Colombian government attempted to revive the previously rejected treaty, this time at a lower price. Not much interested, the Roosevelt administration concentrated its attention on negotiations with the dexterous and omnipresent Bunau-Varilla, who now represented the interests of both newly independent Panama and the New Panama Canal Company. Because of the administration's political concerns, Roosevelt needed favorable terms to assure Senate ratification and got them in the Hay–Bunau-Varilla Treaty of November 18, 1903. This document provided for a perpetual grant of land ten miles wide within which the United States possessed "all rights, power, and authority" as "if it were the sovereign of the territory." In return, the United States agreed to protect Panama's independence, pay $10 million down, and, after nine years, remit an annual fee of $250,000. For the sale of its assets the New Panama Canal Company received $40 million. The prime loser, Colombia, received nothing until 1921, when, under the terms of the Thomson-Urrutia Treaty, the government accepted the loss of Panama and also an indemnity of $25 million from the United States.[48]

Negotiated hastily without benefit of Panamanian representation, the Hay–Bunau-Varilla Treaty distressed officials in the new country's government. They protested "the manifest renunciation of sovereignty" over the Canal Zone, a central issue during the ensuing years, but could not change the provisions. A rejection at this point could have precipitated even worse outcomes. The United States might have seized a canal route without payment or moved the site to Nicaragua, leaving Panama without protection against Colombia. The Panamanians really had no choice. Although the U.S. Senate ratified the treaty by a large margin on February 23, 1904, the acquisition of Panama as a second protectorate in the Caribbean region left a legacy of bitterness and ill will. Colombian leaders objected to the U.S. role in bringing about the loss of the rebellious province. Panamanian nationalists disliked the loss of sovereignty. In each instance, the issue created difficulties for the future.

In the annual message to Congress in December 1904, Roosevelt enunciated his most comprehensive statement of policy toward Latin America. As an expression of preferred assumptions and favorite techniques, his corollary to the Monroe Doctrine uncompromisingly affirmed U.S. responsibility to stand against European intervention in the Western Hemisphere and also to take corrective action when Latin Americans reneged on international debts. Roosevelt advised preventive intervention by which the United States would step in and set things right. Such measures inverted the original intent of the Monroe Doctrine. Initially a prohibition on European intrusion into the New World, it now became a sanction for U.S. intervention when, in Roosevelt's words, "chronic wrongdoing" or "impotence" caused a breakdown of "the ties of civilized society" and forced intercession "by some civilized nation." In the Western Hemisphere the United States, "however reluctantly, in flagrant cases," should assume the responsibility by carrying out "the exercise of an international police power." As Roosevelt explained to secretary of state Elihu Root, a decision "to say 'Hands off to the powers of Europe'" meant that "sooner or later we must keep order ourselves."[49]

A test occurred soon afterward: An international debt exceeding $32 million threatened the Dominican Republic with bankruptcy and the possibility of European intervention. When Dominican leaders asked the United States for help, Roosevelt first hesitated and then, after his reelection in 1904, accepted a commitment. An agreement in January 1905 engaged the United States to manage the foreign debt in such a way as to "restore the credit, preserve the order, increase the efficiency of the civil administration and advance [the] material progress and welfare of the Republic." Senate opponents, mainly Democrats, delayed ratification until February 1907, but Roosevelt characteristically worked around the problem by obtaining authority through an executive agreement. It enabled U.S. officials to take over the collection of Dominican customs receipts, the principal source of revenue, and also to arrange for a new schedule of payments.[50]

Roosevelt employed strong measures in Cuba as well. Following a presidential election denounced by critics as coercive, corrupt, and fraudulent, Liberal party opponents of president Tomás Estrada Palma rebelled in 1906, hoping thereby to provoke U.S. intervention on their behalf. As required by the Platt amendment, Roosevelt responded to the breakdown of public order by sending in occupation troops. This time they stayed until 1909, retiring finally after U.S. authorities supervised another election resulting in a Liberal party victory. As Louis Pérez notes, "That the United States intervened . . . to displace a government held in disfavor by the opposition . . . suggested that there was more than one way to redress grievances and obtain political ascendancy" in Cuba. The United States became a mediator of local disputes, in this instance "with almost unlimited entree into Cuban internal affairs."[51]

Such affirmations of power and prerogative established the principal attributes of U.S. hegemony in the Western Hemisphere. Though Roosevelt annexed no new territory and, indeed, denied any interest in doing so, he upheld his definition of U.S. interest by vigorous means. Through the exercise of a self-proclaimed international police authority, supposedly sanctioned by the Monroe Doctrine, Roosevelt created not colonies but protectorates, using intervention as a major instrument of control. For him, such methods probably suggested paternalism rather than outright imperialism. Yet for many Latin Americans the prospect of domination—political, commercial, and cultural—seemed threateningly real. Among intellectuals especially, suspicion of the United States ran deep and appeared in expressions of

Yankeephobia. In 1900, for example, José Enrique Rodó, a Uruguayan, published *Ariel*, a book in which he defended Latin American spirituality against North American materialism, for him a prime distinction between the two cultures. In 1904, similarly, Rubén Darío, a Nicaraguan, incorporated anti-imperial themes into his poem "To Roosevelt," which represented the president as a symbol of arrogant condescension toward Latin America.[52]

Although historians generally have depicted negative reactions to Roosevelt among Latin Americans, Frederick W. Marks III has argued to the contrary that "American prestige south of the border was exceptionally high under Roosevelt." If correct, this assessment probably pertains to ruling elites who appreciated the U.S. president's techniques as a defense against forcible European debt collections. But Latin American resentment of U.S. intervention appeared at a succession of Pan American conferences: at Mexico City in 1901, Rio de Janeiro in 1906, and Buenos Aires in 1910. Even though these were mainly ceremonial occasions to celebrate appearances of hemispheric unity, the rituals could not disguise the differences. The Argentines especially pressed for formal endorsements of the Calvo and Drago doctrines, both favorite projects. Carlos Calvo, an Argentine expert on international law, upheld the inviolability of national sovereignty, opposed the Roosevelt corollary, and insisted on the principle of nonintervention on grounds that no state should intervene in the affairs of another for any reason. Luis María Drago, an Argentine diplomat, similarly argued against the use of force in collecting international debts.[53]

Roosevelt's handpicked successor, William Howard Taft, shifted the bases of policy somewhat during his single term in the White House. He too ascribed importance to the Caribbean region but for different reasons. A lawyer by training, Taft had scant understanding of Roosevelt's power politics and grand strategy. He thought of diplomacy as an extension of the law. Arbitration treaties impressed him as a means of maintaining peace. He also defined diplomatic aims in more explicitly economic terms. Much like other contemporaries, he accepted overproduction and underconsumption as explanations for economic instability and regarded economic expansion into Asia and Latin America as an appropriate response.

For such reasons, the Taft administration encouraged innovation. Secretary of state Philander C. Knox tried to court Latin Americans as prospective customers, even though he disliked them on racial grounds. He also experimented with more effective forms of bureaucratic organization. During his tenure, State Department specialization brought into existence the Division of Latin American Affairs. This change created some measure of professionalization, although political patronage remained the principal means of filling diplomatic appointments until the 1920s. Similarly, the creation of the Bureau of Foreign and Domestic Commerce within the Commerce Department in 1912 aimed at the promotion of trade.[54]

In Latin America the Taft administration employed the techniques of "dollar diplomacy," modeled on what the leaders regarded as a successful experience in the Dominican Republic. Much like Roosevelt, Taft and Knox worried about disorder in the Caribbean and tried to mitigate bad effects through the application of expert administration. When troubles occurred, they put U.S. officials in charge of running the customs houses, seeking honesty, efficiency, solvency, and reform. Moreover, they encouraged private loans from U.S. banks as supplemental revenues. Through the application of dollar diplomacy, defined as the substitution of dollars for bullets, they sought incentives for responsible behavior, attempting to move Latin Americans into modern times.[55]

Aided by the advantage of hindsight, historians have assessed such policies as failures. Efforts to apply them in the Dominican Republic, Nicaragua, Honduras, and Guatemala encountered ornate complexities, almost never susceptible to easy solution. As U.S. experts discovered, the causes of instability and turmoil were more difficult to address than anticipated. Indeed, the effects of economic expansion often compounded those conditions by destabilizing other kinds of customary relationships.[56] In traditional societies all over the world, capitalist infusions showed remarkable capacity to precipitate dramatic change sometimes tending toward revolution. Moreover, displays of U.S. paternalistic condescension had the counterproductive consequence of arousing nationalist responses. Latin Americans disliked efforts "to make them over in the North American image."[57]

As a result of the New Diplomacy, the United States created protectorates, practiced intervention in the Caribbean region, and established, if not an empire, something very much like one. Within this sphere of influence, successive administrations affirmed a need for stability and invoked the authority of a self-proclaimed international police power based on the assumption that the United States was the racial, political, and cultural superior of the poor republics to its south. This practice, a form of hegemony, required the subordination of Latin American sensibilities to U.S. preferences, sometimes justified on grounds of serving lesser peoples. U.S. policies aimed at peace, order, and predictability but could not sustain such conditions. During the second decade of the twentieth century, the violent disorder of revolution and war assailed U.S. interests all around the world.

NOTES

1. A. Curtis Wilgus, "James G. Blaine and the Pan American Movement," *Hispanic American Historical Review* 5 (November 1922): 695–97.

2. Homer E. Socolofsky and Allan B. Spetter, *The Presidency of Benjamin Harrison* (Lawrence: University Press of Kansas, 1987), chap. 7; Clifford B. Casey, "The Creation and Development of the Pan American Union," *Hispanic American Historical Review* 13 (November 1933): 437–56.

3. Socolofsky and Spetter, *Presidency of Benjamin Harrison,* 112; Robert L. Beisner, *From the Old Diplomacy to the New, 1865–1900,* 2d ed. (Arlington Heights, IL: Harlan Davidson, 1986), 2, 34; David M. Pletcher, *The Diplomacy of Trade and Investment: American Economic Expansion in the Hemisphere, 1865–1900* (Columbia: University of Missouri Press, 1998), chap. 8.

4. John K. Thornton, *A Cultural History of the Atlantic World, 1250–1820* (Cambridge: Cambridge University Press, 2012); Kris E. Lane, *Pillaging the Empire: Piracy in the Americas, 1500–1750* (Armonk, NY: M.E. Sharpe, 1998).

5. John J. Johnson, *A Hemisphere Apart: The Foundations of United States Policy toward Latin America* (Baltimore: Johns Hopkins University Press, 1990), 80–81.

6. Johnson, *Hemisphere Apart,* 83, 85; Brenda Gayle Plummer, *Haiti and the United States: The Psychological Moment* (Athens: University of Georgia Press, 1992), chaps. 1–3.

7. James W. Gantenbein, ed., *The Evolution of Our Latin-American Policy: A Documentary Record* (New York: Octagon Books, 1971), 323–25; Dexter Perkins, *A History of the Monroe Doctrine* (1941; reprinted, Boston: Little, Brown, 1963).

8. Johnson, *Hemisphere Apart,* 86; Walter LaFeber, *The American Age: United States Foreign Policy at Home and Abroad since 1750* (New York: W. W. Norton, 1989), 81, 85.

9. LaFeber, *American Age,* chaps. 3–5.

10. Walter LaFeber, *The New Empire: An Interpretation of American Expansion, 1860–1898* (Ithaca, NY: Cornell University Press, 1963), 61.

11. LaFeber, *New Empire,* chaps. 1, 4; LaFeber, *American Age,* chap. 6; Charles S. Campbell, *The Transformation of American Foreign Relations* (New York: Harper & Row, 1976).

12. Beisner, *From the Old Diplomacy to the New,* 19, 21, 24; David M. Pletcher, *The Awkward Years: American Foreign Relations under Garfield and Arthur* (Columbia: University of Missouri Press, 1962). In *Diplomacy of Trade and Investment,* Pletcher also warns against overstating the coherency of U.S. goals and methods. For a commentary, see James A. Field Jr., "American Imperialism: The Worst Chapter in Almost Any Book," *American Historical Review* 83 (June 1978): 644–83.

13. Michael H. Hunt, *Ideology and U.S. Foreign Policy* (New Haven: Yale University Press, 1987), 18, 58–68; Emily S. Rosenberg, *Spreading the American Dream: American Economic and Cultural Expansion, 1890–1945* (New York: Hill and Wang, 1982); Lars Schoultz, *Beneath the United States: A History of U.S. Policy toward Latin America* (Cambridge, MA: Harvard University Press, 1998).

14. Greg Grandin, *Empire's Workshop: Latin America, the United States, and the Rise of New Imperialism* (New York: Metropolitan Books, 2006); Kristin L. Hoganson, *Fighting for American Manhood: How Gender Politics Provoked the Spanish-American and Philippine-American Wars* (New Haven: Yale University Press, 2000).

15. Beisner, *From the Old Diplomacy to the New,* 74, 77–8; Richard Hofstadter, "Cuba, the Philippines, and Manifest Destiny," in *The Paranoid Style in American Politics and Other Essays,* ed. Richard Hofstadter (New York: Vintage Books, 1967), 145–87.

16. Thomas J. McCormick, *China Market: America's Quest for Informal Empire, 1893–1901* (Chicago: Quadrangle Books, 1967).

17. V. G. Kiernan, *America: The New Imperialism, from White Settlement to World Hegemony* (London: Zed Press, 1978), 1, 120; William Appleman Williams, *The Tragedy of American Diplomacy,* rev. ed. (New York: Delta, 1962), chap. 1.

18. David Bushnell, *Simón Bolívar: Liberation and Disappointment* (New York: Pearson Longman, 2004).

19. Wilgus, "Blaine and the Pan American Movement," 662–67; Graham H. Stuart and James L. Tigner, *Latin America and the United States,* 6th ed. (Englewood Cliffs, NJ: Prentice-Hall, 1975), chap. 2.

20. Russell H. Bastert, "A New Approach to the Origins of Blaine's Pan American Policy," *Hispanic American Historical Review* 39 (May 1959): 375–412; Socolofsky and Spetter, *Presidency of Benjamin Harrison,* chaps. 7–8.

21. William F. Sater, *Chile and the United States: Empires in Conflict* (Athens: University of Georgia Press, 1990), chap. 3; Thomas F. McGann, *Argentina, the United States and the Inter-American System, 1889–1914* (Cambridge, MA: Harvard University Press, 1961), chaps.

1–2; J. Lloyd Mecham, *The United States and Inter-American Security, 1889–1960* (Austin: University of Texas Press, 1967), chap. 3; Joseph S. Tulchin, *Argentina and the United States: A Conflicted Relationship* (Boston: Twayne, 1990), chap. 2.

22. Socolofsky and Spetter, *Presidency of Benjamin Harrison,* 119; LaFeber, *New Empire,* 119.

23. Socolofsky and Spetter, *Presidency of Benjamin Harrison,* chap. 8; William F. Sater, *Chile and the War of the Pacific* (Lincoln: University of Nebraska Press, 1986); Sater, *Chile and the United States,* chap. 3.

24. Joyce S. Goldberg, *The "Baltimore" Affair* (Lincoln: University of Nebraska Press, 1986), ix–x.

25. Gantenbein, *Evolution of Our Latin-American Policy,* 348, 355–58; Richard E. Welch, Jr., *The Presidencies of Grover Cleveland* (Lawrence: University Press of Kansas, 1988), 157, 182–89; Bradford Perkins, *The Great Rapprochement: England and the United States, 1895–1914* (New York: Atheneum, 1968), chaps. 7–8.

26. Louis A. Pérez, *Cuba and the United States: Ties of Singular Intimacy* (Athens: University of Georgia Press, 1990), chap. 3.

27. John L. Offner, *An Unwanted War: The Diplomacy of the United States and Spain over Cuba, 1895–1898* (Chapel Hill: University of North Carolina Press, 1992), 4, chap. 2; Louis L. Gould, *The Presidency of William McKinley* (Lawrence: University Press of Kansas, 1980), 62–63; Pérez, *Cuba and the United States,* 83–84; Welch, *Presidencies of Grover Cleveland,* 194–95.

28. Thomas A. Bailey, *A Diplomatic History of the American People,* 9th ed. (Englewood Cliffs, NJ: Prentice-Hall, 1974), 460; Joseph A. Fry, "William McKinley and the Coming of the Spanish-American War: A Study of the Besmirching and Redemption of an Historical Image," *Diplomatic History* 3 (Winter 1979): 77–98.

29. LaFeber, *New Empire,* 400.

30. Gould, *Presidency of William McKinley,* viii, 59–60; H. Wayne Morgan, *America's Road to Empire: The War with Spain and Overseas Expansion* (New York: John Wiley & Sons, 1965); David F. Trask, *The War with Spain in 1898* (New York: Macmillan, 1981).

31. Gould, *Presidency of William McKinley,* vii–viii, 64–70; Offner, *Unwanted War,* chaps. 3, 4.

32. Offner, *Unwanted War,* chap. 7.

33. Gould, *Presidency of William McKinley,* 79–90; Offner, *Unwanted War,* 174–82, 225; Gantenbein, *Evolution of Our Latin-American Policy,* 465–78.

34. Pérez, *Cuba and the United States,* 94, 96; Gantenbein, *Evolution of Our Latin-American Policy,* 426.

35. Gould, *Presidency of William McKinley,* 88.

36. Gould, *Presidency of William McKinley,* 96; Trask, *War with Spain,* the most thorough military account.

37. Frank Freidel, *The Splendid Little War* (New York: Dell, 1958).

38. John Dobson, *Reticent Expansionism: The Foreign Policy of William McKinley* (Pittsburgh: Duquesne University Press, 1988), 15–16; Robert L. Beisner, *Twelve Against Empire: The Anti-Imperialists, 1898–1900* (1968; reprinted, New York: McGraw-Hill, 1971).

39. Paul A. Kramer, *The Blood of Government: Race, Empire, the United States, and the Philippines* (Chapel Hill: University of North Carolina Press, 2006).

40. Pérez, *Cuba and the United States,* 102–13.

41. Lewis L. Gould, *The Presidency of Theodore Roosevelt* (Lawrence: University Press of Kansas, 1991), 14; Richard Hofstadter, *The American Political Tradition* (New York: Alfred A. Knopf, 1948), 228.

42. Gould, *Presidency of Theodore Roosevelt,* 14; Frederick W. Marks III, *Velvet on Iron: The Diplomacy of Theodore Roosevelt* (Lincoln: University of Nebraska Press, 1979); Richard H. Collin, *Theodore Roosevelt, Culture, Diplomacy, and Expansion: A New View of American Imperialism* (Baton Rouge: Louisiana State University Press, 1985); Collin, *Theodore Roosevelt's Caribbean: The Panama Canal, the Monroe Doctrine, and the Latin American Context* (Baton Rouge: Louisiana State University Press, 1990).

43. Collin, *Roosevelt's Caribbean*, xiii–xiv; Collin, *Roosevelt, Culture, Diplomacy, and Expansion.*

44. LaFeber, *American Age*, 221, 244.

45. Gould, *Presidency of Theodore Roosevelt*, 77–78; Marks, *Velvet on Iron*, chap. 2.

46. Walter LaFeber, *The Panama Canal: The Crisis* in *Historical Perspective*, rev. ed. (New York: Oxford University Press, 1979), 3, 8–9, 17; David G. McCullough, *The Path Between the Seas: The Creation of the Panama Canal, 1870–1914* (New York: Simon and Schuster, 1977); Collin, *Roosevelt's Caribbean*, pt. 2; Ronald H. Spector, *Professors of War: The Naval War College and the Development of the Naval Profession* (Newport, RI: Naval War College Press, 1977).

47. Collin, *Roosevelt's Caribbean*, 167, 169, 242–43; Gould, *Presidency of Theodore Roosevelt*, chap. 7.

48. Collin, *Roosevelt's Caribbean*, 239, 281; Gould, *Presidency of Theodore Roosevelt*, 97; Richard L. Lael, *Arrogant Diplomacy: U.S. Policy toward Colombia, 1903–1922* (Wilmington, DE: Scholarly Resources, 1987), chaps. 4–6; Stephen J. Randall, *Colombia and the United States: Hegemony and Interdependence* (Athens: University of Georgia Press, 1992), chap. 7.

49. LaFeber, *The Panama Canal*, 38; Lael, *Arrogant Diplomacy*, chap. 6, epilogue; Randall, *Colombia and the United States*, chap. 3; Gantenbein, *Evolution of Our Latin-American Policy*, 361–62; Gould, *Presidency of Theodore Roosevelt*, 175.

50. Gould, *Presidency of Theodore Roosevelt*, 176; Collin, *Roosevelt's Caribbean*, chap. 17; Lester D. Langley, *The Banana Wars: An Inner History of American Empire, 1900–1934* (Lexington: University Press of Kentucky, 1983), chaps. 3–4.

51. Pérez, *Cuba and the United States*, 155.

52. Collin, *Roosevelt's Caribbean*, 26–33; Charles A. Hale, "Political and Social Ideas in Latin America, 1870–1930," in *The Cambridge History of Latin America*, vol. 4, c. *1870–1930*, ed. Leslie Bethell (New York: Cambridge University Press, 1986); Gerald Martin, "The Literature, Music, and Art of Latin America, 1870–1930," in *The Cambridge History of Latin America*, vol. 4, c. *1870–1930*, ed. Leslie Bethell (New York: Cambridge University Press, 1986), 414–17, 460–62.

53. Marks, *Velvet on Iron*, 180; Stuart and Tigner, *Latin America and the United States*, chap. 2; Mecham, *United States and Inter-American Security*, chap. 3.

54. Walter V. Scholes and Marie V. Scholes, *The Foreign Policies of the Taft Administration* (Columbia: University of Missouri Press, 1970).

55. Scoles and Scoles, *Foreign Policies of the Taft Administration*, 35–39; Dana G. Munro, *Intervention and Dollar Diplomacy in the Caribbean, 1900–1921* (Princeton: Princeton University Press, 1964); David Healy, *Drive to Hegemony: The United States in the Caribbean, 1898–1917* (Madison: University of Wisconsin Press, 1988).

56. Scholes and Scholes, *Foreign Policies of the Taft Administration*, 105–6; Paolo E. Coletta, *The Presidency of William Howard Taft* (Lawrence: University Press of Kansas, 1973), 190–91.

57. Walter LaFeber, *The American Search for Opportunity, 1865–1913*, vol. 2 in *The Cambridge History of American Foreign Relations* (New York: Cambridge University Press, 1993), preface.

Chapter Two

Revolution, War, and Expansion, 1913–1929

The political and later social revolution against Porfirio Díaz in Mexico signaled the onset of a tumultuous age. During the second decade of the twentieth century, great revolutions in Mexico, China, and Russia overturned established orders, the consequences of which paralleled those of the First World War. In each instance the effects challenged prevailing beliefs and institutions. In response, president Woodrow Wilson articulated an ambitious vision of a new world system, the workability of which entailed two stipulations: The Great Powers must cooperate in defense of stability and peace, and the United States should accept a larger role in international affairs than ever before. For Latin America, meanwhile, an assortment of significant changes altered traditional relations with the outside world. As a consequence of the Great War the United States displaced the European powers as the dominant economic presence. Seeking to consolidate the advantage in the 1920s, Republican administrations under presidents Warren Harding, Calvin Coolidge, and Herbert Hoover experimented with new stratagems in Latin America, anticipating a shift away from interventionist methods and toward the more subtle techniques of the Good Neighbor policy.

LATIN AMERICA AND THE OUTSIDE WORLD

For fifty years after independence in the 1820s, Latin American countries failed to count for much in the international arena. Largely self-contained and self-absorbed, they experienced the disorganizing effects of political turmoil, economic stagnation, and complex diplomatic quarrels over boundaries and territories. Despite being the largest regional bloc of republican governments in the world, the complex legacies of the wars for independence and dependence on primary exports created paralyzing obstacles. These pervasive conditions were exacerbated by civil wars that pitted outward-looking liberals against conservatives who preferred the preservation of colonial institutions in the name of social stability. These visceral differences—often centered on whether or not to preserve the enormous power of the Catholic Church—provided fodder for U.S. observers to characterize Latin Americans as a race incapable of stable self-government. [1]

Such conditions became less pervasive during the latter third of the nineteenth century, following the establishment of more stable, oligarchical, and usually authoritarian regimes in many countries. During the 1870s and after, such governments endorsed an export-led model of economic development. Seeking trade and investment, government leaders opened their countries to foreign goods and capital and embraced the Europeans in a kind of a neocolonial economic relationship. Unlike the colonized regions of Asia and Africa, Latin America required no formal devices of imperial subjugation. Instead, an informal system came into existence, characterized by specialization of functions. Performing much like colonials, Latin Americans produced raw materials and agricultural commodities for the industrializing Europeans in return for capital and finished goods, thereby experiencing integration into the world market system. [2]

Among the largest countries, Argentina featured livestock and cereal products for export, especially wheat, maize, frozen and chilled beef, wool, hides, and linseed. Between 1875 and 1914, Argentine exports expanded impressively at an estimated rate of 5 percent per year. By 1914 the 7.8 million Argentines relied more heavily on overseas sales than any other group of Latin Americans and enjoyed the highest living standards. Their capital, Buenos Aires, stood out as a testimony. Affluent, cosmopolitan, and European in style and taste, the city symbolized Argentina as the embodiment of wealth, culture, and promise for the future.

Exports similarly served Brazil. A functioning monarchy until 1889–1890, then a republic after a virtually bloodless revolution, Brazil relied upon coffee as the mainstay of profit. In the years before the First World War, coffee often accounted for more than half of its overseas sales and made the economy vulnerable to cyclical tendencies within the world market. Periodic, often abrupt contractions in demand led to oversupply and low prices. In response, Brazilians experimented with "valorization" plans to restore higher prices by holding coffee off the market. Brazil, a nation of twenty-five million people in 1914, also sold tobacco and cotton in foreign markets and for a time experienced a rubber boom in the Amazon. Overall, the export trade affected different parts of this vast country unevenly, most of the benefits accruing to the coastal regions and the capital city, Rio de Janeiro.

Chile, inhabited by three million people in 1914, relied on copper exports. At the same time, the country avoided some of the dangers of monoculture—undue dependence on one product—by promoting the sale of wheat, wool, and nitrates. The last, especially important in balancing shifting demands for copper, counted heavily in trade with Europe and the United States. During the early twentieth century the proceeds from nitrate sales totaled around 14 percent of the gross national product and provided the central government in Santiago with more than 50 percent of its operating revenues.[3]

In Mexico too, a country of twelve million people in 1910, economic dependencies characterized the links with the outside world. During the so-called Porfiriato, the era dominated by president José de la Cruz Porfirio Díaz from 1876 to 1910, foreign investments centered on such crucial sectors as transportation, mining, and petroleum. Meanwhile, growth patterns typified Mexican overseas sales of silver, gold, rubber, hides, coffee, minerals, cattle, vegetables, and petroleum. The oil industry, controlled by British and U.S. companies, assumed special significance during the first decade of the twentieth century. In Mexico as elsewhere, bad effects occurred when declining demand within the world economy reduced export prices and income from exports.[4]

In the other countries of Central and South America, export economics typically featured monocultures. Colombia depended upon coffee, as did Venezuela until the petroleum boom beginning in the 1920s. In Central America and the Caribbean the pursuit of tropical agriculture produced bananas, coffee, sugar, and tobacco. Everywhere in Latin America the export trade rendered the participants susceptible to downward shifts in demand and price, underscoring unmistakably the risks of involvement in an unstable international economic environment.[5]

Financial relations, another form of dependency, also entailed a mixture of advantages and risks. In the view of many historians, "the era of high capitalism" before the First World War constituted "a golden age for foreign investment in Latin America." Great Britain was the largest investor, followed by Germany and France. Until the 1890s, small-scale U.S. investments centered on railroads and mines in Mexico, sugar plantations in Cuba, and a few railroads and landed estates in Central America. During the early years of the twentieth century, U.S. investors also acquired a stake in Chilean and Peruvian mining. By 1914 some 87 percent of the direct, U.S. overseas investments were concentrated in Mexico, Cuba, Chile, and Peru. From around $300 million in 1897 the total increased to almost $1.6 billion in 1914, including direct investments of nearly $1.3 billion.

European investments, estimated at $7 billion in 1914, differed in some respects. More dispersed, they affected every country. In addition, a larger portion appeared in the construction of infrastructure, such as railways, ports, power companies, and utilities. Also, about a third went into government bonds. British investments of nearly $5 billion touched every country but had the greatest significance in Argentina, where they amounted to a third of the total foreign investments; in Brazil, they accounted for about a quarter; in Mexico, about a fifth. French and German investors favored the same three countries. These estimates suggest orders of magnitude and degrees of integration into the world system. The transfer of investment capital into regions without financial resources advanced the European interest in gaining access to Latin American markets and raw materials. The process also enabled Latin Americans to respond to overseas demands with the construction of necessary facilities—railroads, shipping services, and communication systems—without which Latin American producers could not have supplied the consumers. Consequently, more efficient, modern technologies came into existence in the export sectors, including mining, ranching, farming, and milling, and also complex networks of economic dependency. Throughout Latin America, foreign-owned mercantile houses were crucial in organizing the export and import trade, and foreign-owned banks provided the financial means.[6]

Some modern scholars—especially proponents of dependency theory—depict these arrangements as economically debilitating, more attuned to foreign needs than to Latin American interests, and actually a form of exploitation. Not all contemporaries would have agreed with this assessment. According to the historian William Glade, most members of the Latin American elites at the end of the nineteenth century exhibited enthusiasm for "the benefits of what they perceived to be modernization" through engagement with the world economy.[7] This participation in the global economy as producers of primary goods, such as coffee, sugar, and bananas, clearly benefited those who controlled the levers of economic and political power. But as the historian E. Bradford Burns has argued, the economic policies favored by the elite negatively affected the lives of the vast majority of Latin Americans. In most instances, life was worse than it was at the close of the eighteenth century.[8] The general appropriation of the ideas behind revolutionary leaders erected barriers to safeguard against the influence of foreign economic powers.

MEXICO AND OTHER MATTERS

The role of foreign interests in Mexico assumed critical importance during the revolutionary era. According to one view, the integration of Mexico into the world economy contributed to political destabilization in 1910 by making the country more vulnerable to cyclical tendencies and economic downturns.[9] The revolution, sometimes understood in present-day historiography more as a struggle among rival elites than as a popular uprising, successfully ousted the dictator, Porfirio Díaz, in 1911 and then assumed many implications. During the ensuing factional strife, foreign interests, economic and other, came under threat both from the ongoing violence and the processes of reconstruction. The constitution of 1917 specifically introduced new dangers by incorporating the principles of nationalization and expropriation, thereby providing Mexican leaders with new instruments of control over the resources of their nation.[10]

Based on a political call for legitimate elections and no boss rule, the revolt against Porfirio Díaz in 1910 mobilized a broad but unstable constituency, incapable subsequently of sustaining president Francisco I. Madero's reformist regime. A series of uprisings culminated in a military takeover on February 19, 1913, in the course of which Madero was assassinated with the connivance of the U.S. ambassador Henry Lane Wilson. General Victoriano Huerta, the army chief of staff and a principal instigator, then sought to impose order by authoritarian means and provoked an insurrection among dissidents in the northern states. Led by Venustiano Carranza, the governor of Coahuila, the so-called Constitutionalists denounced Huerta as a usurper and demanded his removal from power.[11]

Shocked by such events, Woodrow Wilson, the new president of the United States, reacted with committed determination. A former university professor with a PhD in political science, Wilson had served as the president of Princeton University and also as a one-term, reform-minded governor in New Jersey. As a scholar and a devout Presbyterian—indeed, the son of a clergyman—Wilson preferred the high moral ground, prized the constraints of constitutional provision, and regarded Huerta's seizure of power as illegitimate and unacceptable. Unlike the leaders of Great Britain and the other European powers, Wilson withheld diplomatic recognition from Huerta's regime and tried to encourage mediation as the means to establish a legal government.[12] He insisted Huerta stand aside. Huerta's refusal led to a U.S. military intervention on April 21, 1914.

Meanwhile, secretary of state William Jennings Bryan, a Democrat from Nebraska and a three-time failure as a presidential candidate, launched his own initiatives. Though lacking experience in foreign affairs, Bryan had high ambitions, some of them a bit unconventional. As a peace advocate, he urged the negotiation of "cooling off" treaties with every country in the world. These conciliation agreements required a nonpartisan investigation into the causes of a dispute before a resort to war. Latin American governments consented, except Mexico, still unrecognized under Huerta, and Colombia, still aggrieved over Panama. Bryan also envisioned a reduction of Latin American financial dependence on European bankers. He reasoned that cheap loans from the U.S. government would permit "our country" to acquire "such an increased influence . . . that we could prevent revolutions, promote education, and advance stable and just governments."[13] Bryan's projects stirred some interest within the administration but Wilson, unpersuaded, preferred to rely on conventional means and private bankers.

Another pressing concern for the new administration was the practice of unilateral intervention by the United States in Latin America. A variety of critics denounced the exercise of an international police power. Some lambasted Roosevelt's corollary as a hegemonic pretension, an inversion of the Monroe Doctrine's original intent to safeguard the Western Hemisphere against outside intervention. Others wanted to apply a multilateral definition so that joint measures with other nations could, if necessary, provide the means of safeguarding peace and order. A leader among them, professor Hiram Bingham of Yale University, the discoverer of the Inca ruins at Machu Picchu in Peru, described the Monroe Doctrine as "an obsolete shibboleth." For him, it typified paternalistic condescension toward Latin Americans. As a better approach, he proposed some kind of collective action. In the event of trouble, the United States should call together "a family gathering" among the Western Hemisphere nations and "see what if anything needs to be done."[14]

Such advocacy won support from Progressive era reformers and radicals, including leaders in the peace movement, the labor unions, the churches, the universities, and the guild of international lawyers. For many, the development of a collective security system ranked high as a guarantee of national sovereignty. Similarly, Woodrow Wilson, a committed reformer with messianic instincts, favored exalted purposes among nations, seeking to advance mutual interests. Sometimes described as "a liberal-capitalist internationalist," Wilson aspired to the creation of a world system based on a League of Nations to defend representative democracy and economic capitalism. Presuming universal applicability, Wilson intended to serve humankind by extending U.S. values and models throughout the world.[15]

Sometimes flawed by arrogance and delusion, Wilson's emerging vision of international order drew inspiration from experiences with Latin America. On March 11, 1913, his first statement on foreign affairs set forth basic principles and expectations, central among them his belief in international harmony achieved through mutual respect for rights and obligations. To such ends, he invited "the friendship and . . . the confidence of our sister republics" and "the most cordial understanding and cooperation" in relations with them. With General Huerta presumably in mind, Wilson also insisted upon the rule of law. Accordingly, he opposed "those who seek to seize the power of government to advance their own personal interests or ambition" and favored "those who act in the interest of peace and honor, who protect private rights, and respect the restraint of constitutional provision."

In Mexico, Wilson's positions resulted in confusion and contradiction. On October 10, 1913, Huerta dashed the U.S. hope for mediation by dissolving the Chamber of Deputies and declaring himself a candidate for the presidency. On the following day, Sir Lionel Carden, the new British minister, presented his credentials in Mexico City. His arrival impressed U.S. leaders as a deliberate British affront; to them, Huerta now appeared as both an illicit tyrant and a creature of British imperialism.

Wilson discussed this issue on October 27, 1913, in his celebrated address before the Southern Commercial Congress at Mobile, Alabama. Stating his concern over European economic domination in Latin America, he warned that foreign concessions and special privileges threatened self-determination; Mexico, in his view, already had fallen victim. Nevertheless, Wilson promised "emancipation" if Latin Americans would assist in the promotion of "true constitutional liberty" throughout the world. As a pledge of good faith, he affirmed, the United States "never again" would seek "one additional foot of territory by conquest."

Sometimes regarded as a promise of nonintervention, the Mobile address actually anticipated broader involvement in Latin American affairs. In what verged on a declaration of economic war, Wilson wanted Latin American support in rolling back European presences. Colonel Edward M. House, a trusted friend and adviser, understood the intent. For him, Wilson's speech established "a new interpretation of the Monroe Doctrine": For almost a century the United States had tried "to keep Europe from securing political control of any state in the Western Hemisphere"; now, the Wilson administration had taken a position that it is "just as reprehensible to permit foreign states to secure financial control of those weak unfortunate republics." Similarly, John Lind, a special diplomatic emissary to Mexico, expressed his belief that Huerta's continuation in power would make the country "a European annex, industrially, financially, politically."

Mounting suspicions had the effect of producing a chill in U.S. relations with Great Britain. Although British leaders disparaged Wilson's claim as a consequence of bewildered hypocrisy, historian Friedrich Katz credits the president with a correct understanding of British aims. As Katz shows, the British government consistently opposed revolutionary factions and supported counterrevolutionary groups. Such position, in his view, accurately reflected British concerns for economic stakes and petroleum interests.[16]

The Wilson administration, meanwhile, adopted other ambitious plans. To advance various forms of political and economic integration, the leaders focused attention on Argentina, Brazil, and Chile. As the most populous and influential nations in South America, the so-called ABC countries also contained prospective customers. Close relations already existed in dealings with Brazil. As a matter of conscious design, Brazilians had forged an "unwritten alliance" with the United States early in the twentieth century through the policies of foreign minister José María da Silva Paranhos, also known as the Baron de Rio Branco, who wanted to enlist the United States as a trading partner and a counterweight against Argentina. For the United States, Brazil's diplomatic status also ranked high. Before Wilson, only Brazil had qualified for an ambassadorial appointment; the other South American republics received ministers, a designation of lesser rank. Seeking more cordial ties during the summer of 1914, the Wilson administration established diplomatic parity by exchanging ambassadors also with Argentina and Chile. [17]

Troubled by trade deficits in South America, the Wilson administration also promoted commercial expansion. The Panama Canal, scheduled for completion soon, amplified high expectations. U.S. leaders intended to take advantage by renovating the merchant marine and developing regular steamship routes to South America. The Federal Reserve Act of December 1913 rectified another shortcoming by authorizing national banks of the United States to establish branches in foreign countries. The establishment in Latin America of such facilities would free U.S. commerce from dependencies on British banking institutions. [18] But then new difficulties with Mexico produced an obstruction.

An incident at Tampico, a Mexican port city on the Gulf of Mexico, set the trouble in motion. On April 9, 1914, General Huerta's troops arrested some U.S. sailors who had wandered into a restricted zone. In response, U.S. admiral Henry T. Mayo requested a formal apology. So did Woodrow Wilson. At the same time, another problem impended. The *Ypiranga,* a German commercial vessel carrying weapons for Huerta, soon would arrive at Veracruz, the principal eastern port. Abjuring diplomacy, Wilson obtained authorization from the Congress to force a showdown. On April 21, 1914, he seized Veracuz by sending in U.S. Marines. In this way, he intended to block the arms shipment, cut off customs revenues to Huerta, and avoid damaging the petroleum installations around Tampico. He erred by anticipating only light resistance: The Veracruz defenders lost over two hundred soldiers, and war threatened. Not only Huerta but also his enemies, the Constitutionalists, condemned the invasion as an unacceptable violation of Mexican sovereignty.

At the very least, the episode revealed limitations in Wilson's understanding of harmony among nations. Paradoxically, he conceived of the intervention as a defense of Mexican self-determination against an illegitimate tyranny backed by British imperialists, but in so doing he underestimated Mexican nationalist reactions. Fortunately, his courtship of Argentina, Brazil, and Chile paid off when their mediation offer enabled him to avoid an unwanted conflict. An international conference at Niagara Falls, Canada, facilitated face-saving devices, achieved cosmetic effects, and provided a way out of war. In Mexico, meanwhile, general Álvaro Obregón's Constitutionalist Army advanced on Mexico City during the summer of 1914 and forced General Huerta into exile. [19]

The leaders in the Wilson administration rejoiced that multilateral measures had assisted in keeping the peace. Colonel House indulged in high praise, comparing the actions of the ABC countries with the efforts of friends and neighbors who in times of crisis banded together to fight house fires. Similarly, Robert Lansing, the Counselor of the State Department, called for efforts to build on that achievement. In a June 1914 memorandum, "The Present Nature and Extent of the Monroe Doctrine and Its Need for Restatement," he presented a case against unilateral intervention by the United States and in favor of multilateral approaches to advance "fraternal responsibility" with Latin Americans.

Much like Bryan earlier, Lansing also worried about European encroachments in the Western Hemisphere by means of loans and investments. Specifically, he warned against the "European acquisition of political control through the agency of financial control over an American republic." Similarly concerned, Colonel House addressed this same issue during a European visit in July 1914. In conversations with British, French, and German leaders, House inquired whether they would join with the United States in an agreement to reduce the costs of international borrowing. In his private diary, however, House expressed misgivings, accusing the Europeans of subverting weak, debt-ridden Latin American states through demands for "concessions" and "usurious interest." He wanted to find a better way—but his timing was all wrong. During the summer of 1914 the Great Powers of Europe embarked upon world war. [20]

PAN AMERICAN INITIATIVES

The consequences of the Great War extended into all inhabited regions. In the Western Hemisphere the initial impact injured Latin American economies by obstructing the flow of capital and goods. In response, the United States assumed a larger role as the prime purchaser of raw materials and the main supplier of finished products. During the three years from July 1, 1914, to June 30, 1917, trade between the United States and Latin America increased by more than 100 percent. In contrast, ambitious U.S. political initiatives accomplished much less. For the Wilson administration, the war occasioned both opportunities and rebuffs.

Remaining neutral until the spring of 1917, the United States responded to the war by attempting to insulate the Western Hemisphere against it. As part of this endeavor, it also courted Latin American governments, seeking more intimate political and economic ties. The opening of the Panama Canal in August 1914 served as a powerful symbol. This grand event, knitting the Western Hemisphere more closely together, reduced the distance from Colón on the Atlantic to Balboa on the Pacific from 10,500 nautical miles, the distance around South America, to 45 nautical miles, the actual length of the new passage. The Western Hemisphere had become a smaller place. [21]

The prospect of commercial opportunity encouraged a variety of promotional activities sponsored by leaders in the Wilson administration. On September 10, 1914, a Latin American Trade Conference assembled in Washington, DC, at the behest of secretary of state William Jennings Bryan and secretary of commerce William C. Redfield. Delegates representing the U.S. Chamber of Commerce, the Southern Commercial Congress, and the National Foreign Trade Council enthusiastically called for improved transportation and banking facilities and also for more effective sales techniques, conforming more closely to Latin American tastes and preferences. Elsewhere across the United States the prospect of commercial expansion into Latin America stimulated similar growing interest among local chambers of commerce, boards of trade, and business associations. Even President Wilson became a booster. In his annual message to the Congress on December 8, 1914, he urged the United States "as never before, to serve itself and to serve mankind; ready with its resources, its forces of production, and its means of distribution."

Wilson also experimented with peacekeeping devices. Inspired mainly by Colonel House, these efforts eventuated in a proposed Pan American treaty that among other things called for a regional collective security system, featuring compulsory arbitration, and a multilateral definition of the Monroe Doctrine. House initiated the discussions late in November 1914 by urging Wilson to pay "greater attention" to issues in foreign affairs. Specifically, he wanted the president to devise "a constructive international policy" demonstrating "that friendship, justice, and kindliness were more potent than the mailed fist." House criticized the legacies of unilateral intervention. By "wielding the 'big stick' and dominating the two Continents," he averred, the United States had "lost the friendship and commerce of South and Central America and the European countries had profited by it." A better approach could have more desirable consequences by bringing "North and South America together in a closer union" and "welding together . . . the two western continents."

Three weeks later, in December 1914, House again raised the issue, this time exhorting Wilson "to play a great and beneficent part in the European tragedy." Declaring that "there was one thing [Wilson] could do at once," establish a "model" for peace based on "a policy that would weld the western hemisphere together," he sketched out a draft proposal for collective security arrangements to guarantee territorial integrity, political independence, and republican forms of government. Much impressed, Wilson authorized House to engage the ambassadors of Argentina, Brazil, and Chile in conversations.

The ensuing discussions elicited favorable responses from Rómulo S. Naón of Argentina and Domicio da Gama of Brazil but not from Eduardo Súarez Mújica, the Chilean ambassador. For him, the implementation of such arrangements suggested the possibility of embarrassment over Tacna and

Arica, the nitrate-rich provinces taken from Peru in the War of the Pacific. According to the Treaty of Ancón in 1884, a plebiscite should decide the question of ownership of these regions, but none ever had taken place. Chileans also described the proposed commitment in defense of republican institutions as a limitation on national sovereignty and possibly an invitation for U.S. intervention. Undeterred, House pressed on, including in later drafts other requirements for arbitration of territorial and boundary disputes and endorsing Bryan's "cooling off" formula.[22]

Meanwhile, a new civil war was ravaging Mexico. After defeating Huerta the victorious Constitutionalist coalition dissolved into feuding factions, pitting Carranza and his ally Obregón against Francisco (Pancho) Villa and Emiliano Zapata. Wilson again sought peace through reconciliation but without much positive effect. House espoused joint action with the ABC countries as the best means of solution. He also rejoiced when Secretary of State Bryan resigned his position in June 1915 as a protest over the handling of the *Lusitania* crisis. In House's view, Bryan was a fool and a bungler who had obstructed the pursuit of wise and workable policies, whereas his successor, Robert Lansing, the former State Department counselor, shared some of House's convictions and appeared more manageable. Lansing too believed that Germans were "utterly hostile to all nations with democratic institutions" and were hatching plots in Mexico, Haiti, Santo Domingo, and "probably in other Latin American republics." As a counter, he favored "a Pan American doctrine" and the maintenance of "friendly relations with Mexico." In his view, the latter required the diplomatic recognition of Carranza, now regarded as "the stronger."

Beginning in August 1915, Secretary of State Lansing orchestrated moves in conjunction with six countries. Together with representatives from Argentina, Brazil, Chile, Bolivia, Guatemala, and Uruguay, Lansing exhorted the contending Mexican factions to settle their differences. In response, Villa and Zapata took conciliatory positions, supposedly ready for a compromise. But Carranza, an intransigent, would not bend; he insisted that only his government possessed the attributes of sovereignty. Ultimately, Lansing and the other diplomats arrived at the same conclusion. On October 9, 1915, they extended diplomatic recognition on a de facto basis, accepting the existence of Carranza's regime as stable and functioning.

Wilson construed the decision as a triumph for his adherence to high principle. For him, Mexico's right to self-determination had survived the test; in a report to the Congress on December 7, 1915, he claimed, "Her fortunes are in her own hands." He also applauded the good effects of his Pan American policy, choosing to interpret the outcome as a vindication of international cooperation, "a full and honorable association as of partners." To build on this achievement, he publicly endorsed the proposed Pan American Treaty on January 6, 1916, at the Second Pan American Scientific Conference in Washington, DC. By such means, he asserted, the nations of the Western Hemisphere could uphold "the principles of absolute political equality among the states" and "the solid, eternal foundations of justice and humanity."[23]

This pledge notwithstanding, Wilson's policies in the Western Hemisphere never really achieved much coherence. Instead, they manifested inconsistencies and contradictions, as subsequent interventions in Caribbean countries confirmed. In a phrase, Wilson had extreme difficulty reconciling his presumed commitment to self-determination with other U.S. interests in upholding peace, order, and security. In 1915, political turmoil caused violence and disorder in Haiti. Similarly in 1916, instabilities threatened the Dominican Republic. In each instance, the Wilson administration responded by sending in military forces. U.S. leaders justified such measures on grounds of wartime exigency, claiming that threats of German subversion and defense of the Panama Canal required them. In each instance, derogatory racial stereotypes and cultural assumptions provided additional incentives by disparaging the alleged inability of the inhabitants, especially those of African descent, to govern themselves. Once the marines had moved in, U.S. occupation authorities managed government functions and finances. In response, Dominican and Haitian resistance movements precipitated hard-fought guerrilla struggles. Called the "banana wars" by the historian Lester D. Langley, they featured small-scale but brutal violence in which native contingents waged something like "wars of national liberation" against the soldiers of the United States.[24]

Meanwhile, the Wilson administration launched other kinds of programs to win over Latin Americans. On May 24, 1915, the first Pan American Financial Conference assembled in Washington, DC, featuring delegates in attendance from eighteen Latin American countries. The main organizer, secretary of the treasury William Gibbs McAdoo, intended to focus on trade and finance. Specifically, he called for consideration of the principal economic problems emanating from the Great War. McAdoo anticipated that the United States would have to step in, replacing the Europeans as the main supplier of goods and capital. To coordinate the pursuit of practical solutions, the conference brought into existence a body known as the International High Commission. It consisted of finance ministers and other specialists from each country who in future years would meet periodically to issue recommendations and advisements—most of which, as things turned out, eluded implementation.

For leaders in the Wilson administration, commercial statistics bolstered high spirits. Between August 1914 and August 1915, U.S. exports totaled $3 billion, at that time the largest amount ever in a single year. Indeed, the United States surpassed Great Britain as the world leader. In South America, U.S. exports rose from $38.7 million during the first six months of 1914 to

$60.6 billion during the first six months of 1915, while South American sales in the United States expanded from $105.5 to $153 million. Although these figures marked an undesirable deficit in the balance of payments, they failed to dissipate the optimism over long-term expectations: The National City Bank of New York created branches in Montevideo, Buenos Aires, Rio de Janeiro, Santos, São Paulo, and Havana; the Caribbean and Southern Steamship Company initiated regular voyages from the United States to Argentina and Brazil; and President Wilson accepted a commitment to build a modern merchant marine, fully capable of carrying increased trade.

Though encouraged by such gains in Latin America, U.S. leaders still worried about resumed European competition after the war. They expected that Great Britain and France especially would not submit readily to a permanently weakened economic position in the New World. Indeed, British and French behavior at the Paris Economic Conference in June 1916 intensified such concerns, when the Allies established plans to punish their enemies, mainly the Germans, through the adoption of a mercantilist, state-directed system. The main features included a variety of restrictive devices such as trade preferences, state subsidies, government protection of foreign markets, pooling agreements, and cooperative purchases of raw materials. In 1915 the Central Powers had devised their own *Mitteleuropa* plan, intended to promote economic consolidation through the exclusion of the British, the French, and the Russians. To officials in the Wilson administration, all this portended ill, and they anticipated the possibility of drastic measures. Secretary of State Lansing, for example, reasoned that "the best way to fight combination is by combination." He wanted "some definite plan to meet the proposed measures of the allies" in conjunction with Latin Americans. Similarly, Henry P. Fletcher, then U.S. ambassador to Chile and later to Mexico, advised collective arrangements with the ABC countries to hold "our market position in South America." Somewhat fantastically, he also suggested the establishment of "an American Economic League for mutual protection."[25]

Meanwhile, mounting political difficulties destroyed the negotiations over Wilson's proposed Pan American treaty. At first, Chilean opposition accounted for delays. Later, the U.S. punitive expedition into Mexico in 1916 ruined the plan completely by calling Woodrow Wilson's good faith into question. Pancho Villa precipitated the crisis on March 9, 1916, by attacking the border town of Columbus, New Mexico, probably in an effort to demonstrate Carranza's incapacity to safeguard the international frontier. In response, the Wilson administration sent in military forces commanded by general John J. Pershing. By insisting upon a right of "hot pursuit," the president created an impasse. Carranza for his own political reasons could not sanction Pershing's presence and wanted him out of Mexico as soon as possible; Wilson insisted upon guarantees against future border violations. Subsequent armed clashes between Mexican and U.S. troops in the northern towns of Parral and Carrizal caused more trouble, even a likelihood of war. Argentina's offer of mediation presented the Wilson administration with a dilemma bearing directly on the president's credibility in the rest of Latin America. Robert Lansing understood the issue and dreaded the prospect of a full-scale intervention in Mexico. Any such action would have "a very bad effect on our Pan-American program"; indeed, "all Latin America" would regard it as "extremely distasteful." Yet border security also had importance, especially in 1916, a presidential election year. Even suggestions of weakness along the border could demolish Wilson as a viable candidate. [26]

Thus constrained by political imperatives, U.S. leaders spurned the Argentine offer and kept the punitive expedition in Mexico; at the same time, they sought direct negotiations. In this way, the Wilson administration retained a free hand but simultaneously wrecked the Pan American pact. During the summer and fall of 1916, while the United States maintained the pressure by refusing to withdraw and insisting upon Carranza's responsibility for border defense, a joint Mexican-American commission sought solutions. The United States also tried to broaden the scope by including discussions of foreign property rights in Mexico, an issue that assumed ever greater importance during the latter part of 1916 during the proceedings of the Mexican Constitutional Convention.

This assembly promulgated the Mexican constitution of 1917 on February 5 and sanctioned the inclusion of radical provisions. From the U.S. viewpoint, article 27 was an object of special concern: It allowed for the expropriation of privately owned property and for the nationalization of mineral resources. To Mexican leaders, these claims affirmed the prerogatives of national sovereignty and permitted no complaint from other countries through the agencies of international diplomacy. Among outraged U.S. critics, such expressions of hyperinflated nationalism aroused fears over the sanctity of foreign property rights in Mexico; U.S. property holders demanded protection from their government. Unable to reconcile competing interests, Wilson simply withdrew the punitive force on February 5, 1917—coincidentally the same day the constitution took effect. Soon afterward, the United States became a participant in the First World War. [27]

WAGING WAR, MAKING PEACE

In 1917–1918 the Wilson administration entered the First World War, cultivated cordial connections with Latin Americans, and envisioned an independent role in shaping the postwar world. As a safeguard against subsequent European competition, U.S. leaders still advocated Pan American solidarity but elicited centrifugal tendencies. Notably, Mexico and Argentina espoused Pan Hispanic alternatives, calling for Latin American unity against the United States, while Brazil remained the centerpiece of Wilson's policy in South America.

The German resumption of unrestricted submarine warfare on February 1, 1917, precipitated the U.S. entry into the war. Seeking a quick decision through decisive boldness, German leaders revoked the *Sussex* pledge of May 1916, making Allied merchant ships and passenger liners once again the objects of attack and endangering neutral vessels in the war zone around the British Isles. For the Germans, loans from private U.S. banks to the Allies already had created an informal alliance, but they gambled on a British collapse before U.S. participation could make much difference. Hoping to force a reconsideration by the Germans, Wilson severed diplomatic relations on February 3, 1917.

The German U-boat offensive compelled Latin American governments to decide whether to follow the U.S. lead. The first reactions predictably affirmed support from Cuba, Panama, Haiti, Nicaragua, and Brazil. Chile, in contrast, wanted no trouble with any of the belligerents; Mexico remained aloof; and Argentina pursued an independent course. Under president Hipólito Yrigoyen, the Argentines endorsed a call for ending the war through neutral mediation. The Wilson administration responded with suspicions of German intrigue in each country.

Though probably inflated, U.S. apprehensions over German activities in Latin America had some basis in fact. In the summer of 1915, German agents supported general Victoriano Huerta's unsuccessful bid to regain power in Mexico. Though frustrated by U.S. Department of Justice agents who arrested the deposed dictator as he moved toward the border, the scheme implied a German interest in diverting the United States from Europe by provoking trouble with Mexico. For similar reasons, Francisco Villa's raid on Columbus, New Mexico, encouraged unproven but much discussed allegations of German incitement. For Germany, foreign minister Arthur Zimmermann's clandestine courtship of Carranza's government resulted in a disaster. The details appear most fully and accurately in Friedrich Katz's *The Secret War in Mexico*. In broad outline, Zimmermann sent coded messages to Heinrich von Eckhardt, the German minister in Mexico City, on January 15, 1917, informing him of plans to resume unrestricted submarine warfare. Zimmermann also proposed the possibility of an alliance with Carranza. Under its terms the two countries would make war and peace together, and Mexico as a reward would recover its lost provinces of Texas, New Mexico, and Arizona. The plan went awry when British intelligence intercepted the transmissions and then, after appropriate deceptions, turned the information over to the United States. When published in the newspapers on March 1, 1917, the Zimmermann telegram appeared proof positive of German duplicity. Meanwhile, the German refusal to rescind the U-boat decision moved Wilson closer to war. Convinced that only his vision of harmony among nations contained the mechanism of peace for the future, Wilson paradoxically asked the Congress for a declaration of war on April 2, 1917, believing that only by taking part in the war could he later have a voice in establishing peace.

The U.S. entry into the conflict elicited sympathetic but diverse responses in Latin America. Most governments applauded the U.S. defense of neutral rights but otherwise reacted according to their own interests. Within two weeks, ten countries affirmed neutrality: Argentina, Chile, Colombia, Costa Rica, Mexico, Paraguay, Peru, El Salvador, Uruguay, and Venezuela. Seven others broke relations: Bolivia, Brazil, the Dominican Republic, Ecuador, Guatemala, Haiti, and Honduras. Two declared war: Cuba and Panama. Later in 1917, Brazil, Costa Rica, Guatemala, Haiti, Honduras, and Nicaragua also followed with war declarations. These countries went along with the United States in part because of expected rewards. Cut off from European markets and capital, Brazil supported the United States with a war declaration in October 1917 after a series of torpedo attacks on Brazilian ships; its actual participation consisted of naval deployments in the South Atlantic. The others played no part at all. As neutrals, Mexico and Argentina caused worry by urging mediation to stop the fighting. Such efforts failed but encouraged U.S. leaders to look for other signs of pro-German sympathies. In Mexico the already-suspect Carranza produced more irritation by upholding antiforeign provisions in the constitution of 1917. In Argentina, Yrigoyen similarly aroused mistrust because of his allegedly pro-German nationalism. Nicknamed "El Peludo" after "a hairy kind of subterranean armadillo," also secretive and reclusive, Yrigoyen pugnaciously pursued his own course, independent of the United States.[28]

While preparing for war, the Wilson administration also got ready for peace. To establish a planning agency, early in September 1917 the president created the Inquiry. Consisting of experts, mainly professors and journalists, the members formulated peace terms based upon their understanding of history, geography, economics, and ethnography. In regard to Latin America the recommendations typically incorporated hegemonic and paternalistic assumptions. One report, for example, assigned to the United States "a dominating influence in peace discussions so far as the Americas and Mexico are concerned." The reason was obvious: a simple acknowledgment of the U.S. "historical position" and "special relation to all the nations of the western hemisphere."[29]

After the fighting the planners expected a resumption of "economic warfare." Consequently, the Wilson administration perceived the British mission to South America in the spring of 1918 as an alarming portent. Headed by Maurice de Bunsen, a special ambassador, the delegates had instructions to promote British commerce and goodwill for the future. U.S. observers viewed such initiatives as dangers. To counter them, Colonel House called for international commitments in support of free trade, nonaggression, and representative democracy. In other words, he wanted to adopt a set of rules favorable to the United States.

The Mexican constitution of 1917 remained a source of ongoing difficulty. On June 6, 1918, addressing a group of visiting Mexican journalists, President Wilson ill-advisedly told them of his "sincere friendship" for their country, and compounded the error by recalling the provisions of the failed Pan American treaty. According to him, the proposed agreement had placed a laudable emphasis on multilateral endeavors so that "if any one of us . . . violates the political independence or the territorial integrity of any of the others, all the others will jump on her." Mexican critics immediately spotted the inconsistency, and newspaper editorials in Mexico City attacked U.S. opposition to article 27 of the new constitution. On April 2, 1918, the State Department had filed an official protest, warning against the infringement of U.S. property rights. Mexican officials regarded the act as a threat of intervention and devised an ideological defense under the terms of the so-called Carranza Doctrine. Consistent with the national requirements of the Mexican Revolution, Carranza depicted article 27 as an affirmation of Mexican sovereignty, taking precedence over foreign conceptions of property rights. He also invoked nonintervention as an absolute principle and exhorted the rest of Latin America to join with him in repudiating the Monroe Doctrine.

These responses unsettled U.S. officials. The ambassador to Mexico, Henry P. Fletcher, warned of dire consequences. In his alarmist view, Carranza wanted to eliminate "the financial, economic, and political influence of the United States in Mexico" and "to isolate the United States and destroy its influence in this hemisphere." Fletcher warned, "Under the shibboleth of this Carranza Doctrine," Mexico would "enforce Article 27 . . . and justify its disregard of the elemental principles of justice and fair dealings in treatment of foreigners."[30] Big trouble was brewing. However overblown, Fletcher's perceptions expressed the fears of oil men and politicians who opposed the Mexican constitution and were spoiling for a showdown at the end of the First World War.

At the Paris Peace Conference, Woodrow Wilson assumed the statesman's role. In pursuit of peace, he called for a purge to rid the European system of autocracy, imperialism, and militarism: that is, those practices he regarded as causes of the war in the first place. According to his plan the Central Powers, perceived as the aggressors, unquestionably required an array of changes to bring about reform and rehabilitation. But the same held true for the Allies. Wilson had never identified very closely with Allied war aims and opposed the division of the spoils among the victors, as envisioned by the so-called secret treaties. He preferred "a peace among equals." His Fourteen Points statement of January 8, 1918, established his principal goals. Appropriately described by some historians as a "liberal-capitalist internationalist," Wilson regarded representative democracy, free trade, and international cooperation as essential parts of a durable peace settlement. Other points centered on specific territorial issues, emphasizing the right of national self-determination. The fourteenth point, his most cherished, called for the creation of a League of Nations.[31]

Wilson's plan for world peace incorporated devices with which he had already experimented in Latin America. The proposal for defense of national self-determination through collective security drew upon many of the same assumptions as the Pan American treaty. Latin American critics immediately identified discrepancies. They described Wilson's hegemonic practices in the Western Hemisphere as contradictions of high-blown principles. How could the Monroe Doctrine coexist with the Fourteen Points? Was not the exercise of a self-proclaimed hemispheric police power by the United States inconsistent with conceptions of self-determination and international responsibility?

Latin American issues possessed only peripheral importance at the Paris conference. Dominated by European concerns, the peacemaking centered on the consequences of the Great War, the collapse of the Russian, Turkish, and Austro-Hungarian Empires, and the threat of Communist revolution emanating from the newly created Union of Soviet Socialist Republics. But Latin Americans wanted to play a part and eleven nations sent delegations: Bolivia, Brazil, Cuba, Ecuador, Guatemala, Haiti, Honduras, Nicaragua, Panama, Peru, and Uruguay. Mexico contributed an unofficial envoy, Alberto J. Pani, who lobbied against the influence of the big oil companies and the possibility of intervention in his country.

The official proceedings began on January 12, 1919. As various committees and commissions exercised authority over routine matters by conducting investigations, assembling information, and devising recommendations, competition for seats produced high levels of rivalry among the smaller states. The big decisions came about in other ways. Wielding primary authority at first, the Supreme Council, or the Council of Ten, comprised the heads of state and the foreign ministers of the five Great Powers: Great Britain, France, Italy, Japan, and the United States. Later, the Council of Four functioned as the power center, featuring prime minister David Lloyd George of Great Britain, premier Georges Clemenceau of France, premier Vittorio Orlando of Italy, and president Woodrow Wilson of the United States. The top priority for the Europeans was the restoration of stable and functioning political and economic systems in their domains. For them, the threat posed by the Russian Bolshevik Revolution required immediate attention as did the definition of German peace terms, the disposition of German colonies, the settlement of territorial issues in Central and Eastern Europe, and the arrangement of continental security. For Wilson, in contrast, the creation of the League of Nations became the first obligation, transcending all others. Upon completion of the League of Nations covenant, he presented the provisions to the assembled delegates on February 14, 1919, exclaiming, "A living thing is born." For Latin Americans, Great-Power dominance over the proceedings caused mistrust and bitterness. Although most favored a League of Nations as a means of keeping the United States under control in their part of the world, they disliked the insignificance of the roles assigned to them. Their principal concerns, mainly trade issues and border disputes, figured only tangentially in the peacemaking process, and then usually as diversions.

Such was the case with the Monroe Doctrine. At the peace conference, the leaders of the United States insisted upon formal international recognition of what for them had become a hallowed creed. Consequently, under authority of article 21, the peace treaty endorsed the doctrine by upholding "the validity of international engagements, such as treaties of arbitration or regional understandings . . . for securing the maintenance of peace." Alberto J. Pani, the unofficial Mexican observer, sounded warnings, cautioning that such a stipulation might serve the United States as a justification for military intervention in Mexico. For the same reason, Carranza, an international outsider, repudiated the Monroe Doctrine altogether, calling it a "species of tutelage" unacceptable to Latin Americans.

After the war, during the year 1919, difficulties with Mexico provoked growing criticism in the United States. Ambassador Henry P. Fletcher played a leading role by complaining repeatedly of mistreatment of foreigners and came close to advocating the transformation of Mexico into a U.S. protectorate something like Cuba. In his words, he wanted to issue a "call upon the recognized Government of Mexico to perform its duties as a government" or else "accept disinterested assistance from the United States." This hard-line position obtained support from such powerful interest groups as the Oil Producers Association and the National Association for the Protection of American Rights in Mexico and from many Republicans. Senator Albert Bacon Fall of New Mexico, a border-state politician with long-standing interests in Mexican affairs, abominated Carranza's regime and regarded Wilson's policies toward it as contemptible. To force a change, he proposed measures that included the withdrawal of diplomatic recognition from Carranza, the encouragement of a military revolt against him, and the installation of a new government more friendly to the United States. On August 8, 1919, Fall instigated a Senate investigation into Mexican affairs by means of which he intended to weaken both Wilson and Carranza.

Wilson's foreign policies were in deep trouble after the Paris conference. For reasons of politics and principle, Republicans in the Senate spurned collective security by rejecting the provisions of the Versailles treaty and the responsibilities of the League of Nations. Wilson responded by undertaking an exhausting speaking tour to mobilize public support, in the course of which he suffered a personal catastrophe. On September 25, 1919, he collapsed after a speech in Pueblo, Colorado, and then experienced the effects of a cerebral thrombosis. The illness deprived his pro-League supporters of leadership at a critical time and may have made him more intransigent. He ruled out a compromise with his opponents when votes in the Senate went against him and thereby doomed the larger endeavor: The defeat of the treaty also meant rejection of the League.

The crisis in Mexican affairs took place during a showdown early in December 1919. Using his investigation as a forum, Senator Fall introduced a resolution calling for a break in diplomatic relations with Mexico. From his sickbed in the White House, President Wilson managed to frustrate the plan by stating his absolute opposition to it. He then moved to rebuild his shattered administration by naming a new secretary of state. Robert Lansing resigned early in 1920 after losing the president's confidence, presumably for insubordination; Wilson regarded him as a usurper of presidential prerogatives because of differences over the peace treaty and Mexico. His successor, Bainbridge Colby, a New York lawyer and former Progressive party member, had no diplomatic experience but nevertheless creditably served out the remainder of the term. Among other things, he tried to improve relations with Latin America, mainly by opposing the practice of U.S. intervention. For that reason, he has been characterized as a precursor of the Good Neighbor policy, the less direct, more accommodating approach favored by president Franklin D. Roosevelt in the 1930s. Though probably exaggerated, this view correctly underscores Colby's more discerning appreciation of Latin American affairs. Notably, he questioned the wisdom of sustaining Caribbean protectorates and undertook a goodwill tour of South America in 1920. His voyage was a symbolic gesture signifying the ailing president's ongoing but unfulfilled efforts in the Western Hemisphere. Overall, Wilson's emphasis on Pan American political initiatives had failed.[32]

THE REPUBLICAN RESTORATION

Warren G. Harding's election to the presidency in 1920 restored the Republicans to power after an eight-year absence and initiated a set of alternative approaches in foreign affairs. Republicans embraced a more "independent," or "limited," version of internationalism than Wilson's. For them, the former president's conception of collective security implied unacceptable risks. They too favored peace, order, and liberal capitalism but employed more restricted forms of international engagement. Specifically, they rejected prior military commitments in defense of other countries. Instead, they sought to keep the peace through political accommodations and the application of international law. Employing the former at the Washington conference in 1921–1922, they tried to freeze the status quo among the Great Powers in China and to keep naval arms competition under control. Using the latter in

1928, they endorsed the Kellogg-Briand Pact to outlaw war as an instrument of national policy.

Under President Harding's unobtrusive and maladroit style of leadership, secretary of state Charles Evans Hughes assumed a primary role. An accomplished jurist and a seasoned politician—former Supreme Court justice and New York governor—Hughes had failed in his run for the presidency in 1916. As secretary of state, his background in international law disposed him to favor juridical processes, such as arbitration, and the sanctity of treaties. His successor under president Calvin Coolidge, Frank B. Kellogg, a small-town lawyer and former senator from Rochester, Minnesota, was less cosmopolitan and more temperamental. He reacted with special vehemence to allegations of Bolshevik infiltration in Mexico and Nicaragua.[33]

Secretary of commerce Herbert C. Hoover also ranked among the influential policy makers of the 1920s. A wealthy and famous mining engineer and humanitarian, he symbolized Republican ideas of individual integrity and responsibility. As commerce secretary, he assigned special importance to economic foreign policies. By coordinating endeavors in the public and private sectors, Hoover worked for a close association of government and business interests in promoting investment and trade.[34] His efforts sometimes trespassed on the secretary of state's domain, where, under the Rogers Act of 1924, a new professionalism had boosted salaries, emphasized merit, and combined the functions of the diplomatic and consular corps into the U.S. Foreign Service.

During the 1920s, Republican administrations enjoyed advantageous international circumstances, many of which benefited U.S. interests in Latin America. For one thing, wartime fears of renewed economic competition from Great Britain never materialized; instead, the British decline in trade and finance opened up new opportunities for the United States. For another, the German defeat eliminated all danger of European intrusions into the Western Hemisphere and removed a principal justification for U.S. intervention under the Roosevelt corollary. At the end of the war the United States possessed greater power and influence than ever before. It was no longer a debtor nation but as a consequence of wartime loans, a creditor nation to which other countries owed large outstanding balances. Moreover, it led the world in trade and industrial production. As the historian Melvyn P. Leffler explains, these changes meant that "economic considerations" had become primary "in the shaping of American foreign policy," in part because of "the absence of strategic apprehensions." Ironically, the Monroe Doctrine remained "the cornerstone" of U.S. policy in the Western Hemisphere but, in the absence of a European threat, had ever less use as "a viable guide to action."[35]

In the postwar period, U.S. trade and investment expanded at British expense. High demand for U.S. machine products, automobiles, farm implements, typewriters, and cash registers created incentives for aggressive selling. In South America, U.S. imports accounted for growing market shares, from 16.2 percent in 1913 to 25.9 percent in 1918 to 26.8 percent in 1927. In Brazil, Chile, Colombia, Ecuador, Paraguay, Peru, and Uruguay, U.S. sales increased impressively. In Mexico, Central America, and the Caribbean, they dominated the market by accounting for 53.2 percent of imports in 1913, 75 percent in 1918, and 62.9 percent in 1927. In contrast, British imports were either stable or in decline, holding smaller parts of the market. Similar patterns appeared with investments. From 1914 through 1919 the total of U.S. foreign investments rose from $3.5 to $6.4 billion, and growth continued in the 1920s. Specifically in Latin America, U.S. investments expanded from $1,641.4 billion in 1914 to $5,369.7 billion in 1929, whereas British investments barely increased at all. As the economic historian Rosemary Thorp explains, such stagnation resulted from a variety of circumstances, notably British indifference, North American vigor, and U.S. government support for trade and investment.

Thorp illustrates the theme with various examples. Between 1924 and 1928, Latin America absorbed 24 percent of the new U.S. capital issues for foreign accounts and 44 percent of new direct foreign investment. The biggest amounts went into minerals, oil, public utilities, and industrial development in the largest countries. During the 1920s, Chile attracted more U.S. investment in mining than did any other country. By 1926, U.S. national banks were operating more than sixty branches in Latin America, often by contentious means. At one point, U.S. financial houses in Colombia had twenty-nine representatives in competition with one another to peddle loans. Intense rivalry sometimes became unscrupulous when lenders used bribery and sought favors, for example, by paying commissions and retainers to the relatives of government officials.

In a standard work, the historian Victor Bulmer-Thomas depicts the U.S. role as "a mixed blessing for Latin America." To be sure, U.S. investments compensated for "the shrinking capital surplus available from traditional European markets," but "the new borrowing was only achieved at a price." As Bulmer-Thomas notes, "In the smaller republics the new lending was intertwined with U.S. foreign-policy objectives, and many countries found themselves obliged to submit to U.S. control of the customs house or even national railways to ensure prompt debt payment." Nevertheless, the money poured in. In the larger countries "the new lending reached such epidemic proportions that it became known as 'the dance of the millions.'" Consequently, neither the lenders nor the recipients made much effort "to ensure that the funds were invested productively in projects that could guarantee repayment in foreign exchange." In Bulmer-Thomas's view, "the scale of corruption in a few cases reached pharaonic proportions."[36]

Latin American governments welcomed foreign investments and also put up with the economic advisers who came along. One of them, Edwin W. Kemmerer, a Princeton economist known as "the money doctor in the Andes," showed up in Colombia, Chile, Ecuador, Bolivia, and Peru. Working independently of the U.S. government but with its consent, Kemmerer presented himself as a scientific expert. Through the application of precise methods, he sought to produce modernization in South America by creating financial environments more conducive to foreign investment. When a compatibility of interest developed among Latin American elites, private U.S. bankers, and Republican political leaders, the ensuing approach to economic growth resembled what the historian Michael J. Hogan has characterized in another setting as "corporatist." Kemmerer specifically encouraged the reform of monetary institutions and the establishment of central banks patterned on the U.S. Federal Reserve system. When necessary, he also facilitated the negotiation of foreign loans.[37] But to qualify for them, Latin American governments usually had to accept outside supervision. In 1922, U.S. bankers oversaw a Bolivian arrangement in which customs revenues went into payments on a $33 million loan. Similarly, in Peru U.S. officials watched over the customs houses and the central bank. As Thorp remarks, such "typical" examples suggest at the least an "obtrusive" interest in financial control.[38]

The most pressing political issues included the legacies of intervention in the Dominican Republic, Haiti, and Nicaragua. The unintended consequences of such acts aroused dismay among Republicans. The establishment of protectorates in those countries had presumed a purpose of upholding peace and order; instead, the ensuing U.S. military occupations had provoked nationalist resistance and guerrilla war. Republican leaders worried about cost ineffectiveness and public relations: Why encourage Latin American nationalists with interventionist practices when no Europeans posed a threat to U.S. interests? During the 1920 presidential campaign, Republicans subjected Democrats to strong criticism for taking over Haiti and the Dominican Republic during the war, and they urged military withdrawal.[39]

Once in power, Republican administrations succeeded in removing military forces from the Dominican Republic in 1924 but encountered difficulties elsewhere. In Nicaragua a small U.S. Marine legation guard had served since 1911, and for the most part the ruling Nicaraguan elites had not objected. Indeed, they saw the U.S. presence as a way for them to keep their hold on power. In the proposed Bryan-Chamorro Treaty of 1914, for example, Nicaraguan leaders had offered an option on a canal route in return for cash payments and also had indicated their readiness to accept something like the Platt amendment allowing for intervention. Opponents in the U.S. Senate blocked the treaty, and the revised version that passed in 1916 omitted mention of intervention.

For Republicans, military extrication posed a problem. In August 1925 the Coolidge administration removed the marines from Nicaragua and then sent them back in January 1927, following the outbreak of a civil war. This elite struggle over power and patronage pitted Conservatives against Liberals and took on international implications when Mexican president Plutarco Elías Calles supported the Liberals with money and arms. In response, secretary of state Frank B. Kellogg and ambassador to Mexico James F. Sheffield issued overwrought warnings of war unless Mexico stopped exporting revolution to Nicaragua. According to Kellogg, Calles intended his Nicaraguan meddling to advance a Bolshevik conspiracy in the Western Hemisphere.

In a show of resolution, the Coolidge administration dispatched two thousand troops to Nicaragua and also a diplomatic emissary, Henry L. Stimson. This Republican stalwart, who had served President Taft as secretary of war, persuaded Conservative and Liberal leaders to accept a truce, followed by an election. But he failed to win over Augusto C. Sandino, the head of a recalcitrant faction. A Nicaraguan, Sandino had experienced anti-U.S. nationalism while living as an exile in Mexico. As an anti-imperialist, he wanted to rid his nation of the Yankees. According to historian Thomas M. Leonard, his intransigence was "symptomatic" of a growing nationalist response against the United States. Sandino's resistance to the U.S. occupation was informed by his understanding of history: The American freebooter and white supremacist, William Walker, had invaded Nicaragua and declared himself president in the late 1850s. The U.S. president Franklin Pierce extended diplomatic recognition to the sham government. Walker immediately legalized slavery (illegal in Nicaragua since 1824) and declared English as the official language. Sandino feared and fought against an "avalanche of Walker's descendants" in the form of U.S. soldiers acting as "hired thugs of Wall Street bankers."[40]

Sandino's Nicaraguan struggle lasted six years. His army, no more than a thousand soldiers, employed guerrilla tactics to frustrate and outmaneuver government forces and U.S. Marines. In the United States, meanwhile, opposition to the Nicaraguan intervention encouraged president Herbert Hoover to end it. Early in 1931, the administration developed a strategy for removing the troops after sponsoring still another presidential election. When the marines withdrew on January 2, 1932, the State Department proclaimed an end to "the special relationship" with Nicaragua. A year later on February 2, 1933, a Nicaraguan truce ended the Sandinista revolt with promises of amnesty and reform. Sandino himself later was assassinated on February 21, 1934, probably the work of Anastasio Somoza, an emerging strongman whose family would dominate the country for two generations.[41]

Related issues caused trouble with Mexico over the constitution of 1917, regarded by U.S. critics as a dangerously radical precedent. Among other things, it called for land and labor reform and placed limits on foreign property rights. By endorsing expropriation and nationalization supposedly on behalf of the public good, article 27 overturned the more traditional conceptions of property rights favored by the United States. Carranza's intractability posed problems for the Wilson administration until his death by assassination during a military uprising in the spring of 1920. His elected successor, general Álvaro Obregón, sought normal relations but encountered stiff demands as the price. The Harding administration wanted guarantees in defense of foreign property rights—in effect, the abandonment of article 27. When Obregón declined, the United States withheld diplomatic recognition.

For Mexican revolutionary leaders, the consequences deepened an already difficult dilemma. Though resentful of economic dependencies on the United States, they needed money to reconstruct their shattered country after a violent decade, but without diplomatic recognition their government could not qualify for loans. When the Harding administration insisted upon a treaty to nullify article 27, a diplomatic standoff developed.

The big oil companies with properties at risk were well served by the U.S. policy of nonrecognition but other economic interest groups—exporters seeking sales in Mexican markets, U.S. bondholders hoping to collect on previous debts—obtained few benefits. In many ways, diplomatic recognition could advance their interests more effectively. Thomas W. Lamont, a high-level financier with J. P. Morgan and Company and an associate of the International Committee of Bankers on Mexico, previously had negotiated with Mexican officials a new schedule for repaying old debts. On the basis of that experience, he persuaded Harding and Hughes that they could place some trust in Obregón's good faith without risking too much. Subsequently, during the summer of 1923, they sought a negotiated compromise at the so-called Bucareli Conference, named for the location of the Mexican Foreign Ministry at No. 85 Avenida Bucareli in Mexico City. As a consequence of these proceedings, U.S. officials abandoned the demand for a treaty in defense of foreign property rights and accepted instead a ruling by the Mexican Supreme Court. Called "the doctrine of positive acts," this ruling assured foreigners that they would not experience retroactive enforcement of article 27—that is, the loss of their property—if they had engaged in "positive acts" to develop their holdings before the constitution took effect on February 5, 1917. In addition, a claims convention provided reassurance for foreigners seeking compensation for injuries and losses suffered during the era of revolution. As a seal on the agreement, on August 31, 1923, three weeks after Harding's sudden death, the Coolidge administration extended diplomatic recognition to Obregón's government, seeking thereby to inaugurate a period of more normal relations.[42]

Despite such hopes, new difficulties arose under Obregón's successor, president Plutarco Elías Calles. When he took office in 1924, Calles broke with Obregón's policy and rejected "the doctrine of positive acts." Instead, he threatened to enforce article 27 retroactively by placing a fifty-year limit on foreign ownership of petroleum lands, followed by nationalization proceedings. For Kellogg and Sheffield, such behavior smacked of Bolshevism. Kellogg wanted to put Mexico on trial before the world. When Thomas Lamont once again stepped in, urging a less belligerent stance, President Coolidge picked a new ambassador, a friend from college days. Dwight Morrow, another financier connected with J. P. Morgan, was a good choice. Indeed, by means of skill and discretion, he moved Calles along toward more moderate views. Specifically, he emphasized the dangers of intransigence, suggesting the likelihood of bad effects and the loss of future loans. When at last Calles came around, he accepted "the doctrine of positive acts" as assurance against outright nationalization. [43]

For Latin Americans the U.S. practice of intervention remained a pressing issue during the 1920s. Unlike their northern neighbor, they joined the League of Nations—in part to devise multilateral constraints against the United States—and also exerted pressure in other ways. At the Sixth International Conference of American States at Havana in 1928, for example, Latin American delegates introduced a resolution calling for adherence to the principle of nonintervention and declaring that "no state has a right to intervene in the internal affairs of another" for any reason. [44] On this occasion the United States succeeded in blocking any action but could not abolish the idea. Nonintervention retained strong appeal for Latin Americans. Somewhat embarrassed by the circumstance, U.S. leaders in the 1920s preferred the use of economic incentives rather than force as the best means of influencing Latin American behavior, but still they regarded intervention as a right authorized by international law. Whenever necessary, they would use it in defense of U.S. citizens and property.

In 1928, undersecretary of state J. Reuben Clark addressed the issue by establishing important distinctions that overturned the rationale for Theodore Roosevelt's corollary to the Monroe Doctrine. In a State Department memorandum, Clark defended the practice of U.S. intervention in Latin America as legitimate when sanctioned by international law as a means of safeguarding the well-being of U.S. citizens and their property, but he found no similar justification in the Monroe Doctrine. As he described its original meaning, the terms established a prohibition on European intervention in the New World but not a rationale for U.S. intervention. The publication of the Clark memorandum in 1930 marked a shift toward greater subtlety. [45] During the Great Depression, the United States gave up direct interventionist practices in the Western Hemisphere by embracing the policy of the Good Neighbor.

NOTES

1. James Sanders, *The Vanguard of the Atlantic World: Creating Modernity, Nation, and Democracy in Nineteenth-Century Latin America* (Chapel Hill: Duke University Press, 2014).

2. Victor Bulmer-Thomas, *The Economic History of Latin America since Independence* (New York: Cambridge University Press, 1994), chaps. 1–3; William Glade, "Latin America and the International Economy, 1870–1914," in *The Cambridge History of Latin America*, vol. 4, *c. 1870–1930*, ed. Leslie Bethell (New York: Cambridge University Press, 1986), chap. 1.

3. Glade, "Latin America," 10–16; Bill Albert, *South America and the First World War: The Impact of the War on Brazil, Argentina, Peru, and Chile* (New York: Cambridge University Press, 1988), chap. 1.

4. Friedrich Katz, "Mexico: Restored Republic and Porfiriato, 1867–1910," in *The Cambridge History of Latin America*, vol. 5, *c. 1870–1930*, ed. Leslie Bethell (New York: Cambridge University Press, 1986); Glade, "Latin America," 16–17.

5. Bulmer-Thomas, *Economic History*, chap. 3.

6. Glade, "Latin America," 39–41; Bulmer-Thomas, *Economic History*, 161.

7. Ronald H. Chilcote and Joel C. Edelstein, eds., *Latin America: Capitalist and Socialist Perspectives of Development and Underdevelopment* (Boulder, CO: Westview Press, 1986), provides an introduction to dependency theory; Glade, "Latin America," 47.

8. E. Bradford Burns, *The Poverty of Progress: Latin America in the Nineteenth Century* (Berkeley: University of California Press, 1980).

9. John Mason Hart, *Revolutionary Mexico: The Coming and Process of the Mexican Revolution* (Berkeley: University of California Press, 1987), chaps. 6–7.

10. Notable works include Hart, *Revolutionary Mexico;* Ramón Eduardo Ruíz, *The Great Rebellion: Mexico, 1905–1924* (New York: W. W. Norton, 1980); Friedrich Katz, *The Secret War in Mexico: Europe, the United States, and the Mexican Revolution* (Chicago: University of Chicago Press, 1981); and Alan Knight, *The Mexican Revolution*, 2 vols. (New York: Cambridge University Press, 1986).

11. Mark T. Gilderhus, "Carranza and the Decision to Revolt, 1913: A Problem in Historical Interpretation," *Americas* 33 (October 1976): 298–310; Kenneth J. Grieb, *The United States and Huerta* (Lincoln: University of Nebraska Press, 1969), chap. 4; Michael C. Meyer, *Huerta: A Political Portrait* (Lincoln: University of Nebraska Press, 1972), chaps. 4–5; Douglas W. Richmond, *Venustiano Carranza's Nationalist Struggle, 1893–1920* (Lincoln: University of Nebraska Press, 1983), chap. 3.

12. Mark T. Gilderhus, *Diplomacy and Revolution: U.S.-Mexican Relations under Wilson and Carranza* (Tucson: University of Arizona Press, 1977), 3.

13. Mark T. Gilderhus, *Pan American Visions: Woodrow Wilson in the Western Hemisphere, 1913–1921* (Tucson: University of Arizona Press, 1986), 14–16.

14. Thomas L. Karnes, "Hiram Bingham and His Obsolete Shibboleth," *Diplomatic History* 3 (Winter 1979): 39–57.

15. N. Gordon Levin, Jr., *Woodrow Wilson and World Politics: America's Response to War and Revolution* (New York: Oxford University Press, 1968), chap. 1.

16. Gilderhus, *Pan American Visions*, 7–19; Katz, *Secret War*, chap. 5.

17. Gilderhus, *Pan American Visions*, 28–29; Albert, *South America and the First World War*, chap. 1; E. Bradford Burns, *The Unwritten Alliance: Rio-Branco and Brazilian American Relations* (New York: Columbia University Press, 1966); Joseph Smith, *Unequal Giants: Diplomatic Relations between the United States and Brazil, 1889–1930* (Pittsburgh: University of Pittsburgh Press, 1991), chaps. 2–3.

18. Gilderhus, *Pan American Visions*, 20, 28–29; Burton I. Kaufman, *Expansion and Efficiency: Foreign Trade Organization in the Wilson Administration, 1913–1921* (Westport, CT: Greenwood Press, 1974), chaps. 1–2; Jeffrey J. Safford, *Wilsonian Maritime Diplomacy, 1913–1921* (New Brunswick, NJ: Rutgers University Press, 1978), chaps. 1–2.

19. Gilderhus, *Diplomacy and Revolution*, chap 1; Hart, *Revolutionary Mexico*, chaps. 8–9; Robert E. Quirk, *An Affair of Honor: Woodrow Wilson and the Occupation of Vera Cruz* (New York: McGraw-Hill, 1964).

20. Gilderhus, *Pan American Visions*, 33–45.

21. Albert, *South America and the First World War*, chap. 2.

22. Gilderhus, *Pan American Visions*, 44–52; William F. Sater, *Chile and the United States: Empires in Conflict* (Athens: University of Georgia Press, 1990), 75.

23. Gilderhus, *Pan American Visions*, 64, 67–70; Gilderhus, *Diplomacy and Revolution*, chap. 2.

24. Bruce J. Calder, *The Impact of Intervention: The Dominican Republic during the U.S. Occupation of 1916–1924* (Austin: University of Texas Press, 1984); Hans Schmidt, *The United States Occupation of Haiti, 1915–1934* (New Brunswick, NJ: Rutgers University Press, 1971); Frederick S. Calhoun, *Uses of Force and Wilsonian Foreign Policy* (Kent, OH: Kent State University Press, 1993), chap 4; Brenda Gayle Plummer, *Haiti and the United States: The Psychological Moment* (Athens: University of Georgia Press, 1992), chaps. 5–6; Plummer, *Haiti and the Great Powers, 1902–1915* (Baton Rouge: Louisiana State University Press, 1988); G. Pope Atkins and Larman C. Wilson, *The Dominican Republic and the United States: From Imperialism to Transnationalism* (Athens: University of Georgia Press, 1998), chap. 2; Lester D. Langley, *The Banana Wars: An Inner History of American Empire, 1900–1934* (Lexington: University Press of Kentucky, 1983).

25. Gilderhus, *Pan American Visions*, 61, 70–74, 77–80; Kaufman, *Expansion and Efficiency*, 165–75; Carl Parrini, *Heir to Empire: United States Economic Diplomacy, 1916–1923* (Pittsburgh: University of Pittsburgh Press, 1969), chap. 2.

26. Gilderhus, *Diplomacy and Revolution*, chap. 3; Linda B. Hall and Don M. Coerver, *Revolution on the Border: The United States and Mexico, 1910–1920* (Albuquerque: University of New Mexico Press, 1988), chap. 5.

27. Gilderhus, *Diplomacy and Revolution*, chap. 3.

28. Ernest R. May, *The World War and American Isolation, 1914–1917* (Cambridge, MA: Harvard University Press, 1959); Gilderhus, *Pan American Visions*, chap. 3; Katz, *Secret War*, chaps. 9–10.

29. Lawrence E. Gelfand, *The Inquiry: American Preparations for Peace, 1917–1919* (New Haven: Yale University Press, 1963).

30. Gilderhus, *Pan American Visions*, 113, 125–27; Gilderhus, *Diplomacy and Revolution*, 96.

31. Levin, *Wilson and World Politics*, chaps. 5–7.

32. Gilderhus, *Pan American Visions*, 142–56; Gilderhus, *Diplomacy and Revolution*, chap. 6; Dimitri D. Lazo, "Lansing, Wilson, and the Jenkins Incident," *Diplomatic History* 22 (Spring 1998): 177–98; Daniel M. Smith, *Aftermath of War: Bainbridge Colby and Wilsonian Diplomacy, 1920–1921* (Philadelphia: American Philosophical Society, 1970), 10–31.

33. Joan Hoff Wilson, *American Business and Foreign Policy, 1920–1933* (Lexington: University Press of Kentucky, 1971); L. Ethan Ellis, *Republican Foreign Policy, 1921–1933* (New Brunswick, NJ: Rutgers University Press, 1968); Warren I. Cohen, *Empire without Tears: America's Foreign Relations, 1921–1933* (Philadelphia: Temple University Press, 1987), esp. chap. 1.

34. Eugene P. Trani and David L. Wilson, *The Presidency of Warren G. Harding* (Lawrence: Regents Press of Kansas, 1977), chap. 5; Joan Hoff Wilson, *Herbert Hoover: Forgotten Progressive* (Boston: Little, Brown, 1975), chap. 4.

35. Melvyn P. Leffler, "Expansionist Impulses and Domestic Constraints, 1921–32," in *Economics and World Power: An Assessment of American Diplomacy since 1789*, ed. William H. Becker and Samuel F. Wells, Jr. (New York: Columbia University Press, 1984), 225–26, 242.

36. Rosemary Thorp, "Latin America and the International Economy from the First World War to the World Depression," in *The Cambridge History of Latin America*, vol. 4, *c. 1870–1930*, ed. Leslie Bethell (New York: Cambridge University Press, 1986), 59–66; Bulmer-Thomas, *Economic History*, 160–61.

37. Paul W. Drake, *The Money Doctor in the Andes: The Kemmerer Missions, 1923–1933* (Durham, NC: Duke University Press, 1989); Drake, ed., *Money Doctors, Foreign Debts, and Economic Reforms in Latin America from the 1890s to the Present* (Wilmington, DE: Scholarly Resources, 1994), chaps. 5; Michael J. Hogan, "Corporatism," in *Explaining the History of*

American Foreign Relations, edited by Michael J. Hogan and Thomas G. Paterson (New York: Cambridge University Press, 1991), chap. 16.

38. Thorp, "Latin America," 72–73.

39. Thomas M. Leonard, *Central America and the United States: The Search for Stability* (Athens: University of Georgia Press, 1991), chap. 5; Plummer, *Haiti and the United States,* chap. 6; Atkins and Wilson, *Dominican Republic,* chap. 2.

40. Quoted in Donald C. Hodges, *The Intellectual Foundations of the Nicaraguan Revolution* (Austin: University of Texas Press, 1986).

41. Calder, *Impact of Intervention,* chaps. 8–9; Leonard, *Central America,* 70–71, 88, 91, 99–100; Neil Macaulay, *The Sandino Affair* (Chicago: Quadrangle Books, 1971); Paul H. Boeker, ed., *Henry L. Stimson's American Policy in Nicaragua: The Lasting Legacy* (New York: Markus Wiener, 1991).

42. Trani and Wilson, *Presidency of Warren G. Harding,* chap. 5; Robert Freeman Smith, *The United States and Revolutionary Nationalism in Mexico, 1916–1932* (Chicago: University of Chicago Press, 1972), chaps. 6–8; Linda B. Hall, *Oil, Banks, and Politics: The United States and Postrevolutionary Mexico, 1917–1924* (Austin: University of Texas Press, 1995), esp. chaps. 5–7; Lorenzo Meyer, *Mexico and the United States in the Oil Controversy, 1917–1942,* trans. Muriel Vasconcellos (Austin: University of Texas Press, 1977), chaps. 4–5.

43. Smith, *The United States and Revolutionary Nationalism,* chap. 9.

44. Walter LaFeber, *The American Age: United States Foreign Policy at Home and Abroad Since 1970* (New York: W. W. Norton, 1989), 341; Samuel Flagg Bemis, *The Latin-American Policy of the United States: An Historical Interpretation* (1943; reprinted, New York: W. W. Norton, 1967), 251.

45. Frank W. Fox, *J. Reuben Clark: The Public Years* (Provo, UT: Brigham Young University Press, 1980), 514–21.

Chapter Three

Depression, War, and the Good Neighbor, 1929–1945

Between 1929 and 1945 the United States experienced a global depression and another world war. During this time of grave calamity almost everywhere, economic collapse called forth political instability and nationalist movements. In Europe and Asia the rise of Italian fascism, German Nazism, and Japanese militarism intensified economic competition over markets and scarce resources, resulting in conflict and war. In the countries of Latin America the Great Depression led to commercial breakdowns and political difficulties, the consequences of which encouraged the United States to respond in distinctive ways by fashioning a Good Neighbor policy.

The term "good neighbor," a kind of commonplace in diplomatic language, took on actual meaning during the presidencies of Herbert C. Hoover and Franklin D. Roosevelt. For Latin Americans the term signified the end of an era of direct intervention by the United States in Latin American affairs. For the Roosevelt administration the Good Neighbor policy also functioned significantly in other ways: It served as an international counterpart of the New Deal by attacking the economic effects of the Great Depression and later as a means of mobilizing resistance among the nations of the New World against the Axis powers during the Second World War. As the historian Robert Freeman Smith explains, taken together the various components formed "a massive, although ill-defined government effort" under U.S. direction to create "an integrated hemisphere system" characterized by high levels of "political, economic and military cooperation."[1]

Though often as paradoxical and contradictory as the New Deal itself, the Good Neighbor policy introduced important changes. Notably, the United States sacrificed its self-proclaimed international police power for economic reasons and for "hemispheric solidarity" against the Nazis. The main ingredient of Good Neighborliness consisted of nonintervention and other initiatives to promote commercial expansion and regional collaboration. Historians still debate whether the effects constituted a partnership with Latin Americans or a subtle means of imperial domination. David Green, for example, published the book *The Containment of Latin America* in 1971; Professor Green adopted an economic/dependency approach (very much in vogue at that time, in academic circles) to understanding the relationship between the United States and Latin America and his conclusions focused attention on trade, investment, economies of scale and other metrics, all of which tended to benefit the United States at the expense of the Latin American republics.

HOOVER AND LATIN AMERICA

Herbert C. Hoover, the former secretary of commerce, won election to the presidency as a Republican in 1928. While claiming, ironically as it turned out, that his party best understood the means of ensuring prosperity for the future, Hoover pledged his support to traditional Republican positions in favor of high tariffs, low taxes, and minimal government spending. During his career as an engineer working in other countries, he had acquired more international experience than any president since John Quincy Adams. During the campaign, he upheld the values of his Quaker ancestors by affirming his preference for peaceful solutions in the conduct of world affairs. He also espoused an interest in Latin America.

A few weeks after his election, Hoover undertook a goodwill tour into Central and South America. As he explained, "Our trip . . . was conceived for the purpose of paying friendly calls upon our neighbors to the south." He saw the venture as "the first step in what was to be a reorientation of policy toward Latin America." After departing from San Pedro, California, on November 19, 1928, aboard the battleship USS *Maryland,* Hoover's ten-week journey took him to Honduras, El Salvador, Nicaragua, Costa Rica, Ecuador, Peru, Chile, Argentina, Uruguay, and Brazil. In a speech at Amapala, Honduras on November 26, he declared as his purpose "the friendly visit of one *good neighbor to another."* In other public orations, he emphasized the importance of common welfare, mutual respect, and shared understanding among the nations of the Western Hemisphere. For example, before an audience of skeptical Argentines in Buenos Aires, Hoover criticized the condescension typically built into U.S. policy toward Latin America, especially the stereotype depicting his country as "big brother." He affirmed his belief in the principle of equality among states. Such words, followed by actual deeds, established some claim for Hoover as a founder of the Good Neighbor policy.[2]

Once inaugurated as the president, Hoover reaped the whirlwind. Contrary to Republican expectations the Great Depression descended upon the United States and the rest of the world, causing economic crisis, chaos, and calamity. As a consequence, the international political order as conceived by the Republicans in the 1920s entered into a process of disintegration, signaled initially by Japan's seizure of Manchuria in 1931–1932. Herbert Hoover, in some ways a tragic figure, served only one term in the presidency as a result; nevertheless, historians have described his policies in the Western Hemisphere as "highly successful." According to Martin Fausold, Hoover produced positive changes by advocating nonintervention; and according to Robert Freeman Smith, under Hoover "the government came closer to a truly nonintervention policy than at any other time in the 20th century." During this period the United States disengaged militarily from Nicaragua and developed similar plans for Haiti. Moreover, when uprisings and revolts swept Latin America between 1929 and 1933, "the administration refused all requests for armed intervention and constantly admonished diplomats and businessmen to refrain from political meddling." On one occasion, secretary of state Henry L. Stimson "bawled out" the head of the United Fruit Company in Costa Rica for allowing his subordinates to interfere in politics.[3] Unwilling to wield a big stick like Theodore Roosevelt, neither Hoover nor Stimson intended to use the marines in foreign interventions. They wanted to establish no parallels with Japanese military actions in Asia. As Stimson observed, to land "a single soldier among those South Americans now . . . would undo all the labor of three years" and "would put me in absolutely wrong in China."[4] As peace proponents, Hoover and Stimson also tried—unsuccessfully, as it turned out—to settle border disputes in South America between Paraguay and Bolivia over the Gran Chaco and between Peru and Colombia over Leticia.[5]

The Great Depression, of course, had many bad effects and economic dependence on trade made Latin America particularly vulnerable. Although the larger countries had moved toward industrialization and diversification in the 1920s, heavy reliance on the export sectors remained characteristic. According to the economic historian Victor Bulmer-Thomas, "the composition of exports by the end of the decade was very similar to what it had been on the eve of the First World War." Nearly all export earnings resulted from the sale of primary products, such as coffee, sugar, bananas, tin, and oil. Moreover, almost 70 percent of the foreign trade involved only four countries—the United States, Great Britain, France, and Germany—which meant that Latin America was acutely susceptible to shifts in the world market.

For Latin Americans, economic difficulties began before the Wall Street crash in October 1929. Heavy demand for credit and high interest rates during the boom years in the 1920s had had the effect of "raising the cost of holding inventories" and "reducing demand for many of the primary products exported by Latin America." The crash compounded such problems, further diminishing demand in the world market. The result was that exports fell between 1928 and 1932, in some instances by more than 50 percent. To be sure, import prices for foreign finished goods also fell but, in Latin America, neither as fast nor as far. Bolivia, Chile, Mexico, and Cuba ranked among the hardest hit. Venezuela, protected by oil, suffered somewhat less. [6]

Political changes soon followed. The destabilizing effects of the depression overturned incumbent regimes and installed new parties and personalities in power, sometimes by violent means. In Ecuador, Chile, and Cuba, such political transitions took place after periods of near anarchy; in Peru and El Salvador, they came about through sudden coups. Typically, the new governments moved toward nationalistic, centralized, and authoritarian alternatives. Strongmen such as Getúlio Vargas in Brazil, Rafael Trujillo in the Dominican Republic, and Jorge Ubico in Guatemala stood out. An exception, the Venezuelan dictator Juan Vicente Gómez maintained his regime until his death in 1935. Similarly in Mexico, the ruling Partido Nacional Revolucionario, later called the Partido Revolucionario Institucional, retained its hold on power, featuring behind-the-scenes maneuvers by former president Plutarco Elías Calles. [7]

For Latin Americans, rejuvenation of the export sector encountered formidable obstacles. To safeguard domestic markets against foreign competition the Great Powers resorted to protection, that is, high tariffs and other such barriers. Under Hoover the Republican-controlled Congress enacted the Hawley-Smoot tariff of 1930, the highest in U.S. history. Similarly under the "imperial preference" system the British discriminated against outsiders such as Latin Americans, and under the Nazis the Germans introduced the aski mark—nonconvertible currency that provided a means of paying foreign sellers for goods and services but could apply only to the purchase of German goods.

Latin Americans had few alternatives. In better times, international borrowing on credit might have gotten them out of trouble but not in this instance; as a consequence of the depression surplus capital dried up in the United States and Europe. The unavailability of additional loans by 1931 forced a cruel choice upon Latin American governments. While export earnings went into decline, the interest payments on existing debts remained the same, placing ever larger demands on shrinking sources of national income. At first, Latin Americans tried to make payments on their debts, hoping to retain access to international money markets. But to reduce growing deficits as the squeeze continued, they reluctantly accepted default on international interest payments as a necessary resort and then stopped making them. When Roosevelt and the New Dealers took office early in 1933, stringent economic conditions existed everywhere. [8]

THE NEW DEAL AND NONINTERVENTION

For Roosevelt and the Democrats the presidential victory in 1932 turned principally on domestic issues. In his comments on foreign relations, Roosevelt suggested his opposition to high tariffs and a personal preference for friendly relations with other countries. His inaugural address underscored a popular theme: "In the field of world policy," he would "dedicate this nation to the policy of the good neighbor—the neighbor who resolutely respects himself and, because he does so, respects the sanctity of his agreements in and with a world of neighbors."[9] This bland formulation implied nothing specific, but in later years the term "good neighbor" acquired very special meanings for Latin Americans.

Cosmopolitan, sophisticated, and well-to-do, Roosevelt engaged in the practice of politics throughout his adult life. He served first as a New York state legislator and then as assistant secretary of the navy under Woodrow Wilson. In 1920, he ran unsuccessfully as the Democratic candidate for the vice presidency and in 1928 won election as governor of New York state. In 1921 he had become ill with infantile paralysis, or polio, a dread affliction that left him dependent upon heavy leg braces and a wheelchair.

In foreign affairs, Roosevelt's views initially took shape during the Wilson presidency. During the First World War, he supported Caribbean interventions, worried about German intrusions, and favored order and stability within the U.S. sphere of influence. Later, he shifted his ground as a consequence of misgivings over the Nicaraguan intervention. His 1928 article "Our Foreign Policy" in the journal *Foreign Affairs,* published by the Council on Foreign Relations, contained recommendations reminiscent of Wilson's Pan American treaty. Roosevelt too favored broadly conceived definitions of international police power and preferred cooperative approaches with Latin Americans. Speaking as president before the Pan American Union on April 12, 1933, he called for a multilateral understanding of the Monroe Doctrine, in this way asserting his preference for group action and the avoidance of unilateral enforcement.

In Latin American affairs, Cordell Hull, the secretary of state, and Sumner Welles, the assistant secretary of state, played important roles. Hull, a diplomatic amateur from Tennessee, had served in the Congress, where he possessed a strong political base. A champion of low tariffs and free trade, he had strong ideas about combating the depression with an expanding commerce. In contrast, Welles had aristocratic antecedents. A diplomatic professional and a Roosevelt family friend, he had joined the Foreign Service in 1915, consciously picking Latin America as his regional specialty. In 1928 he published a two-volume history of the Dominican Republic titled *Naboth's Vineyard,* in which he advised that the United States identify "its interest both political and material, on a basis of absolute equality, with the interests of its sister republics of the continent." Often rivals, Hull and Welles competed for Roosevelt's favor. According to the historian Irwin Gellman, Roosevelt had a preference for Welles because of his "brilliance, penetrating analysis, and quick reactions" but also appreciated Hull because of his "circumspection" and his "patience" while seeking "a complete examination of the issues." Hull also knew how to cultivate support in the Congress.[10]

When the new administration took over, an impending revolution in Cuba caused immediate concern. The first U.S. protectorate in the Caribbean, Cuba also ranked among the first Latin American countries to experience the effects of economic depression. Beginning in the mid-1920s, sugar prices went into eclipse, producing widespread distress among sugar workers, professionals, merchants, and white-collar employees. In response, president Gerardo Machado negotiated loans from international bankers and employed strong-arm techniques to keep order while he sought reelection in 1928. Calamity ensued nevertheless. Because of the Hawley-Smoot tariff, Cuban sugar exporters lost 25 percent of the U.S. market. Consequently, Cuban sugar production dropped by 60 percent, and Cuban exports declined by 80 percent. As businesses failed, wages fell, and unemployment soared, Cuban dissidents in growing numbers came to regard Machado as expendable.

U.S. citizens had invested over a billion dollars in Cuba. They wanted protection, but under Hoover, nonintervention prevailed. The administration justified inaction, supposedly, out of respect for Cuban sovereignty. But in this instance, nonintervention hardly differed from intervention. In the view of most Cubans, Louis A. Pérez suggests, U.S. support sustained Machado's authoritarian regime. Ironically, "political repression and economic depression" in combination arrayed "vast sectors of the Cuban population against a government that seemed to be supported only by foreigners."[11]

In the spring of 1933, Roosevelt sent Sumner Welles as a special emissary with instructions to halt the turmoil through "friendly mediation." In the process, Welles came to view Machado as a liability and hoped for a replacement candidate among "responsible leaders" in the opposition parties. At first defiant, Machado resisted the pressure to leave office until other Cuban political and military leaders also withdrew their support. Unwilling to risk another U.S. military intervention, the Cuban army on August 12, 1933, forced Machado into exile. As Pérez explains, Welles's role "set in motion a realignment . . . that released Machado's backers to seek a new arrangement with the United States to guarantee their own survival in post-Machado Cuba."

A provisional government then took office under Carlos Manuel de Céspedes, a friend of Sumner Welles. Representing a tenuous compromise among contending groups, this administration lasted only three weeks. On September 3, 1933, army factions consisting of noncommissioned officers and enlisted men under sergeant Fulgencio Batista seized control of the headquarters at Camp Columbia in Havana. Calling for better pay and working conditions, the "Sergeants' Revolt" rallied the antigovernment opposition. Together, soldiers and other dissidents proclaimed a Provisional Revolutionary Government headed by Dr. Ramón Grau San Martín, a physician and university professor. His government was the first in Cuba to take power since 1898 without official sanction from the United States.

Embracing the slogan "Cuba for Cubans," Grau endorsed ambitious reforms: the eight-hour day, protection for rural workers, women's suffrage, and the abrogation of the Platt amendment. Much alarmed, Sumner Welles warned of communist influences and advocated military intervention. U.S. naval contingents were already positioned in Cuban waters, but the Roosevelt administration refrained from sending in the marines. Instead, the leaders withheld diplomatic recognition, thereby sending signals to Batista, now a colonel and the army chief of staff. Encouraged by Welles, Batista, working behind the scenes, shifted military support to Carlos Mendieta at the end of January 1934 and created a new government more acceptable to the United States. A decision in favor of diplomatic recognition followed only five days later.

In this instance the Roosevelt administration avoided military intervention, in part because of public relations. Late in November 1933 a Pan American conference had assembled at Montevideo, Uruguay. As always, nonintervention became an issue. Headed by Secretary Hull, the U.S. delegation preferred a discussion of peace and trade, whereas the Latin Americans wanted to take up such matters as the cancellation of foreign debts and the Cuban question. When Argentina assumed the lead, U.S. officials reacted negatively to foreign minister Carlos Saavedra Lamas—perceived as haughty and condescending in his criticism of the United States—but other Latin Americans joined him in pressing for an endorsement of nonintervention. By insisting that "no state has the right to intervene in the internal or external affairs of another," they forced a tactical change upon U.S. leaders. On this occasion, Secretary Hull accepted the idea in principle; in his words, "no government need fear any intervention on the part of the United States under the Roosevelt administration." At the same time, he employed a kind of diplomatic double-talk by attaching a reservation that could have rendered the commitment meaningless: He retained for the United States a right to intervene militarily if the defense of U.S. citizens and property required it in compliance with treaties or international law.[12]

The qualification notwithstanding, the Roosevelt administration adhered strictly to the pledge. The United States engaged in no more armed interventions and in fact eradicated some of the remnants of previous actions. An executive agreement in August 1933 provided for the withdrawal of U.S. Marines from Haiti but retained financial control until 1941; similar arrangements already existed in relations with the Dominican Republic. A new treaty with Cuba in 1934 eliminated the Platt amendment but preserved for the United States the naval base at Guantánamo Bay. Finally, an agreement with Panama in 1936 produced another modification by affirming joint responsibility for defending the canal.[13]

The United States accepted the principle of nonintervention unconditionally at the Buenos Aires conference in December 1936. Escalating the prestige, Roosevelt himself attended. Mexico introduced the nonintervention resolution, affirming that in the Western Hemisphere the various states regarded as "inadmissible the intervention of any one of them, directly or indirectly, and for whatever reason, in the internal or external affairs of any other."[14] To be sure, the phrase "any one of them" suggested a loophole, leaving open the possibility of collective measures, but the provision conformed with Roosevelt's stated preferences by disallowing unilateral acts.

The principle of nonintervention undergirded the Good Neighbor policy. By embracing it, the Roosevelt administration sanctioned equality among states in the Western Hemisphere and reduced the reasons for Latin American mistrust of the United States. At the same time, nonintervention implied, among other things, readiness to let Latin Americans take charge of their own political destinies. When U.S. military forces subsequently withdrew from the former protectorates, they left behind police contingents, or constabularies, created by U.S. occupation authorities supposedly for purposes of upholding constitutional order. In Nicaragua and the Dominican Republic, such organizations later served the dictators Anastasio Somoza and Rafael Trujillo as institutional foundations for authoritarian rule. Whether these corrupt, repressive regimes came into existence because of inadvertence or conscious design on the part of the United States is an important question. In Somoza's case, the historian Paul Coe Clark, Jr. absolves the United States of primary responsibility. In his view, Somoza stayed in power not so much because of U.S. support as because of his own ruthless political skills. According to this analysis, acceptance of nonintervention entailed an unintended consequence: The Roosevelt administration would have to put up with Somoza.[15]

ECONOMIC DIPLOMACY

U.S. economic diplomacy in Latin America sought commercial expansion through the negotiation of reciprocal trade agreements. To obtain larger market shares, the Roosevelt administration paid the political price for Latin American cooperation by abandoning obsolete forms of military intervention. Viewed in economic terms, the Good Neighbor policy functioned as part of the New Deal's larger attack on the Great Depression.

In the United States the debate over causes, cures, and consequences pervaded political discourse. Divergent views proposed various alternatives.[16] For economic conservatives and Marxists the explanation for the depression resided in the cyclical boom-and-bust patterns inherent in capitalist economies. Economic conservatives saw no ready solutions; the crisis must run its course and bottom out before prosperity could return. Marxists and other radicals thought some kind of anticapitalist revolution could clear the way. According to Herbert Hoover, the problem originated in Europe and then spread to the rest of the world. For the New Dealers, in contrast, the depression was homegrown, a disastrous manifestation of the traditional imbalance between overproduction and underconsumption, rendered all the worse in this instance by Republican policies in the 1920s. According to this view, high tariffs, low taxes, and reduced government spending were to blame. The ensuing maldistribution of income meant that financiers, manufacturers, and industrialists, the main beneficiaries of Republican policies, accumulated too much wealth and too much capability to expand production too rapidly. Lesser folk with smaller incomes—farmers, wage earners, salaried employees—who shared unequally in the wealth were unable to keep up the pace as consumers. Consequently, glutted markets in crucial sectors, notably the construction and automobile industries, generated catastrophic deflation. When producers cut back, slashed wages, and fired workers, they worsened conditions by diminishing purchasing power. Under President Hoover, unemployment reached unimaginable levels during the winter of 1932–1933. An estimated twelve to fourteen million people—about a quarter of the workforce—had no jobs.

Under Roosevelt the New Deal attacked the depression in various ways through trial and error, employing a scattergun approach. The programs that took shape typically relied heavily on centralized planning, government paternalism, and a host of new federal agencies. One such experiment, the National Recovery Administration (NRA), called for cooperation among producers in basic industries to limit output and cut down on overproduction. The effort failed. Well-intended but clumsy, the NRA resulted in a bureaucratic monstrosity, judged unconstitutional by the Supreme Court in 1935. Another initiative, the Agricultural Adjustment Administration (AAA), withstood the test of the Supreme Court and authorized farm subsidies in return for crop reductions—in effect, paying farmers to grow less. Last, a welfare system, a vital New Deal component, made relief payments to the poor and the unemployed. Denounced by Republicans as a "dole," the Civilian Conservation Corps (CCC), the Works Progress Administration (WPA), the Public Works Administration (PWA), and other such programs put federal monies into the pockets of destitute people, turning them into low-level consumers.[17]

The New Deal also sought customers in foreign markets but sometimes had difficulty reconciling interest groups with competing aims and priorities. Economic nationalists, many of them Republicans, preferred to boost sales in domestic markets through the use of protective tariffs. In contrast, economic internationalists, often Democrats, wanted to promote foreign trade through tariff reductions. Financial and commercial groups also disagreed. The former, including lenders and bondholders, regarded timely payments on international debts as important. The latter, including foreign trade expansionists, preferred to defer debt collection until world economic recovery made payment possible. Another difficulty was bureaucratic competition within the U.S. government, producing discord and confusion between the State and Treasury Departments.

As secretary of state, Cordell Hull often bore the brunt.[18] During the fall of 1933 the Roosevelt administration initiated a series of steps. On November 11, the president convened an Executive Committee on Commercial Policy. Consisting of officials from the State and Treasury Departments, the Tariff Commission, and other New Deal agencies, this body advised that Congress allow the downward modification of tariff duties under presidential authority. Subsequently, the Reciprocal Trade Agreements Act of March 2, 1934, addressed the tariff question piecemeal by allowing for the negotiation of tariff reductions with individual countries by as much as 50 percent. Another innovation, the Export-Import Bank, created in the spring of 1934, provided the means for extending government credit to American businesses in foreign counties where commercial banks had closed down or curtailed services. Later, this agency also extended credit to foreign countries.[19]

To U.S. leaders an expanding trade in Latin America became significant for various reasons. For assistant secretary of state Francis B. Sayre, Woodrow Wilson's son-in-law and a former law professor from Yale University, the implications went beyond mere commerce. He feared the collapse of political and social systems, making Latin Americans dangerously susceptible to "anti-foreign and nationalistic programs." For U.S. critics the Latin American default on foreign debts appeared as confirmation. In response, financiers asked for help from Presidents Hoover and Roosevelt, both of whom responded cautiously. As Roosevelt explained, the issue was a private matter "between those republics and . . . the bondholders." Consequently, in December 1933 the latter formed a lobby, the Foreign Bondholders Protective Council, seeking to block new loans and other concessions to those countries already in default.

Overall, the Roosevelt administration attached more importance to trade expansion than to debt collection. Nevertheless, bureaucratic competition over priorities and preferences resulted in confusion and inconsistency, impairing the workability of economic diplomacy. In one episode, Treasury officials promised a loan to Brazil for establishing a central bank and a currency stabilization fund and then encountered obstruction from the State Department, pending an agreement for paying interest on U.S. loans. Such divisiveness also revealed personal antagonism between the two secretaries, Henry J. Morgenthau, Jr. of the Treasury Department and Cordell Hull of State. According to Gellman, the "bickering" interfered with otherwise laudable efforts to pursue "a united approach."

In Latin America, Sumner Welles took charge of reciprocity programs under Cordell Hull's supervision. Described by Gellman as "less dogmatic than his chief" on trade matters, Welles wanted to construct "a firm hemispheric alliance" and looked upon improved economic relations as an appropriate means toward that end. Gellman argues that reciprocal trade agreements with Latin American nations failed to advance commercial expansion very much but in his view "unquestionably moved the signatories toward greater understanding in other endeavors." For example, the effects heightened levels of cooperation during the Second World War. [20]

The first reciprocal trade agreement, signed with Cuba in August 1934, reduced tariff rates and established quotas for Cuban sugar and tobacco. In effect, it provided a guarantee of access to the U.S. market. Though advantageous for Cuba in the short term, the long-term consequences have become the object of controversy. For Cuban nationalists, reciprocity inhibited the economic diversification of their country by perpetuating external economic dependence upon the United States. As Gellman states, "the agreement . . . bound the island's commercial activity closer than ever before to American-made decisions over which Cubans had no control." Other authorities agree, suggesting that the incorporation of Cuba within the protective system of the United States in effect replaced the Platt amendment as a means of wielding influence. Henceforth, U.S. officials could administer rewards and punishments by raising or lowering the import quota, with direct effects upon Cuban well-being. [21]

Brazil, a country more difficult to control, initially engaged in economic maneuvers, playing off one foreign interest against another. In 1930, president Getúlio Vargas, a paternalistic authoritarian, took charge, supported by the military, and engaged both Germany and the United States in commercial relationships. A trade agreement with Germany in 1934 permitted tariff reductions and barter arrangements. A reciprocal trade agreement with the United States in 1935 also reduced tariffs. State Department officials subsequently objected to Brazilian practices, regarding them as double-dealing. They especially disliked barter arrangements with the Germans, claiming that reciprocity with the United States disallowed them, and suggested a penalty, such as increased duties on Brazilian coffee. But Hull resisted because punishing Brazil might have adverse political consequences: Perhaps the country would side more closely with Germany, Italy, and Japan. Meanwhile, Vargas accepted calculated risks. An opportunist, he sought trade with both Germany and the United States, reasoning correctly that the Roosevelt administration would not jeopardize political relations by resorting to commercial retaliation. The published works of the historians Frank D. McCann and Stanley E. Hilton provide full accounts.[22]

As McCann warns, historians should not interpret this "prewar maneuvering" too exclusively in ideological terms. For him, the competition was not so much a matter of "totalitarianism versus democracy" as "a struggle for raw materials and markets" at a time of global depression. Brazilians acted on the basis of economic imperatives. Following the establishment of the Estado Nôvo, or New State—a centralized, personalistic, and authoritarian entity created with the support of the Brazilian army in 1937—Vargas for a time became dependent on Germany for various purchases, including weapons. The United States, meanwhile, courted Brazil with offers of assistance in national defense, economic development, and foreign debt. Finally, after the fall of France to the Nazis in 1940, the United States outbid the Germans by making money available for Brazil's construction of the Volta Redonda steel mill. As McCann notes, this most significant agreement "signaled the beginning of Brazil's industrial coming of age" and "marked the end of the period in which Brazil could gain by playing Germany and the United States against each other." Thereafter, Brazil had "no choice but to enter completely the economic sphere of the United States."[23]

Between 1933 and 1945 the United States signed fifteen Latin American reciprocity agreements, eleven of them before 1940, which served the important purpose of drawing Latin Americans toward U.S. policies at a critical time. Sumner Welles regarded them as "the greatest positive achievement of the first Roosevelt Administration in the realm of international cooperation." In Welles's view, they contributed "greatly . . . in establishing a good neighbor policy in the Western Hemisphere."[24] For many Latin American nationalists, however, the reciprocity agreements had the negative consequence of functioning as impediments to economic diversification, providing yet another means of perpetuating economic dependence on the United States.

No Latin American country escaped the effects of the Great Depression. To stimulate recovery the governments employed various devices, including the promotion of foreign exports; the adoption of import-substitution strategies to diversify production in domestic markets; and the use of public works, road building and the like, to bolster demand at home. Such responses encouraged recuperation in eight countries. By 1934, Brazil, Chile, Costa Rica, Cuba, Guatemala, Mexico, Peru, and Venezuela were experiencing economic upswings. Others lagged behind. For most of Latin America, the export sector was critical. As Bulmer-Thomas explains, Latin Americans benefited from a world trade revival after 1932, in part because of U.S. reciprocity. As total foreign sales in U.S. markets grew by 137 percent between 1932 and 1937, Latin Americans obtained a share of the increase.

Indeed, their "surprisingly robust" performance followed from traditional commitments to the export sector, viewed in most countries as "the engine of growth in the export-led model."

Germany also presented opportunities for Latin Americans. Based on barter arrangements and the aski mark, usable only in the purchase of German goods, German trade practices attracted a growing share from Latin America. In 1938, the last year unaffected by the Second World War, Germany absorbed 10.3 percent of Latin America's exports and sold 17.1 percent of the imports. These figures compared favorably with 7.7 percent and 10.9 percent respectively in 1930. To an extent, Latin American sales in Germany expanded because of higher prices, calculated as inducements for accepting the aski mark. Beneficiaries included Brazil, Colombia, and Costa Rica. Each country found new outlets for coffee sales in Germany but lost them after the outbreak of the war in 1939.[25]

Meanwhile, economic nationalism in Latin America posed other problems for U.S. leaders. First sanctioned in 1917 by article 27 of the Mexican constitution, the principles of expropriation and nationalization threatened traditional conceptions of private property, especially mineral resources. The danger became acute late in the 1930s when the governments of Bolivia and Mexico actually carried out such procedures. For Latin American reformers and radicals, such forms of economic nationalism implied greater hope for modernization and economic growth than the traditional export-led models. Economic nationalism was also a means of combatting foreign domination through assertions of state sovereignty. In contrast, such doctrines impressed U.S. leaders as examples of predatory lawlessness.

In *The Making of the Good Neighbor Policy*, first published in 1961, the historian Bryce Wood develops a discerning analysis. He sees the leaders in the Roosevelt administration as repeatedly displaying their intention to implement a policy of nonintervention. As they understood the term, it meant a refusal "to employ armed force . . . to secure any policy objectives" in Latin America. They also endorsed a parallel effort to uphold a policy of noninterference, signifying their reluctance "to influence in any way the course of domestic political affairs in Latin American countries." Nevertheless, contrary tendencies sometimes got in the way. Seeking some kind of balance, most officials perceived no need for the United States to give up "all methods of influencing all aspects of the foreign relations of its neighbors," especially in defense of U.S. lives and property.

To obtain the requisite leverage, they accepted various techniques as part of the Good Neighbor policy. These included traditional diplomatic instruments—such as "financial inducements, protests, discriminatory practices of an economic or ceremonial character"—and others "to create positive collaboration among the American states." Wood regards "the idea of reciprocity" as central. In this context, the term refers to something broader than New

Deal trade policy, suggesting "a neighborly response to neighborliness." Described as "an essential assumption of the new spirit," reciprocity presumed mutual respect for rights and obligations among states and called for new forms of common understanding. Problems, of course, resided in definitions. What U.S. leaders regarded as a neighborly consideration, that is, a high level of equitable treatment for U.S. citizens and property, sometimes impressed Latin Americans as preferential treatment for foreign interests in their own countries. Diplomatic difficulties arose in dealings with Bolivians and Mexicans who refused to grant the United States unilateral authority to define the term "Good Neighbor"; in their view the United States had to accept "the elimination of what they regarded as an equally offensive interference in their internal affairs" in order to qualify. This position meant abandonment of "that measure of support from Washington" that enabled "certain types of North American business enterprise to maintain the power and status they had secured before 1933."[26]

The Bolivian dispute arose over the holdings of a subsidiary of the Standard Oil Company of New Jersey. For more than a decade the government and the company had squabbled over taxes and royalties. The problem worsened in the mid–1930s during the Chaco War against Paraguay. To obtain revenues the Bolivians asked for a loan that would be, in effect, an advance payment on future taxes. In refusing this request the company also announced plans to shut down the operation and to leave the country. The Bolivian government responded on March 13, 1937, by annulling Standard Oil's contract and confiscating its holdings. The official explanation alleged various illegalities, including nonpayment of taxes, as justification for denying compensation to the company.

Unprecedented in Latin American relations, this convoluted, drawn-out case took on special importance as a test of the Good Neighbor policy. In response to appeals for help from company officials the State Department first advised reliance on Bolivian legal remedies. In the U.S. view this approach failed when Bolivian judges showed hesitation to rule against the preferences of their own government. The United States then applied discreet pressure by withholding loans and achieved some measure of success. Bolivians wanted simultaneously to deny compensation to Standard Oil and to qualify for U.S. aid and credits.

A settlement finally took place in July 1941 after the failure of an allegedly pro-Nazi plot to overthrow president Enrique Peñaranda del Castillo. To stop German encroachments the United States offered economic and military assistance, signaling a shift in priorities: The European war, regional security, and hemispheric solidarity took precedence over the defense of property rights. A negotiated agreement subsequently provided that Bolivia pay $1.5 million to Standard Oil as compensation and also receive $25 million in U.S. aid. All parties could thus claim some satisfaction. Moreover, the Good

Neighbor policy had passed the test. The Roosevelt administration had complied with the requirements of nonintervention, resisted the German threat, and blunted the effects of economic nationalism in Bolivia. [27]

Mexico introduced higher stakes on March 18, 1938, when president Lázaro Cárdenas expropriated the holdings of Dutch, British, and U.S. petroleum companies valued at some $500 million. The U.S. interest amounted to $200 million in land and $60 million in drilling equipment. By taking on foreign-owned oil corporations, Cárdenas accepted exceedingly high risks, the consequences of which he could not accurately predict. As Bryce Wood notes, oil company officials, characterized as "influential and uncompromising," might secure "effective support" from their governments. [28] In politically charged Mexico, moreover, a large-scale failure could arouse strong opposition against Cárdenas, possibly even a revolt.

In 1938, Cárdenas occupied a precarious position. Elected to the Mexican presidency in 1934, he was an authentic revolutionary hero and a former state governor of Michoacán. He was also the protégé of the former president, *el jefe máximo* Plutarco Elías Calles. As president, Cárdenas gradually liberated himself from Calles's tutelage, eventually forcing the former president into exile. Once in control of his own regime, Cárdenas presented himself as a committed heir of the revolution of 1910. Among his goals, he championed the redistribution of land to landless campesinos, the country people, by forming agricultural cooperatives known as *ejidos;* he sought better wages and working conditions for the laboring classes by favoring unions, especially the Confederation of Mexican Workers (Confederación de Trabajadores Méxicanos) under Vicente Lombardo Toledano; and he promoted literacy through advances in secular education. But then a resumption of economic crisis in 1937 threatened Mexico with bankruptcy and collapse.

The emergency had many bad effects. Cárdenas resorted to deficit spending to rescue his government but possessed limited resources for reform. Discontent mounted among country people, workers, and the business classes. Moreover, the Spanish civil war beginning in 1936 conjured "a terrifying preview of Mexico's future." What if Mexico should follow Spain's example and disintegrate into mayhem and violence? For enthusiasts among Mexican conservatives and reactionaries, Spanish general Francisco Franco, a leader of the revolt, personified Hispanic traditions of authority and hierarchy. As William H. Beezley explains, Cárdenas embraced programs of economic nationalism "to unite a people deeply splintered by the economic disruption of the Great Depression" and by "the inability of the government to continue the social programs of the revolution." [29]

A labor-management issue ignited the oil controversy. In May 1937, seventeen thousand petroleum workers went on strike, demanding improvements in wages, working conditions, housing, medical care, and education. When an arbitration decision went against the oil companies, the leaders took the case to the courts, where they experienced another setback: The Mexican Supreme Court ruled in favor of the workers, depriving the companies of further legal remedy. Unreconciled, company officials then escalated the issue by rejecting the outcome and challenging the sovereignty of the Mexican government.

Unable to tolerate such defiance, Cárdenas announced expropriation proceedings against the companies in a national radio address on March 18, 1938. As justification, he invoked not article 27 of the constitution, the restriction on property, but article 123, the labor provision. In his view, the rights of working people and the jurisdictional integrity of the Mexican Supreme Court allowed room for no compromise: he had to defend them at all costs. Patriotic Mexicans rallied in his support. They applauded Cárdenas for his resolve, in effect, declaring economic independence from foreign control. The oil producers, in contrast, issued protests. They depicted the expropriation as a crime against private property, a despicable act probably inspired by Bolsheviks. To combat it, they gave a strong impression of inviting military intervention.[30]

Put to the test in Mexico, the Good Neighbor policy compelled measured responses. As Bryce Wood describes it, U.S. policy unfolded in four phases. First, within a few weeks the United States accepted the expropriation as legal but expected Mexican compensation to the companies for their losses. Second, for the next two years, until April 1940, negotiations went nowhere, culminating in a Mexican refusal of arbitration. Third, discussions until November 1941 revolved around Mexican counterproposals for a joint commission. Fourth, during the spring of 1942 the joint commissioners at last concluded an agreement, leaving the oil companies no choice except acquiescence.

Wood carefully establishes the key propositions. From the outset a dangerous possibility existed. What if a "peremptory" response by the United States ruled out negotiations by forcing Cárdenas into breaking diplomatic relations? U.S. ambassador Josephus Daniels played an indispensable role in heading off any such outcome through the exercise of "a remarkable combination of insubordination and suppression of information." A North Carolina reformer who had served as secretary of the navy under Wilson, Daniels had ordered the occupation of Veracruz in 1914 with Franklin Roosevelt as his assistant secretary. Now an advocate of Good Neighborliness, he toned down State Department objections during the early stages and assured Washington of Cárdenas's "sincere intention" to offer compensation. His role established some measure of mutual understanding. Indeed, Daniels in "his unique and unorthodox fashion . . . had imposed on the Department of State his own judgment of the way the United States should deal with Mexico as a Good Neighbor."

Wood also contends that the State Department never seriously considered the use of armed force. Though oil company press releases and propaganda introduced such possibilities, no doubt causing worry in the Cárdenas government, ambassador Francisco Castillo Nájera of Mexico affirmed his faith in June 1938 in the credibility of the nonintervention commitment. Later, the Roosevelt administration refrained from interjecting the petroleum issue into the Mexican presidential election of 1940. After the victory of the official candidate, general Manuel Ávila Camacho, Roosevelt indicated good faith by sending vice president Henry A. Wallace to the inauguration ceremonies in November 1940.

At the same time, the United States employed economic pressure to encourage prompt settlement. Reduced purchases of Mexican silver inflicted some distress; the oil companies impeded Mexican exports into world markets by denying tankers, pipes, and essential machinery and by discouraging other countries from purchasing Mexican petroleum. Never distinguished by much success, these undertakings also entailed risks: What if Mexico should embrace Germany, Italy, and Japan in bids for overseas markets? The U.S. government also withheld loans from August 1937 until November 1941. But none of these policies ever took the "drastic" form, for example, of denying the legality of the expropriation. The U.S. aim was settlement between the oil companies and Mexico through some kind of compensation.

One possible means of resolution, arbitration proceedings, possessed the sanction of international law. The oil companies and also the governments of Great Britain, the Netherlands, and the United States initially favored this approach. But Mexican leaders regarded arbitration as a function of Great-Power domination, a device more likely to uphold foreign interests than Mexican sovereignty. They preferred to establish a joint commission in which each government would appoint one member and from which no appeal could take place. Once the Roosevelt administration accepted this plan as the best means available to the United States, a settlement followed in the spring of 1942.

U.S. concerns for regional defense and hemispheric solidarity thus assumed priority over property rights, much as in the earlier Bolivian case. Put succinctly, the onset of the Second World War encouraged U.S. officials to perceive "the national interest" as "different from" and "superior to" oil company interests. For example, by the spring of 1941 the War Department urgently wanted access to Mexican air bases as links to Panama. In Wood's words, such considerations became "crucial." Consequently, an agreement on November 19, 1941, approved the use of a joint commission. It also allowed for broad discussion of other issues, including U.S. agrarian property claims against Mexico, the purchase of Mexican silver, the negotiation of a reciprocal trade agreement, and the extension of loans through the Export-Import Bank. The terms fixed the compensation for U.S. oil companies at

$24 million. Lacking other recourse, the oil companies grudgingly accepted this outcome. At least they got something out of the deal.[31]

The episode had great importance. In the 1930s, Mexico had become a preferred model for Latin American nationalists, and the Cárdenas regime possessed high prestige. As a result, some U.S. leaders worried about the dangers of "socialism," "extreme radicalism," and "communism" in other countries. They also feared Axis influence. In this context, as noted by the historian David Green, oil company "intransigence" had the ironic effect of making Germany, Italy, and Japan potential outlets for Mexican oil exports. To avoid "serious consequences," the United States needed "some kind of rapprochement with Latin American nationalists."

Roosevelt acknowledged as much on January 12, 1940, in a statement before newspaper reporters. In uncharacteristically disarranged syntax, he said, "There is a new approach that I am talking about to these South American things . . . Give them a share. They think they are just as good as we are, and many of them are." Whatever the degree of condescension, the president's observation signaled a certain readiness to bestow upon Latin Americans "a share of decision-making authority in inter-American economic concerns" and "a share of the wealth being developed from Latin America's vast resources by private and public capital." Otherwise, as Green observes, private firms might risk the loss of everything, since Latin American strategies for economic development required increasingly national control of economic resources.[32]

A similar issue appeared strikingly in relations with Venezuela. In 1935 the death of long-time dictator Juan Vicente Gómez introduced a period of change. Under Gómez, the head of state since 1908, companies such as Standard Oil of New Jersey, Royal Dutch Shell, and Gulf had obtained easy access to Venezuelan resources while enjoying low taxes and high profits.[33] Subsequently, when a new regime headed by Eleazar López Contreras introduced reforms, including the eight-hour day and collective bargaining, oil company officials worried about the implications. What if Venezuela should follow the Mexican example? By this time the country ranked as the leading petroleum exporter in the world, and U.S. investments in Venezuelan oil in 1940 amounted to $375 million.

For reasons of their own, Venezuelans followed a different model. Less radical in approach, the Venezuelan constitution of 1936 contained no equivalent of article 27 in the Mexican constitution of 1917. Conducting a kind of cost-benefit analysis, Venezuelan leaders recognized their dependence on petroleum exports and chose to avoid the crippling effects of cutting too heavily into the profits. In Venezuela, then, petroleum resources remained under private control but subject to higher taxes and royalty payments. During the Second World War a policy of collaboration with Latin American governments willing to share their resources became for the United States its best means of assuring access.[34]

FROM NEUTRALITY TO WAR

The Second World War occasioned unprecedented diplomatic cooperation among the nations of the Western Hemisphere. Seeking to coordinate regional responses, the United States first tried to uphold neutrality while providing safeguards against other consequences. The participants at a series of inter-American conferences in Lima, Panama, Havana, and Rio de Janeiro proclaimed "continental solidarity," the existence of a war-free zone, and the applicability of the "no transfer" clause. After Pearl Harbor, all the Latin American nations except Argentina and Chile supported the United States, either by declaring war on the Axis nations or by severing diplomatic relations with them. Among other things, U.S. access to Latin American resources was at stake. In the words of the historian R. A. Humphreys, "In 1939 Latin America was the richest raw material producing area in the world free from the control of any Great Power."[35] At a time of global conflict, the prize was well worth having.

Competition over markets and resources had figured prominently in the destabilization of world politics in the 1930s. Economic imperatives drove Japanese expansion in Asia, contributing to the Manchuria crisis in 1931–1932 and to "the China incident"—really a full-scale invasion—in 1937. Similarly, German ambitions in Europe, the incorporation of German-speaking peoples into the Third Reich, and the eastward move into the Slavic domain precipitated confrontations in the middle and late 1930s. These encounters culminated in the onset of the war over Poland in September 1939. U.S. leaders, meanwhile, espoused neutral policies but increasingly embraced pro-British positions.

Beginning in 1935 the U.S. Congress passed a series of three Neutrality Acts. Based on the experience of 1914–1917, these measures disallowed certain practices. They denied loans and arms sales to warring nations and imposed a cash-and-carry provision to reduce the risk of submarine attacks on U.S. merchants ships: Belligerents had to pay "cash" for U.S. goods and "carry" them away in their own vessels. After the fact, these acts ruled out U.S. participation in the First World War. They also hamstrung President Roosevelt by permitting no aid for the victims and no penalties for the aggressors.

U.S. responses to the Axis threat compelled careful maneuvers. Roosevelt presided over a divided country and could not move too far or too fast. One identifiable group, the "internationalists," functioned as Woodrow Wilson's heirs, championing a conception of world organization and collective security. They favored strong measures by the Western democracies in defense of liberal-capitalist institutions but encountered a classic dilemma: How could they calculate the effects of such measures? Would tough policies deter aggression or precipitate a conflict? The internationalists also faced strong opposition from the so-called isolationists, who resisted commitments in defense of other countries and insisted upon "America First." Some feared the consequences of participating in another European war; for them the U.S. entry into the First World War had accomplished no good purpose and was a mistake that did not bear repeating. The disinclination of others to stand against the Axis powers followed from pro-fascist and anti-Semitic proclivities.

These swirling tides within the two parties and the Congress created immense difficulties for Roosevelt. Increasingly, he saw Axis aggression in Europe and Asia as security threats. He defined the issue less as a danger of invasion than as a menace to fundamental interests and ideals or, put another way, to sets of assumptions and commitments upon which larger purposes depended. In modern historiography, some scholars have used the term "Open Door" as a characterization. Understood symbolically, this phrase conveys an impression of the sort of world preferred by U.S. policy makers in the twentieth century and implies fundamental goals and aims, involving some form of obligation—at least rhetorical—in support of liberal capitalism. The goals included free trade, private ownership of property, national self-determination, and representative democracy. U.S. leaders favored such conventions and usages as affirmations of core values, supposedly appropriate for adoption by other peoples and also the means of serving national objectives, which included high levels of prosperity, safety, and ideological integrity. According to this view, the United States could function best in an open world organized much like itself. Conversely, these objectives called forth resistance to the division of the world into spheres of influence, the creation of exclusive trading blocks, and the depredations of militaristic dictatorships.[36]

Franklin Roosevelt's twists and turns, moving the United States toward a policy of aiding Great Britain by measures short of war, have attracted a great deal of scholarly attention. Many historians have noted that for him the shortest distance between two points was seldom a straight line. According to Robert A. Divine, Roosevelt often "moved two steps forward and one back before he took the giant step ahead." Keeping his own counsel, the president employed devious, secretive methods sometimes verging on outright deception. According to vice president Henry A. Wallace, he performed as a juggler who "could keep all [the] balls in the air without losing his own." An important book by Warren F. Kimball employs the same metaphor in its title.[37] Following the outbreak of war over Poland in September 1939, Roosevelt's policies tilted by increments toward the Allies. In response, the

Congress in November 1939 changed the Neutrality Acts so that France and Great Britain could purchase arms and supplies in the United States on a cash-and-carry basis. The French defeat in June 1940 and subsequently the Battle of Britain created new concerns, leading to a destroyers-for-bases deal in September 1940. Devised as an executive agreement between Roosevelt and prime minister Winston Churchill, it allowed a swap of fifty U.S. destroyers in return for U.S. leases on British bases in the Western Hemisphere. Roosevelt defended this profoundly unneutral act as the means of keeping the United States out of the war and Britain in it. Later, he upheld the Lend-Lease proposal on similar grounds. This measure set off a fierce fight in Congress. Once accepted in March 1941, it permitted the United States to lend or lease instruments and commodities of war to Britain and "any country [such as the Soviet Union] whose defense the President deems vital to the defense of the United States."[38] It also exposed U.S. merchant ships to German submarine attacks. During the fall of 1941 an undeclared naval war got under way against the Germans in the North Atlantic.

Between 1938 and 1941, apprehensive leaders in the New World tried to insulate their region against the worst effects. After the failure of the British and French experiment with appeasing Germany at Munich in September 1938, assistant secretary of state Sumner Welles called for vigilance against aggression "from whatever source" and urged the United States "to join with our fellow democracies of the New World in preserving the Western Hemisphere safe from any threat of attack." Considerations of "hemispheric solidarity" figured prominently at the Eighth International Conference of American States at Lima in December 1938, where, happily for U.S. policy makers, the northern power no longer looked quite so much like Latin America's natural enemy. Cordell Hull again led the U.S. delegation and stopped along the way in Panama, Colombia, and Ecuador, focusing attention on unity and friendship. In Lima, he encountered dissent from Argentine foreign minister José María Cantilo, who cautioned against overreaction. Cantilo recalled Argentina's traditional European ties, especially with Italy and Germany, and opposed a regional alliance against either one. In the end, compromises muted Argentine objections and allowed for the Declaration of Lima on Christmas Eve. This statement affirmed continental solidarity against foreign intervention in the Western Hemisphere but refrained from designating any nation as a specific threat.

It also allowed for conferences of foreign ministers to coordinate future policy. After the outbreak of war in Europe on September 1, 1939, the First Meeting of Consultation of Ministers of Foreign Affairs of the American Republics assembled in Panama on September 23. This time Sumner Welles headed the U.S. delegation. In a speech on September 25, he advocated Pan American uniformity in establishing neutral policies. In a sequence of sessions lasting eight days the participants formed committees, discussed common interests, and drafted the Declaration of Panama. This measure—unenforceable, as it turned out—erected a shield against acts of war by establishing a three-hundred-mile security zone around North and South America and instructing the belligerents to keep out. The question was whether the warring countries would abide by the prohibition.

Naval contingents displayed disinclination to do so. In December 1939 the German pocket battleship *Graf Spee* entered the South Atlantic and engaged three British cruisers in battle off the Uruguayan coast. Forced by heavy damage to seek refuge in port at Montevideo, the German captain, Hans Langsdorff, asked for two weeks for repairs; the British stipulated one day, and the Uruguayans settled on seventy-two hours. Faced with an impossibility, Langsdorff scuttled his vessel, arranged for his crew's internment in Argentina, and committed suicide.

How to safeguard the neutrality zone became a source of contention. Diplomatic representations to the Germans and the British had scant effect. Indeed, the United States accepted British "hot pursuit" when German commerce raiders sought safe haven in the zone. Other U.S. practices further bent neutrality in Britain's favor: They allowed the capture of German merchant ships within the zone by the Royal Navy and, in the spring of 1941, aided British operations by providing radio information on German locations. Roosevelt nevertheless kept up a public masquerade, depicting U.S. actions as purely defensive. Ironically, the security zone, initially a function of neutrality and hemispheric solidarity, turned into a cover for aiding the Allies by methods short of war.

Another issue became acute. What if the Germans acquired bases in the Western Hemisphere from conquered countries? Following the French collapse in June 1940 the United States could not rule out such possibilities. To guard against them the State Department formulated a resolution, later endorsed by Congress, based on the "no-transfer" principle. Traditionally associated with the Monroe Doctrine, this tenet withheld U.S. recognition of "any transfer" of "any geographic region of the Western Hemisphere from one non-American power to another non-American power." Though mocked by German officials as delusionary and pretentious, the no-transfer resolution won support from Western Hemisphere diplomats at a conference in Havana on July 26, 1940. In this way, they ruled out the possibility of Germans occupying Dutch, Danish, and French possessions in the New World.[39]

U.S. leaders also worried about Nazi subversion. By 1940 a million German colonists were living in Latin America, most of them in southern South America. Reputedly, the Germans resisted assimilation and affirmed their national identities through schools, newspapers, radio broadcasts, and expatriate organizations. The question of whether they functioned as political affiliates of the Third Reich and promoted Latin American fascism became a source of much discussion. German economic penetration also produced apprehension; for example, the rivalry over Latin American routes between Lufthansa and Pan American Airlines had military implications for air power. Consequently, influential writers such as the journalists Carleton Beals and John Gunther and the historian Samuel Flagg Bemis drew attention to such matters, calling for appropriate safeguards. President Roosevelt, meanwhile, used allegations of aggressive design as justification for British aid. According to his Pan American Day address on May 29, 1941, "Adolf Hitler never considered the domination of Europe as an end in itself"; therefore, "unless the advance of Hitlerism is forcibly checked now, the Western Hemisphere will be within range of the Nazi weapons of destruction." One such disaster scenario imagined German moves from Africa to Brazil to the Caribbean, imperiling the Panama Canal. In another speech on October 27, 1941, Roosevelt claimed to possess a map showing secret Nazi plans for Latin American conquests. When pressed by reporters to display it, he refused, invoking confidentiality to protect his sources. Such statements, unsubstantiated by evidence, underscored his growing pro-British convictions.[40]

Japan's assault on Pearl Harbor brought the United States into the Second World War. Best understood as a desperate act, the attack followed a period of fruitless negotiation in the course of which neither country showed much interest in accommodation. Japanese leaders insisted upon a free hand in what they called a Greater East Asia Co-Prosperity Sphere, described as an equivalent of the Monroe Doctrine. Unconvinced, Secretary Hull defended the sanctity of the Open Door. To the Japanese, this meant either accepting a status of dependency upon the United States or affirming national prerogatives as a Great Power. Taking a big risk, Japan inaugurated hostilities against the United States with a surprise attack. In a war message to Congress the next day, Roosevelt referred to December 7, 1941, in a famous phrase as "a date which will live in infamy." Following the U.S. declaration of war, Germany and Italy honored the Tripartite Pact with Japan four days later by declaring war on the United States. The undeclared conflict in the North Atlantic had turned into a full-scale shooting war on two fronts.[41]

For other Western Hemisphere nations the U.S. declaration of war entailed pressing urgencies. In December 1941, nine Central American and Caribbean republics declared war on Japan, later on Germany and Italy; Colombia, Venezuela, and Mexico severed relations. In response, Adolf Berle, an assistant secretary of state, set forth an assessment later endorsed by many historians: "The heartening thing . . . is the swift and virtually unanimous support from all the republics of this hemisphere. If ever a policy paid dividends, the Good Neighbor policy has. So far, they are sticking with us with scarcely a break."

Following the procedures established at Havana, the Western Hemisphere nations again assembled for consultations, this time at Rio de Janeiro on January 15, 1942. Given the disaster at Pearl Harbor the delegates had to take into account an act of aggression actually committed against an American state. In preparation, the U.S. State Department sought compliance with Secretary Hull's preferences. The agenda included a resolution requiring all American republics to sever relations with the Axis powers but not necessarily to declare war. The distinction was based on an understanding of limited capability. The United States could not defend the entire Western Hemisphere.

On this occasion, Hull, worn out from the Japanese negotiations, had allowed Sumner Welles to take over as head of the U.S. delegation. Welles understood Hull's objective but anticipated resistance. Chile reportedly feared Japanese hit-and-run attacks along the coast, and Argentina favored neutrality. Welles hoped for support from Brazil but could not accomplish Hull's goal. Neither Chile nor Argentina would sever relations. On his own authority, Welles accepted a compromise, recommending but not requiring a break in relations with the Axis. In a fury, Hull upbraided Welles for sabotaging State Department policy, but Welles had Roosevelt's support; the recommendation stood. Soon afterward, Peru, Uruguay, Bolivia, Paraguay, Brazil, and Ecuador broke relations, making the total eighteen. As a consequence, most historians bestow high marks on the Roosevelt administration for achieving multilateral cooperation with Latin America during the Second World War.[42]

WARTIME RELATIONS

Latin American leaders supported the United States during the Second World War for various reasons. Usually, their decisions centered on questions of political and economic advantage more than on abstract notions of hemispheric solidarity. Latin American governments feared for their own security if the Nazis or the Japanese made a move into the Western Hemisphere, but more significantly, they recognized the U.S. capacity to reward and punish. By severing ties or declaring war, Latin Americans might secure the means for coping with inimical circumstances. The Axis powers controlled Europe, and the Allies dominated the high seas. Taken together, these geopolitical configurations cut off Latin Americans from the continent and accentuated dependencies upon the United States. In response, Mexico and Brazil accepted high risks and declared war, whereas Chile and Argentina for much of the war stayed neutral for reasons of their own.

Specific judgments varied from country to country. Overall, the Caribbean and Central American republics fashioned their responses to please the United States. Among other things, they wanted economic outlets and political support against internal dissidents. By declaring war, they advanced each goal. In Cuba, colonel Fulgencio Batista, formerly the power behind the scenes, won the presidential election of 1940, depending on the army as a base of support. As president, he qualified for U.S. economic and military assistance from the Export-Import Bank and the Lend-Lease Program. In Haiti, president Élie Lescot's government acted on ideological imperatives by going on record in opposition to Nazi racial doctrines, and in the Dominican Republic, generalissimo Rafael Leónidas Trujillo Molina somewhat fantastically depicted his dictatorial regime as a bastion of liberty in defense of the Western Hemisphere. In these countries, war declarations meant modest U.S. economic and military aid.[43]

Central American reactions developed similarly. In Costa Rica, president Rafael Calderón Guardia aligned his democratic country with the United States on ideological grounds. Elsewhere, the authoritarian regimes of presidents Maximiliano Hernández Martínez of El Salvador, Anastasio Somoza of Nicaragua, Tiburcio Carías Andino of Honduras, and Jorge Ubico of Guatemala went along with the United States in anticipation of assistance for their economies and their police forces. The United States especially prized order in regions close by the Panama Canal Zone. In Panama itself, sensitive questions of national sovereignty complicated U.S. efforts to secure air bases and other installations. In return for granting access to them, president Arnulfo Arias required various forms of compensation and also assurances in defense of Panamanian national prerogatives.

When obliged to pick between Germany and the United States, most Latin American leaders opted for the latter. In politically factionalized Mexico after the election of 1940, president Ávila Camacho wanted to consolidate his country politically and also to develop more regular relations with the United States. The petroleum issue presented a potential obstacle; nevertheless, a wartime alliance took shape between the two nations. Consequently, Mexico permitted the use of air bases in its territory; the United States purchased Mexican products and strategic materials at high prices; and on May 30, 1942, after German submarine attacks on Mexican tankers, the Mexican government formally entered the war. Later, in March 1945, the Mexican air force participated in attacks against the Japanese in the Philippines and Formosa.

Most South American countries also developed pro-U.S. policies by cutting ties with the Axis. Their reasons included economic advantage and national security. In Venezuela the defense of oil exports compelled such action from president Isaías Medina Angarita. In Colombia, president Eduardo Santos believed that the national interests of his country corresponded with those of the United States. Similar perceptions prevailed in the governments of Carlos Arroyo del Río in Ecuador, Manuel Prado y Ugarteche of Peru, Enrique Peñaranda del Castillo of Bolivia, Higinio Moríñigo of Paraguay, and Alfredo Baldomir of Uruguay. They all broke relations with the Axis powers.

Brazilian leaders actually declared war. Under authority of the Estado Nôvo, Getúlio Vargas constructed an "entirely personal" dictatorship. Described by R. A. Humphreys as "a master of the arts of political manipulation and persuasion," Vargas employed "a Machiavellian astuteness" to maintain "a delicate balance" between civilian and military interests. Supposedly standing above partisan strife, he presented himself with some measure of accuracy as "a paternal statesman devoted to his country, the development of its resources, and the welfare of its people." The most comprehensive study of the complex Vargas regime remains Robert M. Levine's *Father of the Poor? Vargas and His Era* published in 1998.

For Latin Americans during the war, adherence to pro-U.S. policies generally paid some kind of dividends. For Brazil a "steady" economic recovery in 1941 reflected "the great expansion of trade with the United States," regarded by Humphreys as "the prime cause." Various economic devices contributed. For example, the Inter-American Coffee Agreement in April 1941 halted "ruinous competition among the coffee-producing countries" and guaranteed Brazil "a fair share of the North American market at enhanced prices." Other agreements channeled the sale of strategic materials to the United States, increasing Brazilian mineral exports.

The country also possessed geopolitical significance. The great Brazilian "bulge" extending eastward from Natal and Recife made the Atlantic narrows the shortest route to the New World from Africa. Because this largely defenseless region appeared as a potential invitation to German invasion, the United States constructed air bases in Brazil and developed other forms of military and naval cooperation. Though reluctant to admit U.S. troops, Vargas did want military aid through Lend-Lease. Consequently, Brazil broke Axis relations on January 28, 1942, and declared war in August. In 1944, Brazilian army contingents took part in the Italian campaign, the only Latin American military force so engaged in Europe.

Different considerations governed decisions elsewhere. In Argentina, neutrality functioned as the guide. According to Humphreys, pro-Axis sympathies affected the officer corps in the German-trained Argentine army. Moreover, fascist and ultranationalist doctrines appealed, as Humphreys explains, "to arch-conservatives, to upper-class young men-about-town, to right-wing intellectuals, and others who sought to rehabilitate the reputation of the greatest and worst of Argentine tyrants": that is, the nineteenth-century strongman Juan Manuel de Rosas. Nevertheless, "the majority of Argentines, if they feared that Britain would lose, hoped that she would win." The "public mind was confused"; the "barometric pressure tended to move up and down according to events in Europe," suggesting a large measure of "uncertainty." British markets absorbed large quantities of Argentine beef and mutton but could not compensate for the loss of continental sales. Mounting surpluses heightened economic insecurity, and the succession of military officers moving in and out of high political offices suggested impending instability. After Pearl Harbor the civilian president, Ramón S. Castillo, officially declared neutrality as "the best and the safest policy." Unlike Vargas, who decided that "he must stand or fall with the United States," neither President Castillo nor the Argentine foreign minister, Enrique Ruiz Guiñazú, invested much faith in the credibility of Pan American alignments under U.S. leadership. Moreover, neither one anticipated an Allied victory at the end of the war.

Chile also stayed neutral at first. Beset by "strikes, rising living costs, and administrative incompetence," a Popular Front government dissolved in January 1941, ripped to pieces by the competition among Radical, Conservative, Socialist, and Communist parties. Deeply divided, the country tried to avoid international complications. At the same time, as Humphreys notes, "there was little doubt where the preponderance of Chilean sympathies lay in 1941." Characterized as "hard-headed, cautious and independent," Chileans favored the Allies but feared an outbreak of war in the South Atlantic and the possibility of an Allied defeat. They also worried about Japanese raids along their lengthy, exposed coastline. Chile consequently remained neutral until January 20, 1943, when at last president Juan Antonio Ríos embraced a pro-Allies position by breaking off diplomatic ties with the Axis powers. At this point, he feared the effects of political and economic isolation in the Western Hemisphere more than the Germans and the Japanese. [44]

Although during the Second World War the United States forged closer military, cultural, and economic links with Latin America than ever before, questions of interpretation pose a problem. Some historians argue that the establishment of close ties ranked as a significant form of Pan American achievement, part of a praiseworthy effort to transform "the Western Hemisphere idea" into reality.[45] More skeptical historians depict the wartime Pan American partnership as something of an illusion, perhaps even a deception to obscure hegemonic designs. According to this interpretation, U.S. leaders used the war as a means of consolidating previous gains under the Good Neighbor policy, thereby guaranteeing access to Latin American resources and perpetuating U.S. dominance.[46]

In the years before the war, military collaboration between the United States and Latin America hardly existed at all. Latin American armies typically relied on European professionals and arms suppliers for training and equipment. As late as 1939, German advisers were operating in about half the countries of Latin America. (Brazil, an exception, had hosted small U.S. military and naval missions since the First World War.) During the 1920s and 1930s, U.S. officials displayed little interest in cultivating Latin American military connections. When in support of the Good Neighbor policy Sumner Welles argued in favor of such measures, he encountered mainly indifference and prejudice toward Latin Americans among the U.S. military, naval, and foreign policy elites.

Following the catastrophic French defeat in June 1940, an abrupt change took place in U.S. thinking. The so-called Rainbow strategic war plans anticipated the possibilities of fighting on various fronts and in different combinations in the Atlantic, the Pacific, or both. The planners assumed a vital interest in defending the Western Hemisphere region, especially the Caribbean, and, for such purposes, assigned the primary responsibility to U.S. military and naval forces. Other parts of the plans called for the cultivation of Latin American cooperation to assure access to strategic materials and the acquisition of land, sea, and air bases. U.S. officials showed scant appreciation for Latin American sensitivities over issues of national sovereignty; they wanted long-term leases with full jurisdiction but typically settled for less, since few host governments wanted U.S. troops stationed outright in their countries. As a subterfuge in Brazil, the authorities described them as unarmed technicians who would manage U.S. bases for the duration and get out once the war ended.

The early German successes elicited alarm and pessimism. During the Battle of Britain in 1940, U.S. observers fully expected German attacks in the New World if British forces should suffer a defeat. Although the German invasion of the Soviet Union on June 22, 1941, dissipated the immediacy of that fear, defensive preparations took many forms. The U.S. Navy kept close watch by multiplying the number of seagoing patrols in the Atlantic; the U.S. Army courted military counterparts in Latin America by developing new means of cooperation such as the Inter-American Defense Board created at the Rio conference early in 1942; and the distribution of aid and supplies in conjunction with the Lend-Lease Program proffered an assortment of rewards for compliant Latin Americans. The Panama Canal, vulnerable to either sabotage or air attack, posed special problems in defense. U.S. officials never fully solved them but used air patrols to guard against surprises. [47]

Following Hitler's declaration of war on the United States in December 1941, German submarines inaugurated deadly assaults against merchant ships in the Caribbean. Oil tankers moving precious cargoes from Mexico and Venezuela became favorite targets. The sinkings escalated in number from twenty-four in February 1942 to sixty-six in June of the same year. Such attacks concentrated in the sea-lanes around Trinidad, the Panama Canal, the Yucatan Channel, and the Windward Passage between Cuba and Haiti, where a total of 336 ships went down. The worst of the carnage ended early in 1943, once U.S. authorities had learned how to minimize the effects through the proper use of naval convoys, air patrols, and other forms of antisubmarine warfare. [48]

The defeat of the German U-boats extinguished the enemy naval presence in the Western Hemisphere and raised other questions. At a time of fierce fighting around the world, some U.S. leaders, such as secretary of war Henry Stimson, wondered why Latin American countries that were uninvolved in actual combat should qualify for military assistance under Lend-Lease. In the State Department, Sumner Welles raised the same issue and worried about the effects of an impending Latin American arms race. Also causing criticism was the belief that dictators such as Somoza, Trujillo, and Ubico were using military aid to keep themselves in power. Irwin F. Gellman observes that only small amounts—about 1.1 percent of all Lend-Lease aid—went to Latin America, mainly to Brazil and Mexico. In his view the "hemispheric despots," though admittedly beneficiaries of U.S. military aid, relied more heavily on other means to maintain their control. Paul Coe Clark, Jr.'s study of the United States and Somoza arrives at a similar conclusion, showing that the dictator's survivability depended more on his own unscrupulous political skills than on U.S. support.

For the United States, military cooperation with Latin American officials paid off in various ways. The Inter-American Defense Board advanced a sense of goodwill and common purpose. As Gellman explains, it functioned something like "a hemispheric war college" in which Latin Americans could acquire instruction in the use of U.S. methods and equipment. Such forms of military collaboration also had political significance. Although under the terms of most agreements the United States would lose access to Latin American bases at the end of the war, the War Department intended "to extend inter-American comradeship into the postwar era" through the cultivation of the Latin American officer corps. For proponents of U.S. air power the maintenance of bases in Latin America had particular significance.[49]

The Roosevelt administration also employed cultural diplomacy to combat the Nazis. Wartime propaganda emphasized likenesses and affinities with Latin Americans. Its purpose was to underscore "the mythical ideological unity of the nations of the New World" and draw sharp distinctions between totalitarian powers and the "democratically oriented nations of the Western Hemisphere." A typical State Department memorandum in September 1939 listed the "distinguishing ideals and beliefs which bind us together," including "faith in republican institutions, loyalty to democracy as an ideal, reverence for liberty, acceptance of the dignity of the individual, . . . aversion to the use of force [and] adherence to the principles of equal sovereignty of states and justice under international law." Such formulations played down the prevalence of authoritarian regimes. If necessary for purposes of public relations, U.S. leaders could depict Batista, Somoza, Trujillo, and Ubico as old-fashioned military strongmen who differed in important ways from the European totalitarians.[50]

Negative stereotypes everywhere distorted popular perceptions on all sides. In the United States, pervasive images depicted Latin American males as indolent and licentious. In political cartoons, they took long naps under enormous sombreros during the siesta hour or lustily pursued long-haired, dark-eyed señoritas. Similarly flawed, Latin American renditions depended too heavily on clichéd versions of the Yankee capitalist, notable for his greed and crass materialism. To combat misconceptions and promote goodwill, the Roosevelt administration became "culture conscious." U.S. government officials believed that "economic and political cooperation" would follow from "intellectual and cultural understanding" and consequently emphasized "a sympathetic understanding of tradition, history, literature, and the arts."[51] On August 6, 1940, the Roosevelt administration created the Office of the Coordinator of Inter-American Affairs (OCIAA). Headed by Nelson A. Rockefeller, the talented and ambitious scion of an oil-rich Republican family, this agency assumed the responsibility of promoting a coherent Pan American system, seeking thereby to attain an omnibus purpose "to prevent revolutions in the Americas, fight Axis agents, and increase United States trade." In order to work the OCIAA had to avoid the impression of "interfering in any way with the internal affairs of those sovereign states." Rockefeller devised "a multifaceted program of ideological, cultural, and financial persuasion." Budgeted initially at $3.5 million from Roosevelt's emergency fund, the OCIAA by 1942 became a $38 million operation, attempting to present the United States to Latin America as "the beneficent, philanthropic, understanding, yet humble sister nation in the hemispheric family of free and equally idealistic republics."

As distribution outlets the agency employed radio broadcasts, newspapers, magazines, and motion pictures, all the while encouraging favorable, upbeat treatment of the United States and Latin America. The office would not sanction criticism of imperfections in the U.S. political system and blocked the distribution of the movie *Mr. Smith Goes to Washington* in Latin America because it reflected negatively on the activities of the U.S. Congress. Similarly, the office compelled changes to eliminate offensive stereotypes in the film *Down Argentine Way:* a smarmy Argentine gigolo who spoke with a Mexican accent and a crooked horse race rigged by elites at the Buenos Aires Jockey Club. In contrast, the Walt Disney Studio in conjunction with OCIAA produced an animated film called *Saludos Amigos*. Properly perky, it featured a peppy little anthropomorphic airplane with human characteristics and a dapper Brazilian parrot, José Carioca, who swapped wisecracks with Donald Duck. [52]

Wartime economics initially played havoc with Latin Americans. Actually the third in a sequence of external shocks to strike them in twenty-five years, the Second World War entailed consequences that "were quantitatively and qualitatively different" from those of the First World War and the Great Depression. The war not only devastated the traditional Latin American export trade by cutting off the markets of continental Europe and diminishing the British demand but hastened "growing disillusionment" with the export-led model of economic growth in Latin America. The result was "a growing sense of nationalism in a number of Latin American republics" and "a greater commitment" to "an inward-looking" approach to economic development and industrialization. Such tendencies, already present in Bolivia and Mexico during the 1930s, accelerated during the war years. According to Bulmer-Thomas, "State intervention in support of industry, particularly in the larger republics, now became direct, with important investments in basic commodities as well as in the infrastructure needed to support a more complex industrial system."

The Roosevelt administration, "more sensitive to Latin American needs than its predecessors," understood "the importance of avoiding economic collapse in the region," if for no other reason than "to secure supplies of raw materials and strategic commodities." Consequently, a system of inter-American economic cooperation took shape after the outbreak of war in September 1939. For example, the Inter-American Development Commission (IADC), established in 1940, sought to stimulate trade between the United States and Latin America, to promote trade among the Latin Americans, and to encourage industrialization. Because access to strategic materials was a priority for the United States, in 1940 the Roosevelt administration originated the Metals Reserve Company and the Rubber Reserve Company to stockpile essential supplies. As it turned out, Latin America became the prime beneficiary. After the Japanese conquered raw materials–producing regions in Asia, the United States relied on its southern neighbors for a vast range of materials such as abaca, antimony, asbestos, cinchona, industrial diamonds, kenaf, mica, quebracho wood, quartz crystals, rubber, and zirconium. Direct U.S. foreign investment in Latin America, much of it in strategic materials, "soared during the war to levels not seen since the late 1920s," and "official U.S. loans through the Export-Import Bank and Lend-Lease—though not restricted to the extraction of strategic materials—became increasingly important." Cooperation developed in other areas as well. Recognizing "the crucial role played by coffee exports in a dozen republics," the United States promoted the Inter-American Coffee Convention (IACC) in 1941. By establishing quotas, higher prices, and guaranteed market access, it became "a lifeline for the smaller republics and a great boon for the larger republics—many of which had become heavily dependent on the German market in the 1930s."

Still, although U.S. purchases of Latin American exports became critically important, they "could not fully compensate for the loss of Japan, continental Europe, and the shrinking British market." Latin Americans increasingly sought trade with one another to sustain the volume of exports. Previously, this kind of commerce had never amounted to much; in 1938 it had accounted for only 6.1 percent of the region's exports. As Bulmer-Thomas notes, "All this changed as a result of both war and the system of inter-American economic cooperation."

Indeed, proliferating bilateral agreements reduced economic barriers and allowed for a significant expansion of interregional trade, amounting to 16.6 percent of the total in 1945. Inter-American cooperation was "the major factor preventing a collapse of exports after 1939."

The war also encouraged industrial growth in the larger republics for three main reasons. First, "the sharp decline in the volume of imports after 1939 allowed domestic manufacturers to expand production even with an unchanged level of real consumption." Consequently, the adoption of an import-substitution plan permitted modest increases in the growth of manufacturing in Argentina, Brazil, Chile, and Mexico. Second, intra–Latin American trade allowed manufacturers to sell their products in neighboring countries. As examples, Brazil increased textile exports; Argentina sold more manufactured goods; and Mexico expanded industrial sales in the United States. Third, "the rise of firms not dependent on consumer demand" also provided a stimulus. They produced capital goods for other productive sectors and the state. For example, the U.S.-financed Brazilian steel mill, Volta Redonda, sold its output to construction and manufacturing enterprises, thereby providing a substitute for previously imported steel. Similarly, in Argentina, Chile, and Mexico, cement works, chemical plants, oil refineries, and operations in plastics, rayons, and machinery relieved existing dependencies upon imports.

Such changes in the industrial sector had links with "the rise of a more interventionist state in Latin America." As Bulmer-Thomas notes, "Even deeply conservative governments could not avoid an increase in state responsibilities during the war years." For one thing, "free markets could not handle the problems posed by dollar inflation, import shortages, and unsold agricultural surpluses." For another, the war effort placed "additional demands on the state through the need for infrastructure and public works." Such developments had huge implications for the immediate postwar period and ran counter to U.S. preferences by moving away from reliance on private capital and free enterprise as the means of economic development. In the short term the Second World War marked a transition from the traditional export-led model of growth toward an alternative, inward-looking approach based on import-substitution industrialization. This change "weakened the link between the external sector and aggregate economic performance," "increased the importance of the nonexport sectors," and "shifted the composition of industrial output toward intermediate and capital goods."[53] In combination, the effects altered important parts of the traditional economic relationship between the United States and the countries of Latin America.

How should historians evaluate the impact of the Good Neighbor policy, the depression, and the war? This large, difficult, and multifaceted question allows for no single answer. Much depends on angles of vision and value systems. In a book published in 1943, Samuel Flagg Bemis praises the wartime partnership with Latin America, claiming that creative changes in the 1930s made it possible. Irwin F. Gellman's 1979 account follows Bemis in looking upon the political achievements of Good Neighbor diplomacy as beneficial. In contrast, David Green underscores the importance of U.S. economic interests and the difficulty of reconciling them with the demands of Latin American nationalism. George Black, in 1988, focused on advertising, travel and tourism, and cultural relations between the United States and Central America and the Caribbean in his assessment of the Good Neighbor policy.[54] Too often, according to Green, U.S. leaders displayed arrogance and insensitivity toward legitimate Latin American concerns.[55]

Such differences are probably irreconcilable. Michael Grow explicitly addresses the problem in *The Good Neighbor Policy and Authoritarianism in Paraguay*. Using familiar categories, he characterizes the leaders in the Roosevelt administration as "heirs of Woodrow Wilson's 'liberal internationalist' world vision" and explains their behavior on the basis of such convictions. For them, a "world order of capitalist democracies," led by the United States and "linked interdependently through mutually profitable free trade," would constitute "the surest path to international peace and prosperity." From a liberal perspective the expansion of U.S. power and influence during the period might appear as the consequence of "an altruistic and pragmatic campaign to construct a prosperous, stable new hemispheric order mutually beneficial to the United States *and* the nations of Latin America." But for Grow, any such conclusion would be an error. He endorses a more skeptical view, depicting Roosevelt's Latin American policy less as an example of "liberal inter-nationalism" than as a product of "liberal imperialism," that is, "a concerted drive to achieve informal United States hegemony" for reasons of "national economic self-interest."[56]

Frederick B. Pike's important work, *FDR's Good Neighbor Policy: Sixty Years of Generally Gentle Chaos,* provides a more sympathetic account. Pike begins by asking a fundamental question: Have we been good neighbors? His brutally realistic reply says yes, some of the time, but really "no better . . . than we had to be." For him, "that seems the most one could expect. We might, after all, have been a good deal worse." That sage point establishes a main theme, emphasizing that whatever its shortcomings, the Good Neighbor policy did rank in some ways as a success. Pike intriguingly and effectively depicts Roosevelt as a "trickster," a kind of political magician who obtained successes through the reconciliation of opposites. In this case, he brought together the defense of vital U.S. interests with some kind of regard for the requirements of Latin American sovereignty. Roosevelt, according to Pike, will always be "an enigma and a source of controversy." Nevertheless, his "enigmatic qualities served him well as a hemispheric statesman." Roosevelt earned respect and admiration from Latin Americans. He was in Pike's account "a gringo in the Latin mold, a man they could understand . . . as a projection of their own political and social style." He was "aristocratic," "patronalistic," "personalistic," and also an affable "populist" who supposedly could intuit the people's will. He was seldom preachy, condescending, or racist in his treatment of Latin Americans and seemed willing to let them count for something by giving them a share. His death on April 12, 1945, deprived the Good Neighbor policy of an essential part. His successor, Harry S. Truman, "an archetypical gringo" in the White House, possessed none of the skills and sensitivities necessary to maintain it. [57]

NOTES

1. Robert Freeman Smith, "The Good Neighbor Policy: The Liberal Paradox in United States Relations with Latin America," in *Watershed of Empire: Essays on New Deal Foreign Policy,* ed. Leonard P. Liggio and James Martin (Colorado Springs: Ralph Myles, 1976), 66–67.

2. Alexander DeConde, *Herbert Hoover's Latin-American Policy* (Palo Alto: Stanford University Press, 1951), 13–15, 18–24; Martin L. Fausold, *The Presidency of Herbert Hoover* (Lawrence: University Press of Kansas, 1985), 32.

3. Fausold, *Presidency of Herbert Hoover*, 183; Smith, "Good Neighbor Policy," 66–67.

4. Bryce Wood, *The Making of the Good Neighbor Policy* (New York: Columbia University Press), 45.

5. Fausold, *Presidency of Herbert Hoover,* 185–86; Bryce Wood, *The United States and Latin American Wars, 1932–1942* (New York: Columbia University Press. 1966).

6. Victor Bulmer-Thomas, *The Economic History of Latin America since Independence* (New York: Cambridge University Press, 1994), 194–99.

7. Peter H. Smith and Thomas E. Skidmore, *Modern Latin America,* 2d ed. (New York: Oxford University Press, 1992), chap. 3; Rosemary Thorp, ed., *Latin America in the 1930s: The Role of the Periphery in World Crisis* (New York: St. Martin's Press, 1984).

8. Bulmer-Thomas, *Economic History*, 208–09, 216–17.

9. Irwin F. Gellman, *Good Neighbor Diplomacy: United States Policies in Latin America, 1933–1945* (Baltimore: Johns Hopkins University Press, 1979), 11.

10. Gellman, 14, 17, chap. 2; Gellman, *Secret Affairs: Franklin Roosevelt, Cordell Hull, and Sumner Welles* (Baltimore: Johns Hopkins University Press, 1995), chap. 1.

11. Louis A. Pérez, Jr., *Cuba and the United States: Ties of Singular Intimacy* (Athens: University of Georgia Press, 1990), 180, 183, 185.

12. Pérez, *Cuba and the United States*, 186, 191–92, 194, 200–1; Gellman, *Good Neighbor Diplomacy,* 25.

13. Gellman, *Good Neighbor Diplomacy,* 33; Brenda Gayle Plummer, *Haiti and the United States: The Psychological Moment* (Athens: University of Georgia Press, 1992), chaps. 6, 8; G. Pope Atkins and Larman C. Wilson, *The Dominican Republic and the United States: From Imperialism to Transnationalism* (Athens: University of Georgia Press, 1998), chap. 2; Michael L. Conniff, *Panama and the United States: The Forced Alliance* (Athens: University of Georgia Press, 1992), chap. 5.

14. Gordon Connell-Smith, *The United States and Latin America: An Historical Analysis of Inter-American Relations* (New York: John Wiley & Sons, 1974), 167.

15. Paul Coe Clark, Jr., *The United States and Somoza, 1933–1956: A Revisionist Look* (Westport, CT: Praeger, 1992), esp. chaps. I, II.

16. Arthur A. Ekirk, *Ideologies and Utopias: The Impact of the New Deal on American Thought* (Chicago: Quadrangle Books, 1969), chaps. 1–2; William E. Leuchtenberg, *The FDR*

Years: On Roosevelt and His Legacy (New York: Columbia University Press, 1995); chaps. 1–2.

17. William E. Leuchtenberg, *Franklin D. Roosevelt and the New Deal* (New York: Harper & Row, 1963), chaps. 3–4.

18. Dick Steward, *Trade and Hemisphere: The Good Neighbor Policy and Reciprocal Trade* (Columbia: University of Missouri Press, 1975), 10; Lloyd C. Gardner, *Economic Aspects of New Deal Diplomacy* (Madison: University of Wisconsin Press, 1964), chaps. 2–3, 6, 10.

19. Frederick C. Adams, *Economic Diplomacy: The Export-Import Bank and American Foreign Relations, 1934–1939* (Columbia: University of Missouri Press, 1976), 65–66, chaps. 5, 7.

20. Gellman, *Good Neighbor Diplomacy*, 40, 43, 47.

21. Gellman, *Good Neighbor Diplomacy*, 47–49; Pérez, *Cuba and the United States*, 122–23; David Green, *The Containment of Latin America: A History of the Myths and Realities of the Good Neighbor Policy* (Chicago: Quadrangle Books, 1971), 20.

22. Frank D. McCann, *The Brazilian-American Alliance, 1937–1945* (Princeton: Princeton University Press, 1974); Stanley E. Hilton, *Brazil and the Great Powers, 1930–1939: The Politics of Trade Rivalry* (Austin: University of Texas Press, 1975).

23. Frank D. McCann, "Brazil, the United States, and World War II: A Commentary," *Diplomatic History* 3 (Winter 1979): 63–64, 66–67; Gellman, *Good Neighbor Diplomacy*, 48; R. A. Humphreys, *Latin America and the Second World War*, 2 vols. (London: University of London Athlone Press, 1982), 113–46, chap. 1.

24. Gellman, *Good Neighbor Diplomacy*, 48.

25. Bulmer-Thomas, *Economic History*, 201, 212, 217, 219–20, 222–23.

26. Wood, *Making of the Good Neighbor Policy*, 159–60, 162.

27. Gellman, *Good Neighbor Diplomacy*, 49–50; Wood, *Making of the Good Neighbor Policy*, chap. 7.

28. Wood, *Making of the Good Neighbor Policy*, 203.

29. William H. Beezley and Colin M. MacLachlan, *El Gran Pueblo*, 2 vols. (Englewood Cliffs, NJ: Prentice-Hall, 1994), 309, chap. 2.

30. Beezley and MacLachlan, *El Gran Pueblo*, 309–11, 322–24; Friedrich E. Schuler, *Mexico between Hitler and Roosevelt: Mexican Foreign Relations in the Age of Lázaro Cárdenas, 1934–1940* (Albuquerque: University of New Mexico Press, 1998), chaps. 4–5; E. David Cronon, *Josephus Daniels in Mexico* (Madison: University of Wisconsin Press, 1960), chaps. 1, 7, 8–10; Lorenzo Meyer, *Mexico and the United States in the Oil Controversy, 1917–1942*, trans. Muriel Vasconcellos (Austin: University of Texas Press, 1977), chaps. 8–10.

31. Wood, *Making of the Good Neighbor Policy*, 205–6, 208–9, 213, 222, 233, 249, 253, 258–59; Cronon, *Josephus Daniels*, chaps. 7–8; Schuler, *Mexico between Hitler and Roosevelt*, chaps. 5–6.

32. Green, *Containment of Latin America*, 38.

33. B. S. McBeth, *Juan Vicente Gómez and the Oil Companies in Venezuela* (New York: Cambridge University Press, 1983), chaps. 2–3; Judith Ewell, *Venezuela and the United States: From Monroe's Hemisphere to Petroleum's Empire* (Athens: University of Georgia Press, 1996), chaps. 5–6.

34. Wood, *Making of the Good Neighbor Policy*, 263–65, chap. 10.

35. Humphreys, *Latin America*, 1, chap. 1.

36. Thomas G. Paterson, J. Garry Clifford, and Kenneth J. Hagan, *American Foreign Relations: A History*, 2 vols., 4th ed. (Lexington, MA: D. C. Heath, 1995), chaps. 4–6; William Appleman Williams, *The Tragedy of American Diplomacy*, rev. ed. (New York: Delta, 1962), chaps. 4–5; Robert Dallek, *Franklin D. Roosevelt and American Foreign Policy, 1932–1945* (Oxford University Press, 1979), pts. 2, 3; Gardner, *Economic Aspects*, chaps. 7, 8.

37. Robert A. Divine, *Roosevelt and World War II* (Baltimore: Johns Hopkins University Press, 1969), 37; Paterson, Clifford, and Hagan, *American Foreign Relations*, 209–10, chap. 2; Warren F. Kimball, *The Juggler: Franklin Roosevelt as Wartime Statesman* (Princeton: Princeton University Press, 1991).

38. Paterson, Clifford, and Hagan, *American Foreign Relations*, 2:213.

39. Gellman, *Good Neighbor Diplomacy,* 74–79, 83–85, 88–92, 95.

40. Gellman, *Good Neighbor Diplomacy,* 109–15; Stanley E. Hilton, *Hitler's Secret War in South America, 1939–1945: German Military Espionage and Allied Counterespionage in Brazil* (Baton Rouge: Louisiana State University Press, 1981); Leslie B. Rout, Jr. and John F. Bratzel, *The Shadow War: German Espionage and United States Counterespionage in Latin America during World War II* (Frederick, MD: University Publications of America, 1986); Robert C. Newton, *The "Nazi Menace" in Argentina, 1931–1947* (Palo Alto: Stanford University Press, 1992).

41. Waldo H. Heinrichs, *Threshold of War: Franklin D. Roosevelt and American Entry into World War II* (New York: Oxford University Press, 1988).

42. Gellman, *Good Neighbor Diplomacy,* 121, 124–26.

43. Humphreys, *Latin America,* 92–96, chap. 2.

44. Humphreys, *Latin America,* 97–100, 105, 117–19, 136, 138, 143–44, 149–50, 158–59.

45. Samuel Flagg Bemis, *The Latin-American Policy of the United States* (1943; reprinted, New York: W. W. Norton, 1967), chaps. 22–23; Gellman, *Good Neighbor Diplomacy,* chaps. 10–13.

46. Green, *Containment of Latin America,* chaps. 4–5; Gardner, *Economic Aspects,* chap. 10; Adams, *Economic Diplomacy,* chaps. 5, 7; Michael Grow, *The Good Neighbor Policy and Authoritarianism in Paraguay: United States Economic Expansion and Great-Power Rivalry in Latin America during World War II* (Lawrence: University Press of Kansas, 1981), 113–15.

47. Gellman, *Good Neighbor Diplomacy,* 128–29, 134–35, chap. 10; John Major, *Prize Possession: The United States and the Panama Canal, 1903–1979* (New York: Cambridge University Press, 1993), chap. 12.

48. Humphreys, *Latin America,* 2–4, chap. 2.

49. Gellman, *Good Neighbor Diplomacy,* 138–39.

50. Gerald K. Haines, "Under the Eagle's Wing: The Franklin Roosevelt Administration Forges an American Hemisphere," *Diplomatic History* 1, no. 4 (Fall 1977): 373–74.

51. Haines, "Under the Eagle's Wing," 378–79; Frederick B. Pike, *The United States and Latin America: Myths and Stereotypes of Civilization and Nature* (Austin: University of Texas Press, 1992), chap. 8; John J. Johnson, *Latin America in Caricature* (Austin: University of Texas Press, 1980); J. Manuel Espinosa, *Inter-American Beginnings of U.S. Cultural Diplomacy, 1936–1948* (Washington, DC: U.S. Department of State, 1976), chaps. 3, 9–10.

52. Haines, "Under the Eagle's Wing," 380, 382–83.

53. Bulmer-Thomas, *Economic History,* 239, 241–48.

54. See George Black, *The Good Neighbor: How the United States Wrote the History of Central America and the Caribbean* (New York: Pantheon, 1988).

55. Bemis, *Latin-American Policy,* chap. 22; Gellman, *Good Neighbor Diplomacy,* chaps. 10–13; Green, *Containment of Latin America,* chap. 4.

56. Grow, *Good Neighbor Policy and Authoritarianism,* 113–15; Abraham F. Lowenthal, "United States Policy toward Latin America: 'Liberal,' 'Radical,' and 'Bureaucratic' Perspectives," *Latin American Research Review* 8 (Fall 1973): 3–25.

57. Frederick B. Pike, *FDR's Good Neighbor Policy: Sixty Years of Generally Gentle Chaos* (Austin: University of Texas Press, 1995), xi, 138–62, 350–53.

Chapter Four

Cold War, Dependency, and Change, 1945–1959

The onset of the Cold War transformed the conduct of international relations by establishing a new context. For U.S. policy makers the breakdown in relations with the Soviet Union after the Second World War became the central preoccupation. Seeking to build liberal-capitalist systems in as much of the world as possible, U.S. leaders guarded against presumed threats of Soviet expansion by applying the containment principles first in Western Europe and then in other regions. The consequences shaped U.S. dealings with most other countries. Those nations operating outside of the Soviet sphere became significant or not, depending on larger calculations of gain or loss in the Cold War struggle.

In the Western Hemisphere, U.S. leaders initially took much for granted. While working toward the construction of a regional collective security system, they embraced Latin American governments as political and military allies but otherwise looked upon the region as peripheral in importance. For that reason, they placed no equivalent emphasis on programs of economic modernization and development. Latin Americans, meanwhile, resented the neglect, regarding it as a sign of indifference and condescension. Yet for many of them, economic dependence on the United States had gone so far that breaking loose posed complicated problems.

Under Presidents Truman and Eisenhower the Good Neighbor policy lost viability as a guide. Neither president possessed much understanding of Latin America, and personnel changes in the State Department compounded the difficulty. In August 1943, Sumner Welles resigned as undersecretary after allegations of personal misbehavior. In November 1944, Cordell Hull, his health failing, also went into retirement. His successor was Edward R. Stettinius, Jr., a corporate executive who possessed no diplomatic experiences and no special appreciation for Latin American issues. According to Irwin Gellman, those shifts marked "the beginning of the disintegration in Pan American solidarity" by removing from authority the policy makers most committed to it.[1]

FASHIONING A REGIONAL SYSTEM

Questions of regional organization in the Western Hemisphere ranked high as priorities at the end of the Second World War. Drawing on wartime experiences stressing hemispheric solidarity, government leaders fashioned a regional system of collective security at a series of international conferences in Mexico City, San Francisco, Rio de Janeiro, and Bogotá. The system consisted of two parts, the Rio Pact, a military alliance, and the Organization of American States (OAS), a political counterpart. Taken together, these devices perpetuated at least an appearance of cooperation but otherwise elicited divergent appraisals. For enthusiasts, the creation of a regional system was laudable for reasons of national security. For critics, the system emanated from U.S. hegemonic aspirations and functioned essentially as an alliance between the United States and the established elites of Latin America in defense of the status quo.[2]

Serious discussions of regional organization for the postwar period got under way late in the war, prompted mainly by Argentine ambiguities. By remaining neutral, the Argentine government upheld what its leaders regarded as sovereign prerogatives and drove secretary of state Cordell Hull to distraction. He attributed the Argentine position to pro-Axis preferences. He also feared the destabilization of neighboring countries by pro-Nazi influences and wanted a cohesive alignment in support of the Allies. Actually an amalgam of various tendencies, the Argentine policy of neutrality followed from traditional aversions. Argentine nationalists perceived Pan American formulations as instruments of U.S. domination. Moreover, in a sense pro-Axis, neutrality showed the impact of German and Italian immigration; indeed, many Argentines conceived of their country as European. Another consideration was economic. For the most part, the Argentines lacked restrictive dependence on U.S. markets and capital and so possessed some additional room to maneuver. As producers of primary agricultural commodities such as beef, wheat, and mutton, they sold mainly in the British market. The British, for their part, had less concern about Argentine neutrality than about maintaining a reliable food supply.

The Argentine army took over the government in a bloodless coup in June 1943 by installing general Pedro Ramírez as interim president. The leaders, mainly high-ranking officers working through a secret society, the so-called Grupo de Oficiales Unidos, embraced some fascist notions about corporate unity and racial purity and also drew on traditional militarist beliefs in nationalism, hierarchy, and authority. For Argentine military officers the Franco and Mussolini regimes in Spain and Italy served as special inspirations. Nevertheless, the Ramírez government did promise to break with the Axis eventually. In fact, the new foreign minister, admiral Segundo Storni, naïvely asked for patience from the United States in a letter to secretary of state Cordell Hull in which he also urged large-scale military assistance for Argentina through Lend-Lease. To Hull, this request looked like a bribe. In full fury, he excoriated the Argentine government as a pro-fascist presence in South America. Storni had to resign. Replacing him as foreign minister, general Alberto Gilbert engaged in something of a balancing act, seeking to avoid giving offense to either the United States or other high-ranking Argentine officers. Some of them, notably colonel Juan Domingo Perón, an emerging power, opposed any concession to the United States as an insult to Argentine honor. When as a consequence of complicated political maneuvers General Ramírez withdrew from the presidency early in 1944, Hull withheld diplomatic recognition from the new government, headed by general Edelmiro Farrell. The secretary sought in this way to force a change in favor of the Allies; he also employed economic sanctions to escalate the pressure.[3] The effort failed. Later, Hull himself resigned. Ill and exhausted, he retired from the State Department soon after Roosevelt won the presidential election in November 1944.

Meanwhile, cross-purposes in the State Department contributed to other diplomatic confusions. Hull's successor, secretary of state Edward Stettinius, functioned mainly as a figurehead. For a time, he upheld Hull's policy of nonrecognition toward Argentina and thus incurred a challenge from Nelson Rockefeller. Young, smart, rich, and ambitious, Rockefeller became the undersecretary of state for Latin American affairs following Sumner Welles's departure. Unlike Hull and Stettinius, Rockefeller regarded nonrecognition as ineffective and counterproductive. He favored a more conciliatory position toward Argentina, a preference shared by most Latin American diplomats. As a means of clarifying its status the Argentine government requested a special inter-American conference. Disinclined to risk public embarrassment, Stettinius wanted no such gathering but hesitated to oppose it outright. To resolve the dilemma, Mexican foreign minister Ezequiel Padilla then proposed a conference of foreign ministers in Mexico City. This approach allowed for international discussions of the Argentine problem without direct Argentine participation: Under the rules, only those countries that had broken relations with the Axis powers or declared war upon them would receive invitations.[4]

The Mexico City conference met at Chapultepec Palace from February 21 until March 8, 1945. Headed by Secretary Stettinius, the U.S. delegation wanted a carefully controlled agenda to avoid controversy over Argentina and to maintain the appearance of hemispheric solidarity. Other potentially troublesome and divisive issues included the relationship between the nations of the Western Hemisphere and the proposed United Nations organization, one of Franklin Roosevelt's favorite projects. At the Dumbarton Oaks conference in Washington late in the summer of 1944, the Big Three—the United States, Great Britain, and the Soviet Union—had accepted commitments to create a new world organization, conceiving of it as something like a remodeled League of Nations. The idea was popular in the United States, especially among Democrats, who looked upon it as a "second chance": that is, an opportunity to atone for the rejection of the Treaty of Versailles after the First World War. Administration planners wanted the United States to participate in a postwar system of collective security based solidly on the expectation of continued cooperation among the Big Three. Yet unanswered questions produced high levels of uncertainty. What of the impact on existing regional arrangements, such as the Western Hemisphere system? Would this new organization take precedence over them? Could the United Nations sanction interference from the outside in Western Hemisphere affairs, possibly even military intervention?

Among officials in the State Department the discussions ranged around two broad choices. Advocates of the first portrayed the prerogatives of the United Nations as superior to those of regional systems. These "universalists" included Alger Hiss and Leo Pasvolsky, both attached to the State Department's International Organization Division. They worried about the emergence of regional spheres of influence and regarded any such outcome as incompatible with a truly international system. To check such tendencies, they wanted to vest the dominant decision-making authority in the United Nations. Critics saw this approach as expanding the role of the Great Powers too much at the expense of the smaller states. Consequently, a group of "regionalists" in the State Department advocated a second option. Led by Nelson Rockefeller, they called for a self-sustaining, collective-security system in the Western Hemisphere as protection against outside meddling and the possibility of subjugation to the Great Powers. One of the regionalists, Adolf A. Berle, the U.S. ambassador to Brazil, conjured up dire possibilities. Adoption of the universalist option "would mean that the United States and others could not prevent Argentina from seizing Uruguay without the consent of Britain and Russia—who at the moment might be backing Argentina." In short, the universalist alternative "would introduce European diplomacy into every inter-American dispute."[5]

Latin Americans desired a regional system for their own reasons. They wanted protection against external interference and also against the United States. At the same time, they perceived in such arrangements a means of facilitating the infusion of U.S. economic aid into Latin America. During the war, at the third meeting of foreign ministers in Rio de Janeiro in January

1942, Sumner Welles had encouraged this expectation by promising U.S. support for Latin American economic development. He hoped to raise living standards by means of aid and assistance for industrialization, modernization, and diversification. To Latin Americans, such rewards seemed proper responses, given their magnitude of support for the Allies during the war.[6]

The outcome of the Mexico City conference, the Act of Chapultepec, allowed for multiple approaches toward common goals. The measure endorsed Latin American preferences by recommending in favor of a "regional arrangement" to maintain peace and security in the Western Hemisphere. It also affirmed support for "the purposes and principles" of the United Nations.[7] By combining the one with the other, the delegates maintained their options, seeking to accommodate both the universalist and the regionalist position.

For Latin Americans, economic relations in the postwar period took on special significance. During the war, they had benefited from special arrangements assuring extensive sales in foreign markets at good prices. Now they worried about the impact of falling prices and shrinking sales in contracting markets. As safeguards, some favored protective tariffs to nurture infant industries; others advocated commodity agreements to stabilize prices. Most hoped for U.S. aid, specifically in the form of loans and grants to bolster growth and diversification. As Mexican foreign minister Ezequiel Padilla pointed out at Chapultepec, it was "vital for the [Latin] Americans to do more than produce raw materials and live in a state of semi-colonialism." He looked for some form of assistance from the United States.[8]

Instead of assurances, he got statements of high capitalist principle. The speeches by U.S. delegates indicated that prewar suspicion of economic nationalism and state enterprise in Latin America had not gone away. Indeed, according to official U.S. views, restrictive trade and investment practices in the 1930s had contributed to the world crisis by encouraging cutthroat international competition and eventually war. To avoid "shortsighted" policies, undersecretary of state Dean Acheson affirmed his belief in free trade as the best means of expanding commerce, enhancing prosperity, reducing world tension, and promoting peace. These views were established orthodoxy among U.S. leaders. As assessed by the historian R. A. Humphreys, the implications for Latin America meant some measure of U.S. encouragement for economic development but typically "within the context of an expanding, interdependent and liberalized world economy." Overall, the discussion placed the United States in opposition to Latin American efforts to escape from "economic vassalage to the more industrialized countries."

Finally, the delegates at Chapultepec addressed the question of Argentine neutrality by affirming a resolution of censure. It castigated Argentine leaders for possessing pro-fascist sympathies and maintaining Axis ties. It also proposed the means of rectification. To set things right, Argentina would have to adhere immediately to Allied principles and issue a war declaration. This outcome gratified Secretary of State Stettinius, an heir of Hull's anti-Argentine animosity. He extolled the achievements of the Chapultepec conference, however vague and mixed, as splendid things and hyperbolically characterized the experience as "a culmination of the Good Neighbor Policy." Whatever the fissures and cleavages among them, the Western Hemisphere nations had retained an appearance of hemispheric solidarity.

The United Nations conference got under way in San Francisco on April 25, 1945. Forty-six countries sent delegations, including nineteen from Latin America—but not Argentina. The neutrality question still caused friction. The Farrell government in Argentina received no invitation, even though the leaders had complied with the Act of Chapultepec by declaring war upon Germany and Japan on March 27, 1945. The problem now resided in Great-Power politics. The Soviet Union regarded Argentina as a pro-fascist enemy state, undeserving of participation in the San Francisco conference. Somewhat more forgiving, the other Latin American delegations accepted in better faith the Argentine war declaration, however belated. With the support of the United States, they suggested a workable solution. If the Soviets wanted "White Russia" and the Ukraine to have representation at the conference, they could do so, but only if Argentina could take part.[9]

At San Francisco, Latin Americans displayed special interest in the structure of decision-making authority but otherwise exercised scant influence. To head off Great-Power domination, they hoped for a broad allocation of responsibility to the smaller states in the General Assembly and also for a permanent Latin American seat on the Security Council; President Vargas of Brazil thought his country a candidate for such a spot. In these matters, Latin Americans achieved none of their goals. The Security Council fell under the control of the Big Three, each with veto power, and the General Assembly functioned primarily as an international debating society. These outcomes reflected political realities. The United States, Great Britain, and the Soviet Union, having invested the greatest effort in winning the victory over the Axis powers, also wielded the greatest influence when the conflict ended.

Other discussions centered on ways to reconcile regional and universal approaches. For Latin Americans, the Act of Chapultepec remained the guide. They wanted to reconcile the purposes and principles of the inter-American system with those of the world organization, seeking among other things safeguards against outsiders, including the United States. Meanwhile, the U.S. delegation divided into factions. Secretary Stettinius espoused the universalist option while affirming Great-Power prerogatives. In his view, "we must not be pushed around by a lot of small American republics who are dependent on us in many ways—economically, politically, militarily." But different arguments based on other considerations undercut Stettinius's position and prepared the way for a kind of blending process.

The defense of the Monroe Doctrine especially concerned conservative nationalists. They regarded this ancient creed as the embodiment of U.S. tradition and experience and would sanction neither concessions nor compromises which, they warned, would bring dire consequences. What of the prerogative to guard against European intrusions? What of the political implications? Could a failure to uphold the Monroe Doctrine result in rejection of the United Nations in the U.S. Senate? Or conversely, could acceptance of the United Nations mean repudiation of the Monroe Doctrine? These touchy matters required clarification and of course recalled the debate in 1919 over the Versailles treaty. Senator Arthur P. Vandenberg, a Republican from Michigan and a U.S. delegate at San Francisco, had described the Monroe Doctrine in 1926 as "the indispensable bulwark of American independence." As Gaddis Smith explains, his views in 1945 had not changed: "No politician . . . was more steeped emotionally and intellectually in the principles of the Monroe Doctrine."

Under the terms of article 51, the UN Charter, as written at San Francisco, provided the means of reconciling universalist and regionalist views by allowing for a form of coexistence: It sanctioned the exercise of regional prerogatives within the context of the world organization. More specifically, it recognized for each member "the inherent right of individual and collective self-defense," thereby permitting defensive measures to be taken alone or in cooperation with others, pending action by the Security Council. Humphreys calls article 51 "the great compromise." Less positively, he also claims that it established "the legal basis of the post-war blocs that marked the Cold War." This long-term implication, not so clear at the time, caused no bother for Senator Vandenberg. In a celebratory mood, he affirmed, "We have preserved the Monroe Doctrine and the Inter-American system . . . We have retained a complete veto—exclusive in our own hands—over any decisions involving external activities."[10]

Meanwhile, the disintegration of the wartime alliance between the United States and the Soviet Union initiated a Cold War, resulting in mounting levels of acrimony, mistrust, and confrontation. During the early stages, as Walter LaFeber has explained, the rivalry centered on the shape and structure of the postwar world, symbolized for him by the terms "Open Doors" and "Iron Curtains." For U.S. leaders the essential parts of Woodrow Wilson's liberal-capitalist internationalism retained fundamental validity. They wanted an open world based on free trade, liberal democracy, and collective security. For Soviet leaders, however, the Open Door approach had no appeal. To restore their war-ravaged country, they preferred an emphasis on spheres of influence, notably an extension of the Soviet system into the countries of Eastern Europe. An immense historiographical controversy surrounds the causes of the Cold War. In accounting for Soviet behavior and the split with the United States, modern scholars debate among themselves the relative importance of economic and security considerations, Joseph Stalin's distinctive personality, and the impact of Marxist ideology. For a combination of reasons, Stalin chose to seclude the Soviet domains after the war through the creation of a "closed system" sealed off, in Churchill's phrase, by an Iron Curtain. [11]

In response to mounting difficulties around the world, the Truman administration took alarm over the possibility of Soviet expansion into other regions and endorsed the necessity of containing the communist threat. At the same time, U.S. leaders pursued their own spheres-of-influence policies in the New World. Unbothered by the inconsistency, they denied any sort of parallel. Only secretary of commerce Henry A. Wallace perceived an incongruity, noting that the Russians "might feel about the Balkan states in somewhat the same way as we feel about Latin America." In a famous speech in March 1946 at Madison Square Garden in New York City, he stated his conviction that "we should recognize that we have no more business in the political affairs of eastern Europe than Russia has in the political affairs of Latin America." For enunciating such heresy, Truman fired him soon thereafter. [12]

Caught up in a contradiction, the leaders in the Truman administration wanted the Open Door in other regions but regarded Latin America as closed because of special ties with the United States. But then in the famous speech setting forth the Truman Doctrine before the Congress on March 12, 1947, the president found a way of bridging the gap. This speech, the first component in what became the containment policy against Soviet communism, called for extraordinary measures in response to a civil war in Greece. Truman wanted an allocation of $400 million from the Congress to sustain programs of economic and military aid and assistance in the eastern Mediterranean region. In justification, he stressed "the gravity of the situation." In his view, the ideological struggle between democrats and communists in Greece also had geopolitical implications. A communist victory in Greece could threaten Turkey and the rest of the Middle East with Soviet subversion and aggression. To ward off this dread possibility, Truman argued, "it must be the policy of the United States to support free peoples who are resisting attempted subjugation by armed minorities and outside pressures." For good measure, he insisted, "We must assist free peoples to work out their own destinies in their own way." [13]

Through this formulation, as Gaddis Smith explains, "Truman resolved the problem" with Latin America. By extending "to the entire world the definition of American interest in protecting small nations from external coercion," the Truman Doctrine in effect transformed the Monroe Doctrine into a global policy. A contemporary journalist, James Reston of the *New York Times*, drew the same inference. He described Truman's address as the most important statement in U.S. foreign policy since 1823. In Reston's words, "Like the Monroe Doctrine," the Truman Doctrine "warned that the United States would resist efforts to impose a political system or foreign domination on areas vital to our security." For this reason, the Soviets had better keep hands off or risk the consequences.[14]

Meanwhile, Latin American diplomats initiated a process for creating an inter-American collective security system through the implementation of article 51 of the UN Charter. In August 1945, Brazil offered to host a meeting of American republics in Rio de Janeiro to devise a treaty. At first the United States resisted, again because of Argentina. The Truman administration was reluctant to sign a treaty with president Juan Domingo Perón's government. Indeed, U.S. leaders regarded Perón as an unreconstructed pro-fascist and mounted a determined campaign against him.

The anti-Perón movement, eventually a kind of fiasco, followed from wartime suspicions and Spruille Braden's obsessions. A professional diplomat with experience in Latin America, Braden went to Buenos Aires as U.S. ambassador in May 1945 and developed an intense dislike for Perón, then the vice president, because of his pro-fascist reputation and a reportedly anti-U.S. attitude that Braden characterized as "neurotic nationalism."[15] When Braden later adopted the practice of criticizing Perón in public, presumably seeking to bring him down, he went too far. Perón turned the tables, depicting Braden as persona non grata because of his undiplomatic partisanship.

To avoid trouble, the Truman administration recalled Braden to Washington in September 1945, assigning to him responsibilities as assistant secretary of state for American republic affairs. Now, unwisely and ineffectively, he pursued a long distance vendetta. For example, he allowed himself to become identified with a loosely conceived proposal floating about to destroy Perón by means of a joint international intervention. Braden also meddled in Argentine politics. Perón had become the front-running candidate in the presidential campaign. Seeking to block him, Braden instigated the publication of a State Department Blue Book in February 1946, a short while before the election; it consisted of a compilation of documents, reiterating the charge that Argentina had pursued pro-fascist policies during the war. Without much plausibility, U.S. officials denied any political intent. Unpersuaded, the historian Roger Trask explains that "the Blue Book was an effort to influence Argentine votes against Perón," and it failed. Indeed, it enabled Perón to mobilize Argentine nationalism against the United States by brandishing the slogan "Perón or Braden." Given the choice, Argentines voted for Perón. An embarrassing failure on all counts, Braden's obsession with Perón not only demonstrated an incapacity to influence Argentine elections but also aroused concern among Latin Americans elsewhere over resurgent threats of U.S. intervention. The debacle further diminished the legacies of the Good Neighbor policy.

Braden's successor in Argentina, George S. Messersmith, formerly the ambassador to Mexico, favored a more conciliatory approach. This preference ran parallel with those of his superiors in the State Department who wanted to place relations with Argentina on a more regular basis. They also wanted to move ahead with the negotiation of an inter-American defense treaty. From his post in Buenos Aires, Messersmith defended his position by writing long letters to President Truman, secretary of state James F. Byrnes, and undersecretary of state Dean Acheson in which he attacked Spruille Braden for an assortment of misdeeds and misconceptions. At the same time, Messersmith developed an argument based on Cold War assumptions and perceptions for supporting Perón as a strong anticommunist. Seeking support on exactly those grounds, Perón subsequently switched tactics to cultivate leaders in the Truman administration. Now a proponent of diplomatic accommodation, he claimed to foresee an impending war with the Soviet Union, in which case, he vowed, Argentina would side with the United States.

From the Argentine viewpoint, these policy adjustments had good effects by edging the two countries toward the establishment of more normal relations. They also opened the way for the negotiation of an inter-American collective defense treaty at a conference in Rio de Janeiro, beginning on August 15, 1947. Headed by general George C. Marshall, the new secretary of state, the U.S. delegation included senator Arthur P. Vandenberg, the new chairman of the Senate Foreign Relations Committee, who occupied the position as a consequence of Republican victory in the off-year elections of 1946; for the first time since 1928, they controlled the Congress. Also in attendance, Truman arrived ceremoniously aboard the USS *Missouri,* the great battleship on whose decks the Japanese had surrendered in Tokyo Bay two years earlier.[16]

Formally known as the Inter-American Conference for the Maintenance of Continental Peace and Security, this assembly resulted in the negotiation of a mutual defense treaty among nations within the region. In the Inter-American Treaty of Reciprocal Assistance, also called the Rio Pact, the participants accepted three vital provisions. In the first, they promised to seek peaceful settlements in disputes among themselves before appealing to the United Nations. In the second, they embraced the essential feature of collective security by vowing to look upon an attack against any one of them as an attack against all of them. In the third, they agreed that any resort to collective action would depend upon a two-thirds majority vote and that no state ever would have to use force against its will. Senator Vandenberg, a leading player, waxed eloquent in his request for Senate ratification: "We have sealed a New World pact of peace which possesses teeth. We have translated Pan-American solidarity from an ideal into a reality . . . This is sunlight in a dark world." The Senate then passed favorably on the treaty by a vote of 72 to 1. As Gaddis Smith notes, "For Vandenberg the Monroe Doctrine had never been so alive and well."[17]

Among Latin Americans, too, the pact aroused enthusiasm although, as Roger Trask observes, "the motives of the various American republics varied to a considerable extent." Some took the affirmations of anticommunist purpose seriously. The Argentines, for example, expressed their desire for "a completely united front against extra-hemisphere aggressions, particularly against Russia." For others, economic needs assumed importance. As Trask notes, "One gets the impression that the mutual defense treaty was a secondary concern, perhaps looked upon as something to trade to the United States in return for economic assistance." Mexican foreign minister Jaime Torres Bodet candidly remarked that economic development was "the one way to provide [the] only sound basis for hemisphere peace." Brazilian foreign minister Raúl Fernandes urged that the United States instigate a large-scale program of aid and assistance to bring about economic change in the Western Hemisphere. To the extent that such words represented Latin American expectations, Truman effectively squelched them in his address before the assembled delegates. While claiming that he understood "the economic problems common to the nations of North and South America," he stated, "We have been obliged . . . to differentiate between the urgent need for rehabilitation of war-shattered areas and the problems of development elsewhere." To underscore the point, he said, "The problems of countries in this Hemisphere are different in nature and cannot be relieved by the same means and the same approaches which are in contemplation for Europe." Although acknowledging a need "for long-term economic collaboration," Truman assigned "a much greater role . . . to private citizens and groups than is the case in a program designed to aid European countries to recover from the destruction of war."[18] In other words, he envisioned no equivalent of the Marshall Plan for Latin America.

First proposed by the secretary of state in a commencement address at Harvard University in June 1947, the Marshall Plan was the second component in the containment policy, after the Truman Doctrine. It called for the use of large-scale aid and assistance, ultimately $12.4 billion, to promote the economic reconstruction of Western Europe. For the citizens of the United States, it became a subject of "almost limitless self-congratulation . . . then and since." For Latin Americans, it became a cause of resentment and ill will, a "sorry proof of American priorities." When asked at a press conference about a Marshall Plan for Latin America, Truman replied: "Well, I think there has always been a Marshall Plan in effect for the Western Hemisphere. The foreign policy of the United States in that direction has been set for one hundred years, known as the Monroe Doctrine." As Gaddis Smith observes, "It is difficult to say whether that comment demonstrated more confusion about the Marshall Plan or about the Monroe Doctrine."[19]

Meanwhile, the concluding step in bringing about an inter-American collective security system took place at the Ninth International Conference of American States in Bogotá, Colombia. This gathering lasted from March 30 to May 2, 1948, resulting in the transformation of the old Pan American Union into the Organization of American States. Again led by Secretary Marshall, the U.S. delegation embraced a plan to sidestep the issue of economic assistance by mobilizing resistance against what they perceived as an escalating communist menace. During the preliminaries, U.S. planning documents placed great importance on the development of anticommunist measures for implementation within the inter-American system. They described communism in the Western Hemisphere in alarming terms, characterizing it as a "potential danger," a "tool of the Kremlin," "a direct and major threat to the national security of the United States, and to that of all the other American Republics." Marshall himself underscored the issue by warning of "foreign-inspired subversive activities directed against [the] institutions and peace and security of American Republics."[20]

With apprehension running high, U.S. diplomats anticipated trouble at Bogotá. The ambassador, Willard S. Beaulac, cautioned against possible disruptions by "Communists and left wing Liberals." As if in fulfillment of his forecast, on April 9 an assassin killed Jorge Eliécer Gaitán, a Colombian politician and reformer in the Liberal Party. Subsequently, a mob lynched the suspected murderer, Juan Roa Sierra, and put the corpse on display in front of the presidential palace. The ensuing violence, known in Colombian history as the *Bogotazo,* featured several days of killing, rioting, and looting in the course of which the conference site, the Capitolio, came under attack. State Department officials urged General Marshall to come home at once, but he refused. In his view, fleeing would encourage revolutionary movements elsewhere. Marshall attributed the outbreak to communist provocations. Historians with the advantage of hindsight are less categorical. According to Roger Trask, "The riots were essentially an emotional response to the death of a charismatic leader and communist participation was incidental"; Stephen J. Randall points out that CIA observers at the time attributed Gaitán's assassination to an act of personal vengeance. Whatever the cause, the rioting had important consequences. For one thing, it intensified the conflict between Liberals and Conservatives in Colombia and brought about "the virtual collapse" of the political system. For another, it encouraged Latin American support at the conference for an anticommunist resolution favored by the United States. Formally titled "The Preservation and Defense of Democracy in America," the resolution affirmed "that by its antidemocratic nature and its interventionist tendency, the political activity of international communism or any totalitarian doctrine is incompatible with the concept of American freedom." As a safeguard, each nation should adopt "measures necessary to eradicate and prevent activities directed, assisted, or instigated by foreign governments, organizations, or individuals."[21]

Most significantly, the Bogotá conference brought into existence the Organization of American States, which, according to Trask, "provided an institutional framework for the inter-American system and machinery for implementation of the Rio pact."[22] The OAS charter endorsed as goals the pursuit of "peace and justice"; the advancement of "collaboration" and "solidarity" among the states; and the defense of national "sovereignty," "territorial integrity," and "independence." As a fundamental principle, the document affirmed equality among the states; decision making would depend on simple majority rule, whether carried out during inter-American conferences or during meetings of foreign ministers. Unlike the UN Security Council, the OAS gave no government a veto power. Finally, article 15 formally embraced an absolute version of the principle of nonintervention: "No State or group of States has the right to intervene, directly or indirectly, for any reason whatever, in the internal or external affairs of any other State." It also excluded the use of armed force and "any other form of interference or attempted threat" against the state and "its political, economic and cultural elements."[23] Whether such terms actually could constrain the United States remained an issue for decision in the future.

ORDER, STABILITY, AND ANTICOMMUNISM

The legacies of Franklin Roosevelt's Good Neighbor policy faded away during the early Cold War, providing ever less guidance for diplomatic conduct in the Western Hemisphere. Under Presidents Truman and Eisenhower, anticommunism dominated official thinking. The consequences encouraged order and stability as the primary goals and afforded conservative elites in Latin American with incentives to counteract recent political losses. According to the historians Leslie Bethell and Ian Roxborough, the "conjuncture" at the end of the Second World War had important ramifications, among them, a halt in the growth of democratization and a restoration of more traditional forms of authoritarian rule.[24]

This thesis appears more fully in Bethell and Roxborough's *Latin America between the Second World War and the Cold War*. Presented as a series of case studies on a country-by-country basis, the essays argue that from 1944 to 1948 each Latin American republic fashioned "its own history" yet displayed "striking similarities." As the editors explain, late in the war and immediately after, "three distinct but interrelated phenomena" threatened to undermine the political status quo. These consisted of, first, more extensive popular participation in government, second, a shift to the political left and, third, a growing militancy within the labor movement. Seeking to thwart such challenges, conservative elites marshaled resistance, blunted the effects, and reasserted their traditional prerogatives. [25]

Popular parties with mass followings toward the end of the Second World War expanded democratic bases by insisting upon free elections. In some countries the existence of rudimentary democratic forms already existed. In others, authoritarian traditions presented formidable obstacles. In most of Latin America, "reformist" and "progressive" parties became identified with urban interests, including middle- and working-class elements. At the same time, radical groups, often Marxist in orientation, scored political gains, usually in conjunction with the mobilization of labor unions. In some countries, "the incorporation of organized labor into democratic politics" took place for the first time.

Soon after the war the traditional, conservative elites in Latin America struck back, often by repressive means. They targeted for special attention political activists, agitators, union organizers, radicals, communists, and others they looked upon as dangerous. The outcome, a "historic defeat" for the popular parties, marked a lost opportunity "for significant political and social change." Two developments account for the setback: "The shifting balance of domestic political forces in each country" and "the complex interaction between domestic and international politics as the Second World War came to an end." In the latter case, the U.S. role in Latin America took on special importance.

Convincing evidence of increased democratization exists for the mid-1940s. At the beginning of 1944, only Uruguay, Chile, Costa Rica, and Colombia could claim with much veracity to possess functioning democracies: that is, elected civilian governments operating under the rule of law, while respecting civil liberties such as freedom of speech, association, and assembly. Mexico, a special case, conducted regular elections under the tight control of the ruling party, the Partido Revolucionario Mexicano (PRM). Elsewhere, authoritarian governments prevailed. They were "narrowly oligarchical and often repressive regimes," typically "military or military-backed dictatorships, some benevolent, some brutal, and most personalistic."

Democratization took place in Ecuador, Cuba, Panama, Peru, Venezuela, and Mexico, when popular pressure from the people compelled freer electoral procedures and forced transitions away from military or military-backed dictatorships. In Guatemala in July 1944, for example, a popular, urban-based uprising brought down the dictator Jorge Ubico. In Brazil early in 1945, Getúlio Vargas in effect dismantled the Estado Nôvo by making plans for presidential and congressional elections. In the same year, massive street demonstrations in Buenos Aires set in motion a sequence of events leading to democratic Argentine elections in February 1946. And in Bolivia during the summer of 1946 a liberal-left coalition overturned a military government. In the estimation of one contemporary observer, historian Arthur P. Whitaker, these occurrences taken together signified "more democratic changes in more Latin American countries" than at any time since the wars of independence. Notable exceptions, of course, existed in Paraguay, El Salvador, Honduras, Nicaragua, and the Dominican Republic, but even those dictatorial governments had to make "token gestures toward political liberalization."

The Allied victory over the fascist powers functioned as "the principal factor" underlying these changes. To be sure, urban-based, democratic groups, from both the middle and working classes, drew on "a strong liberal tradition" in Latin America while demanding a more open form of politics. At the same time, the triumphant democracies of the United States and Great Britain compelled the "dominant groups in Latin America, including the military . . . to make some political and ideological adjustments and concessions." During the war "an extraordinary outpouring of wartime propaganda" favored "U.S. political institutions, the U.S. economic model, and the American way of (and standard of) life." Democracy emerged as "a central symbol with almost universal resonance," in part because of the role played by the United States.

The democratization process also featured the inclusion of "progressive" parties of the center and the left. Important examples were the Acción Democrática in Venezuela, the Alianza Popular Revolucionaria Americana in Peru, and the Partido Revolucionario Cubano-Auténtico in Cuba. Highly personalist and populist in orientation, these parties secured support from the urban middle classes, the working classes, and in some instances the rural poor. Among other things, they offered "an extension of democracy, social reform, and national economic development." Marxists too, especially communists, made gains, in part because of the Soviet Union's role in the Allied coalition. After years of "weakness, isolation, and for the most part illegality . . . the Latin American Communist parties achieved for a brief period a degree of popularity, power, and influence—which would never be recaptured, except in Cuba after 1959 and (briefly) in Chile in the early seventies."

Communist parties became legal in most Latin American countries during the war years. The total membership, less than 100,000 in 1939, increased to about 500,000 in 1947. The parties claimed 180,000 members in Brazil, 30,000 in Argentina, 50,000 in Chile, 35,000 in Peru, 20,000 in Venezuela, 55,000 in Cuba, 11,000 in Mexico, 10,000 in Colombia, and 15,000 in Uruguay. Though probably exaggerated, these figures indicate "an important presence of Communist parties in the major countries." For a time, they enjoyed a measure of electoral success, especially in coalitions with other parties of the center and the left. The explanation resides "primarily in the war itself and its outcome." Following the German invasion of the Soviet Union in June 1941, Latin American communists advocated a political truce with the pro-Allied governments in power, no matter how authoritarian or reactionary. They also played down conceptions of class conflict and encouraged notions of national unity. At the same time, Latin American governments relaxed their earlier strictures against communists. In the short run, communist parties ranked among "the beneficiaries" of victory and democratization.

Organized labor also benefited, especially in Mexico, Argentina, and Brazil. Mainly because of industrialization, import-substitution strategies, rapid population growth, and mass migrations from rural into urban areas, the working classes grew in numbers, especially in the service and transportation sectors, in mining and light manufacturing, and in textiles and food processing. "For the first time. something approaching a recognizably modern proletariat was coming into existence." Similarly, expanded union membership by 1946 reached 3.5 to 4 million workers. The Confederación de Trabajadores de América Latina (Confederation of Latin American Workers), founded in 1938 and headed by a Mexican Marxist, Vicente Lombardo Toledano, reportedly represented some 3.3 million members in sixteen countries. Moreover, since union membership clustered in key industrial and transportation sectors, labor militancy, strikes, and agitation could exercise the greatest clout in vulnerable areas. Although, as Bethell and Roxborough remark, "democrats, leftists, and labor militants were not always and everywhere on the same side," their efforts—"for the most part linked and mutually reinforcing"—nevertheless, constituted "a serious challenge to the established order, at least in the perceptions of the governments of the time." That challenge, whether real or perceived, also elicited countermeasures from traditional elites.

In the immediate postwar period, conservative shifts effectively curbed democratizing tendencies almost everywhere. More closely policed, labor unions fell under state control, often muzzled by antistrike legislation. Purges removed radical leaders from positions of influence, and communist affiliations again became illegal. Taken together, these actions represented "a marked tendency to restrict or curtail political competition and participation, to contain or repress popular mobilization, and to frustrate reformist aspirations." Within a decade, as a consequence, outright dictatorships existed in eleven Latin American countries: Guatemala, El Salvador, Honduras, Nicaragua, Panama, Cuba, the Dominican Republic, Venezuela, Colombia, Peru, and Paraguay.

Bethell and Roxborough explain these reversals by underscoring "the continuing strength of the dominant classes." Unlike those in other parts of the world, the traditional elites in Latin America, including the military, "had not been weakened, much less destroyed by the Second World War." Instead, they had assumed a defensive posture, intending subsequently "to restore the political and social control that was threatened by the political mobilization of 'the dangerous classes.'" The "most progressive parties" also displayed debilitating, internal weaknesses. Often they lacked such vital prerequisites for success as "deep roots" in society, internal cohesion, and "a vocation for power." Overall, they possessed insufficient means to maintain their gains when traditional oligarchs reasserted their authority and privilege.

Bethell and Roxborough also emphasize the importance of "the international environment" at the beginning of the Cold War. According to them, "the international stance" of the United States "reinforced domestic attitudes and tendencies," providing for "an ideological justification for the shift to the right" and for "the counteroffensive" against labor and the left. In many cases, in the official versions set forth by Latin American governments, "popular political mobilization and strike activity, whether or not Communist-led, suddenly became Communist-inspired, Moscow-dictated, and therefore 'subversive.'" Such ploys catered to U.S. preferences and prejudices.

In addition, "the new international economic order and Latin America's place in it" influenced elite perceptions. During the early Cold War the U.S. refusal of economic aid and assistance in favor of private capital conveyed important messages. To attract foreign investors, Latin American governments had to provide "an appropriate climate for direct investment." This requirement meant "various guarantees and assurances, both symbolic and real," including commitment to "liberal, capitalist development and to an 'ideology of production.'" The necessary conditions allowed for no more "Mexican stunts," to use financier Bernard Baruch's term for the oil expropriation in 1938. For such reasons the elites moved against radicals, communists, and labor leaders. Bethell and Roxborough conclude, "Above all, political stability was essential if foreign capital were to be invested in Latin American industry." The observation highlights the importance of external constraints. "Thus, just as the United States *indirectly* promoted political and social change in Latin America at the end of the Second World War, it *indirectly* imposed limits on change in the postwar years."

During the early Cold War the Soviet Union posed no threat of outright aggression against Latin America or any other place in the Western Hemisphere; Soviet leaders possessed neither the means nor, for that matter, the intent—but U.S. leaders worried about communist subversion and penetration by political and ideological methods. Consequently, the intelligence operations initially set up to monitor Nazi activity shifted attention to the communists. In U.S. embassies the legal attachés (usually FBI agents), the military, naval, and labor attachés, and the CIA operatives who made up the apparatus found scant evidence of a threat. A CIA review of Soviet aims in Latin America in November 1947 denied any possibility of a communist takeover anywhere in the region. But such findings ran counter to official U.S. preferences. At the 1948 Bogotá conference the delegate described the mere existence of communist parties as a menace to regional security.

U.S. leaders worried especially about communism in Latin American labor unions. Presumably, such influence could endanger U.S. interests in vital enterprises, such as petroleum in Mexico and Venezuela, copper in Chile, sugar in Cuba, and industry and transportation everywhere. Moreover, militant unions, whether or not controlled by communists, appeared as destabilizing elements, fundamentally at odds with the requirements of postwar capitalist development. In most countries the United States had no need to intervene, even by clandestine means, to secure action against communists and labor militants. The ruling elites correctly understood U.S. preferences and responded to U.S. political and economic pressures. As the leaders in the Truman administration saw it, the removal of communists strengthened democracy by expunging alien and hostile presences. [26]

Overall, the Cold War diverted U.S. attention away from Latin America. The containment policy initially manifested a Europe-first orientation that culminated in 1949 with the North Atlantic Treaty Organization (NATO), a formal military alliance and collective security system. It rounded out a sequence of impressive victories for the United States. But then, a turnabout ostensibly situated the advantage with the other side. In August 1949, only four years after Hiroshima and Nagasaki, the Soviet Union broke the U.S. atomic monopoly by setting off a nuclear device. In October 1949, another hammerblow fell: Communist forces under Mao Zedong triumphed in the Chinese civil war, and in the following year the People's Republic of China negotiated a mutual defense pact and military alliance with the Soviet Union. Even worse, the onset of a war in Korea in June 1950 threatened to ignite a global conflict.

As viewed from Washington, these calamitous events indicated a shift in the distribution of world power favoring the Soviet Union, and U.S. responses incorporated frightening, perhaps distorted, assessments of Soviet aims and capabilities. One such appraisal by the National Security Council known as NSC-68 took shape early in 1950. A powerful endorsement of prevailing assumptions among U.S. officials, the text remained classified until 1975. Alarmist and hyperbolic in content, it presumed the existence of a grave crisis and a mortal threat. As the historian Walter LaFeber observes, it established "the American blueprint for waging the Cold War during the next twenty years." [27]

NSC-68 began by describing a profound change in the world balance of power. As a consequence of the Second World War the two Great Powers, the United States and the Soviet Union, dominated the globe. The document then spelled out the implications: "What is new, what makes the continuing crisis, is the polarization of power which inescapably confronts the slave society with the free." As LaFeber notes, "It was us against them." NSC-68 attributed the threat of Soviet aggression largely to Marxist ideology. Much in vogue at the time, this analysis claimed that the Soviet Union was "animated by a new fanatic faith, antithetical to our own," which sought "to impose its absolute authority over the rest of the world." The ensuing struggle, "endemic" and "momentous," entailed high stakes. The Soviets presumably would use "violent or nonviolent methods in accordance with the dictates of expediency." By setting forth a "design" seeking total victory, their ambitions called into question "the fulfillment or destruction not only of this Republic but of civilization itself." The Soviets wanted "the complete subversion or forcible destruction of the machinery of government and structure of society in the countries of the non-Soviet world and their replacement by an apparatus and structure subservient to and controlled from the Kremlin." No compromise was possible.

Most historians in the present day probably would tone down these assessments of Soviet motives and goals. Nevertheless, for many contemporaries the prospect of terrible consequences seemed real enough. How could they avert them? Predictably, NSC-68 called upon the United States to take the lead "in building a successful functioning political and economic system in the free world" to deter "an attack upon us" so that "our free society can flourish." It advised against premature negotiations with the Soviet Union, favoring instead the construction of positions of strength based on a buildup of U.S. military forces, both conventional and nuclear. It also affirmed a need for calculated measures to ensure "unity" and "consensus" at home and to maintain strong alliance systems with other anticommunist nations. [28]

Such expansive definitions of the communist menace encouraged U.S. leaders to think of Latin America almost exclusively in a Cold War context. The region ceased to have much significance in its own right; instead, it became an arena of Cold War competition in which the United States and the Soviet Union would play out a contest for power, resources, prestige, and influence. Typically, U.S. leaders looked upon Latin Americans as minor players who should subordinate their wishes, interests, and aspirations to Cold War imperatives as defined by the United States. Indeed, their countries took on importance not because of anything intrinsic to them but because of connections with the larger struggle. U.S. officials tended to regard Latin America mainly as a place in which to turn back communist intrusions for reasons of high policy.

Ignorance of the region compounded the tendency. Those in charge—presidents, secretaries of state, secretaries of defense, national security advisers, CIA directors, and the other inhabitants of the U.S. foreign policy apparatus—never possessed much knowledge and understanding of Latin America. Secretary of state Dean Acheson confessed early in 1950 that he was "rather vague" about its people, unsure "whether they were richer or poorer, going Communist, Fascist or what." President Truman made comparisons based on ethnic stereotypes, claiming that Latin Americans reminded him of the Jews and the Irish: They were "very emotional" and hard to manage. Later, secretary of state John Foster Dulles claimed to know what to do: "You have to pat them a little bit and make them think you are fond of them."

President Eisenhower acknowledged that he had a fondness for the Argentines because they are "the same kind of people we are." This kind of condescension at least hinted of racism.

A remarkable memorandum by George F. Kennan revealed something of official perceptions. A senior Foreign Service officer and State Department counselor, Kennan obtained renown as "the father of containment" for his "Mr. X" article, "The Sources of Soviet Conduct," in *Foreign Affairs* in July 1947. Early in 1950, he undertook his first journey into Latin America. His subsequent report, "Latin America as a Problem in United States Foreign Policy," contained his observations. As Gaddis Smith explains, this report had no direct bearing on the formulation of foreign policy but nevertheless qualified as "a seminal document" because it set forth the "Kennan corollary," following in the tradition of the Richard Olney and Theodore Roosevelt corollaries to Monroe's original message to Congress and the J. Reuben Clark memorandum. As "an unvarnished statement of widely held attitudes," it affirmed a rationale for supporting repressive dictatorships when compelled to do so by the requirements of anticommunism.[29] Kennan, it should be stressed, had no experience in Latin America comparable to his knowledge of the USSR.

Kennan left Washington, DC, by train on February 18, 1950, on his way to Mexico City and then traveled by plane to Caracas, Rio de Janeiro, São Paulo, Montevideo, Buenos Aires, Lima, and Panama City. What he saw and experienced along the way dismayed and distressed him. In Mexico City, he disliked the altitude and the disturbed, sultry, and menacing sounds of "nocturnal activity." In Caracas, he reacted against a "feverish economy debauched by oil money." In Rio, the "noisy, wildly competitive" traffic and "the unbelievable contrasts between luxury and poverty" repelled him. In Lima, he became "depressed" while reflecting "that it had not rained . . . for twenty-nine years." Overall, his memorandum conveyed an impression of distaste for the people, the leaders, and their countries. In Kennan's words, "It seemed unlikely that there could be any other region of the earth in which nature and human behavior could have combined to produce a more unhappy and hopeless background for the conduct of human life than in Latin America." Placing heavy responsibility on the legacies of miscegenation, he wrote, "The handicaps to progress are written in human blood and in the tracings of geography; and in neither case are they readily susceptible of obliteration. They lie heavily across the path of human progress."[30]

Kennan nevertheless attached geopolitical importance to Latin America. In a war against the Soviet Union, he feared catastrophic consequences if "a considerable portion of Latin American society were to throw its weight morally into the opposite camp." Such an association "might well turn the market of international confidence against us and leave us fighting not only communist military power, but a wave of defeatism among our friends and spiteful elation among our detractors elsewhere in the world." For him, communism in Latin America posed a real threat. "Here, as elsewhere, the inner core of the communist leadership is fanatical, disciplined, industrious, and armed with a series of organizational techniques which are absolutely first rate."

How could the United States turn back the danger? Kennan found the answer in the Monroe Doctrine: Soviet efforts to make "pawns" of Latin American countries from "beyond the limits of this continent" clearly ran against Monroe's historic prohibition. The United States needed support from Latin American governments. To enlist it, positive incentives— possibly economic and military aid—could encourage anticommunist measures such as crackdowns on radical agitation. Otherwise, coercion, perhaps diplomatic penalties, could dissuade Latin American governments from engaging in "excessive toleration of anti-American activities." As Gaddis Smith explains, Kennan saw in Latin America "a political culture too weak and selfish to support a democracy strong enough to resist the superior determination and skill of the Communist enemy."

The Kennan corollary articulated a basic premise: "We cannot be too dogmatic about the methods by which local communists can be dealt with." In Kennan's view, everything depended upon "the vigor and efficacy of local concepts and traditions of self-government." If these were as sound and reliable "as in our own country," then "the body politic may be capable of bearing the virus of communism without permitting it to expand to dangerous proportions." He regarded this approach as "undoubtedly the best solution of the communist problem, wherever the prerequisites exist." But lacking them, if "the concepts and traditions of popular government are too weak to absorb successfully the intensity of the communist attack," then "we must concede that harsh governmental measures of repression may be the only answer." He went on to explain "that these measures may have to proceed from regimes whose origins and methods would not stand the test of American concepts of democratic procedures; and that such regimes and such methods may be preferable alternatives, and indeed the only alternatives to further communist success." In short, relying on right-wing military dictators as anticommunist bastions was preferable to risking communist advances. Gaddis Smith remarks that Kennan's position on this matter "is inconsistent with much of his subsequent thought" and attributes it to "the culture shock of a Europeanist who had never visited Latin America before." During his trip, he experienced "an uncharacteristic susceptibility to the views of the American ambassadors with whom he talked" and to "the near-hysterical sense of a worldwide Communist menace in that year 1950." His own preference for "realism" over "moralistic rhetoric" also contributed. Nevertheless, and this is the important point, Kennan's assumptions and observations typified official thinking and undergirded important parts of U.S. policy toward Latin America during the next forty years.[31]

The Korean conflict intensified apprehension over communist expansion and the possibility of a third world war. The causes, much discussed in historical literature, appeared straightforward to U.S. leaders at the time. In their view, the North Korean invasion of South Korea on June 25, 1950, came about because the Soviet Union had willed it, establishing another case in which totalitarian aggression threatened the freedom of peace-loving nations. Recalling Nazi behavior in the late 1930s, Truman acted upon a set of analogies derived mainly from the Munich conference in 1938. Constituting for him and others of his generation the primary lesson of the Second World War, the Munich analogy set forth a simple proposition: Appeasement in the face of totalitarian aggression never works. Indeed, shows of weakness and irresolution merely invite further aggression. Therefore, democratic nations must stand their ground or subsequently run the risk of bigger wars. Scholars have since questioned Truman's analysis, asking whether the Munich analogy holds in this instance. Some recent works depict the conflict less as Stalin's creation than as a consequence of a Korean civil war. North Korean leader Kim Il Sung probably took the initiative on his own to unify the country, and Stalin, for his own reasons, went along. Indeed, some scholars now wonder whether U.S. intervention improved the situation or made it worse.[32]

Taking the lead, the Truman administration resisted Soviet aggression while working through the Security Council of the United Nations. The United States obtained a resolution urging a cease-fire, the withdrawal of North Korean forces, and the restoration of the status quo ante bellum. When North Korea failed to comply, a second UN resolution called upon members to respond with military support for South Korea. During the next three years, until the armistice on July 27, 1953, the United States supplied most of the ground, air, and naval forces from the outside. Other contingents came from the United Kingdom, Turkey, Greece, the Philippines, and Thailand.[33]

The countries of Latin America, whose twenty votes constituted two-fifths of those in the General Assembly in 1950, initially backed the United Nations. Moreover, the Organization of American States went on record on June 28, 1950, declaring its "firm adherence to the decisions of the competent organs of the United Nations" and reaffirming "the pledges of continental solidarity which unite the American States."[34] Latin American republics displayed no equivalent readiness to take part in the fighting, however. Only Colombia sent a token force, an infantry battalion, primarily because the dictator, Laureano Gómez, anticipated payoffs from the United States in return.[35] U.S. leaders tried to recruit the participation of other Latin American ground forces as a sign of commitment, especially after the Chinese intervention late in 1950. These attempts centered on Bolivia, Chile,

Uruguay, Mexico, Peru, and Brazil and failed in each instance. At first, Brazil and Peru indicated some interest but only in return for military and economic subsidies. Most Latin American governments claimed that public opinion in their countries would not accept troop commitments.

The historian William Stueck attributes such "meager results" partly to the fact that Latin America, "a grievously poor region," lacked "any tradition of direct involvement" in overseas conflicts. Only Mexico and Brazil had sent military contingents abroad during the Second World War. In addition, Latin Americans perceived no communist threat to themselves and resented what they understood as U.S. neglect, specifically the absence of a Marshall Plan. In Stueck's phrase, "Tired of being taken for granted by their big brother in the north . . . the Latin republics hedged when asked to provide cannon fodder for a U.S. crusade in a remote land."[36]

Latin American recalcitrance became apparent at the Fourth Meeting of Consultation of Ministers of Foreign Affairs of the American Republics in Washington from March 26 to April 7, 1951. Summoned by the Truman administration "to consider problems of an urgent nature and of common interest to American States," and sponsored by the OAS, the conference revealed deep divisions over questions of hemispheric security and economic development. Latin American delegations denied the existence of a communist threat in the Western Hemisphere and argued that in any case, improved living standards sustained by U.S. aid would provide the best means of defense.[37] Resisting this appeal, the United States emphasized the military requirements of collective self-defense. Later on in 1951, the U.S. Congress implemented a program under the Mutual Security Act, which authorized the negotiation of "mutual defense assistance agreements" with Latin American countries. Beginning with Ecuador in January 1952, twelve such pacts eventually came into existence. Under the terms first established with Ecuador, the United States agreed to make available "equipment, materials, services, and other military assistance designed to promote the defense and maintain the peace of the Western Hemisphere." In return, Ecuador would utilize the aid to strengthen its military defenses and, significantly, "to facilitate the production and transfer . . . of . . . strategic materials required by the United States." From the U.S. standpoint, these provisions contained strong incentives for pact partners to provide adequate supplies of raw materials and to guard against radical subversion. Subsequent military programs also emphasized the training of Latin American officers in "counterinsurgency" techniques, proposing to use them as anticommunist bulwarks.[38]

In the end, the Korean War destroyed the Truman presidency. Weakened politically by the military inconclusiveness of the conflict, his firing of general Douglas MacArthur, and the spurious Republican allegations of softness on communism, Truman lacked the grounds to present himself in 1952 as a candidate for a second full term. Instead, the Democratic nomination fell to

Adlai Stevenson, a former Illinois governor. The Republicans, seeking to gain the presidency for the first time since 1932, took full advantage. Particularly, they assailed the Democrats for perpetuating big government at home and incompetency in foreign policy. Korea supposedly stood as a case in point. While characterizing the Democratic policy of containment as "defensive, negative, futile, and immoral," the Republicans suggested a more dynamic approach by which to seize the initiative, roll back the communist tide, and win victories in the Cold War.[39] Their efforts to advance such goals during Dwight D. Eisenhower's presidency had many implications for Latin America.

ANTICOMMUNISM UNDER IKE:
TRADE, AID, AND INTERVENTION

During the 1950s, Cold War issues preoccupied the leaders of the Eisenhower administration in Latin America. Anticommunism, the hallmark of U.S. policy, required order, stability, and constant vigilance against radical subversion. At the same time, Latin American nationalists, reformers, and homegrown revolutionaries blurred distinctions by insisting upon state activity to instigate economic development. For the United States, how to sort them out from Soviet-style communists posed a real dilemma. Other issues also caused difficulties. A critical one centered on trade, or aid, as the best means of moving Latin America toward modernization. Another concerned the utility of intervention by the United States. A clandestine operation in Guatemala in 1954 toppled a popularly elected government that was perceived in Washington as communist-dominated. This short-term success led later to similar efforts against Fidel Castro in Cuba. Looked upon by the United States as a dangerous precedent, Castro's revolutionary triumph symbolized a repudiation of U.S. tutelage and suggested to the remainder of Latin America the option of following Cuba's lead.

As depicted by Eisenhower during the 1952 campaign, Truman's policies in Latin America had gone dangerously wrong. According to Ike, the U.S. had "frantically wooed Latin America" during the Second World War but then "proceeded to forget these countries just as fast" after the peace. Consequently, a "terrible disillusionment set in," and "Communist agents" who were standing ready "skillfully exploited" economic distress and political unrest for their own purposes. "Through drift and neglect," the Truman administration had embraced what Ike called "a poor neighbor policy," now very much in need of a change.[40]

In an important book on the Eisenhower administration and Latin America, the historian Stephen G. Rabe takes a revisionist stance by arguing that the president "decisively" established and oversaw the policies of his administration. Unlike the earlier body of writing that depicted Eisenhower as a kind of figurehead, the more recent scholarship portrays him as a chief executive truly in charge. According to the political scientist Fred I. Greenstein, Eisenhower often misled observers by employing indirect and obscure methods in a "hidden hand" style of leadership. Operating unobtrusively behind the scenes, he exercised command while allowing subordinates to indulge in appearances.[41]

In the case of Latin America, Eisenhower moved quickly to institute corrective actions. Within two months of taking office, he approved a statement formulated by the National Security Council, "United States Objectives and Courses of Action with Respect to Latin America." This document emphasized the necessity of "hemispheric solidarity" against international communism and called for the enlistment of Latin American support in the struggle against the Soviet Union, especially the threat of internal communist subversion. Recalling the requirements of the Kennan corollary, this approach encouraged the administration to embrace anticommunist leaders in Latin America—including repressive dictators—as allies.

Before becoming president, Eisenhower had had modest experience with Latin America. After graduating from the U.S. Military Academy in 1915, while serving at Fort Sam Houston in San Antonio, Texas, he went on hunting trips into Mexico and acquired a "romantic" if somewhat "patronizing attitude" toward Mexicans. In Panama in the early 1920s, he developed a dislike for the tropics and for the blatant forms of discrimination experienced by Panamanians in the Canal Zone. Early in the Second World War, he worked with Lend-Lease programs for Latin America and later paid official visits to Mexico, Panama, and Brazil. In the main, he thought that military aid to Latin America well served U.S. interests in national security.

Eisenhower's secretary of state, John Foster Dulles, had a reputation as the Republican expert on foreign affairs. As a young man, he had attended the Paris Peace Conference in 1919 in a minor capacity. He built his professional career with the Wall Street law firm of Sullivan and Cromwell, often working out of its Berlin and Paris offices on matters of international investment and finance. In Latin America, he represented U.S. corporations such as the United Fruit Company. Outspoken, acerbic, and assertive, Secretary Dulles played an influential role but never dominated Eisenhower. The "hidden-hand" president allowed subordinates to take credit or blame, depending on his needs, but always kept his own prerogatives intact.

Eisenhower also relied heavily on his youngest brother, Milton Eisenhower, as a source of information on Latin American affairs. Regarded by Ike as "the most knowledgeable and widely informed of all the people with whom I deal," Milton Eisenhower possessed no particular Latin American expertise but a broad understanding based on a variety of career experiences, including stints as a former Foreign Service officer and an Agriculture Department official. He had also served as the president of Kansas State University, Pennsylvania State University, and Johns Hopkins University. Ike corresponded with his brother regularly and often spent weekends in his company. On two occasions, he sent Milton as a special ambassador on fact-finding missions to Latin America.[42]

Top Eisenhower leaders were united in the conviction that communism posed a worldwide danger. During his confirmation hearings before the Senate Foreign Relations Committee, Dulles described the "threat" as "the gravest . . . that ever faced the United States," indeed, "the gravest . . . that has ever faced what we call western civilization, or . . . any civilization which was dominated by a spiritual faith." In Latin America, in Dulles's view, communists had penetrated every country. Animated by "hatred of the Yankee," they sought "to destroy the influence of the so-called Colossus of the North in Central and South America." Distressed by what he regarded as a disturbing parallel, he claimed that "conditions in Latin America are somewhat comparable to conditions as they were in China in the mid-thirties when the Communist movement was getting started." Therefore, "the time to deal with this rising menace in South America is now."

Such rhetoric aptly reflected the administration's apprehensions. Sometimes Eisenhower and his aides used this kind of language for political effect to rally anticommunists in the Republican party, but in the Latin American case "the private discussions and classified policy statements of administration officials differed little from their public positions." For example, the president worried about the consequences of surging nationalism in the Third World, identifying it as a cause of instability and a potential vehicle of communist expansion. For Ike, nationalism "on the move" required special wariness. In his diary, attempting to describe "actually what is going on," he wrote that "communists are hoping to take advantage of the confusion resulting from the destruction of existing relationships and uncertainties of disrupted trade, security, and understanding." He feared that communists would capitalize on nationalist agitation "to further the aims of world revolution and the Kremlin's domination of all people."[43]

Ike's critics have suggested that such anxieties, however overdrawn, should have elicited more imaginative reactions. Specifically, the Eisenhower administration should have tried to neutralize communist appeals by mobilizing pro-U.S. nationalist elements with positive incentives. As it turned out, the leaders never attained such creative levels. Their error resided in apprehending third-world nationalism so exclusively in Cold War terms. As a consequence, the historian Robert J. McMahon argues, the Eisenhower administration "grievously misunderstood and underestimated the most significant historical development of the mid-twentieth century."[44]

How to distinguish third-world nationalism from Soviet communism remained a principal problem for U.S. policy makers in Latin America throughout the Cold War. Among his primary goals, Eisenhower wanted to secure "the allegiance of these republics in our camp in the cold war." But he could not tell whether policies to accommodate Latin American nationalists would win them over or open the way to communist advances. In other words, he was unsure how to calculate the effects of meaningful reforms: Would they undercut communist appeals or encourage revolution by disrupting traditional relationships? Dulles, a pessimist in these matters, feared that "the Communists are trying to extend their form of despotism in this hemisphere." Underscoring what he regarded as the true nature of the threat, he defined communism as "an internationalist conspiracy, not an indigenous movement." "In the old days," Dulles claimed, "we used to be able to let South America go through the wringer of bad times . . . but the trouble is now, when you put it through the wringer, it comes out red."

The National Security Council initiated discussions of these matters in February 1953. Stating the theme, the CIA director Allen Dulles, brother of the secretary of state, spoke of "deteriorating" relations with Latin America, marked by a "Communist infection" in Guatemala, and warned of "an approaching crisis." A month later, on March 18, 1953, the National Security Council established essential aims in a policy document known as NSC-144/ 1. As Stephen G. Rabe notes, the planners "interpreted inter-American affairs solely within the context of the global struggle with the Soviet Union." Essentially, the Eisenhower administration wanted four things from Latin America: support in the United Nations, eradication of "internal Communist or other anti-U.S. subversion," access to strategic raw materials, and military cooperation in defending the hemisphere. Yet the document demonstrated scant faith in the reliability of Latin American leaders and their capacity to comprehend the international danger. NSC-144/1 disparaged as "immature and impractical idealists" such influential figures as Lázaro Cárdenas in Mexico, Juan José Arévalo in Guatemala, José Figueres in Costa Rica, Rómulo Betancourt in Venezuela, Víctor Raúl Haya de la Torre in Peru, and Getúlio Vargas in Brazil. It asserted that these men were "inadequately trained to conduct government business efficiently," lacked "the disposition to combat extremists within their ranks, including communists," and displayed a Latin American penchant for "irresponsible acts." Much like the Kennan corollary, NSC-144/1 invoked "overriding security interests" as a justification for U.S. intervention. Whenever necessary, the United States should employ unilateral measures, even if they might violate "our treaty commitments, . . . endanger the Organization of American States . . . and . . . probably intensify anti-U.S. attitudes in many Latin American countries."

The anticommunist campaign in Latin America also employed political propaganda and military aid. According to Rabe, the U.S. Information Agency spent $5.2 million a year in such efforts to get out the message as, for example, the production and distribution of comic books, cartoon strips, and movie shorts. Intended for mass consumption, these devices warned of totalitarian threats menacing the freedom and property of individuals. Sometimes they elicited faulty inferences; in Mexico, some audiences reportedly thought the danger emanated from their own government. Anticommunist initiatives placed special importance on Latin American trade unions. The military establishments also received special treatment. Viewed by U.S. leaders as anticommunist bulwarks, Latin American armies became the recipients of increased military aid. Rabe questions whether "the strategic benefits of inter-American military cooperation" really amounted to much. At the same time, he acknowledges that "the political advantages of military aid" were "significant," especially when training and assistance programs gave access to the dominant military caste. Military officers wielded power in so many of the countries that U.S. leaders regarded shows of support for them as essential. In dealings with Juan Perón's Argentine government, for example, Cold War considerations ultimately overcame earlier suspicions of his profascism.

As staunch anticommunists, Eisenhower officials displayed no equivalent devotion to democracy and human rights. Some thought the defense of such values might violate the nonintervention principle or, worse, incite radicalism and subversion. Others shared Milton Eisenhower's misimpression. After a trip to South America in the fall of 1953 the president's brother reported with stunning inaccuracy that "most American nations which still have degrees of feudalism and dictatorship are moving gradually toward democratic concepts and practices." As Rabe observes, military dictators at the time controlled thirteen Latin American republics and enjoyed many favors from the Eisenhower administration. Indeed, two military strongmen, Manuel Odría of Peru and Marcos Pérez Jiménez of Venezuela, received from the United States a special award for foreign leaders called the Legion of Merit citation. After all, as Rabe notes, "Communists, not dictators, were the enemies of the United States."[45]

The Guatemalan intervention in 1954 destroyed whatever remained of the Good Neighbor policy. In conformance with the Kennan corollary, Eisenhower officials aided in the overthrow of a government perceived as procommunist. Whether they overreacted or not has occasioned some debate. Most historians have taken a critical stance. Some have emphasized the importance of confusion and misperception: Typically, Eisenhower and his advisers had trouble distinguishing between nationalist reform and communist subversion. Others have perceived a conscious design: To safeguard capitalist interests against radical threats, the United States reverted to interventionist techniques.[46]

Among the Western Hemisphere nations, Guatemala ranked high in misery and hopelessness. The masses of people, descended from the native Mayas, suffered oppression, poverty, and illiteracy; the effects included disease, malnutrition, high infant mortality, and low life expectancy. In contrast, a small, landed elite monopolized political power and economic advantage, usually with the support of army officers and foreign corporations. The United Fruit Company, owned by U.S. investors, was the biggest property holder and employer in the country. It also dominated transportation and communications. Traditionally, military strongmen, or *caudillos,* upheld order and authority on behalf of elite interests. From 1931 until 1944, the dictator Jorge Ubico y Castañeda governed with repressive efficiency. Under his criminal code, death was the penalty for union organizers. Laws supposedly intended to curb vagrancy compelled the rural poor to labor in public works projects in circumstances close to slavery. Ubico, a self-styled Napoleon figure, displayed an exhibitionist need for regal uniforms and public displays. A riding accident had rendered him impotent when he was a young man. Nevertheless, in later shows of prowess, he went into the cages at the Guatemala City zoo to roar at the lions.[47]

Ubico fled the country late in 1944 following an urban-based uprising among middle-class elements: disenchanted schoolteachers, shopkeepers, students, lawyers, and junior military officers. Inspired by Allied ideals during the Second World War and the Mexican example under Lázaro Cárdenas, they joined in marches, demonstrations, and strikes to demand democracy and modernization. An honest election in 1945, probably the first in the country's history, resulted in the victory of Juan José Arévalo, who won 85 percent of the votes cast by literate adult males. A professor of literature and philosophy and a longtime enemy of Ubico, Arévalo had fled into exile in Argentina in 1935. Back in Guatemala after a decade, he found appalling conditions. The majority of people, mainly agricultural workers, earned less than $100 a year; 2 percent of the population owned 70 percent of the land. Backwardness pervaded the rural regions. Hardly any industry existed at all. More than half of the people were illiterate, including almost all the native peoples.

During a six-year term in office, Arévalo fashioned for Guatemala a reformist program reminiscent of the New Deal in the United States. Among other things, it extended voting rights to all adults, abolished forced labor, instituted minimum wages and collective bargaining for workers, redistributed small amounts of land confiscated from Germans during the war, established a social security agency, and launched a literacy campaign. Predictably, members of the privileged elite opposed these changes. In the course of his presidency, Arévalo survived more than twenty attempts to overthrow him.

Nevertheless, a legal election produced a peaceful transition in March 1951, when Jacobo Árbenz Guzmán took over as president. A professional soldier, a graduate of the Guatemalan military academy, and the secretary of defense under Arévalo, Árbenz "accelerated the pace of change in Guatemala." In his inaugural address, he promised to build an independent, modern, capitalist state. Later, his efforts to improve the economic infrastructure through the construction of ports and highways trespassed upon the United Fruit Company's control of such facilities. Similarly, he offended elite interests by supporting an income tax and land reform. Described as "the centerpiece of his program," Árbenz's agrarian reform bill sought to advance progress and modernization by redistributing land more equitably to rural workers. One controversial provision authorized the expropriation of uncultivated portions of large estates, in many instances as much as 75 percent of the land controlled by these plantations. Between 1952 and 1954 the Árbenz government disbursed 1.5 million acres to 100,000 families. As Rabe notes, this reform operated well within "the boundaries set by twentieth-century reform movements in the West." Nevertheless, "the process and pattern of change in Guatemala" collided with the interests of the United Fruit Company.

Based in Boston, United Fruit had operated in Guatemala since the late nineteenth century. Tight linkages connected the company with the traditional ruling elites. Under Ubico the company supported the regime and received tax concessions and vast tracts of land. It owned 550,000 acres, about 85 percent uncultivated, supposedly for reasons of crop rotation and soil conservation. When the Árbenz government initiated expropriation proceedings, offering compensation at three dollars an acre in government bonds, company officials rejected the terms. Instead, they appealed to the Eisenhower administration, claiming that communists had taken over in Guatemala and threatened the Western Hemisphere.[48]

Much as expected, Eisenhower officials responded sympathetically. Indeed, similar suspicions had percolated through the State Department for some time. In 1949, the Assistant Secretary of State for Inter-American Affairs, Edward G. Miller, Jr., had warned of bad effects if Guatemala threatened the properties of United Fruit. In the same year, U.S. ambassador to Guatemala Richard Patterson pledged his personal opposition to the "cancerous doctrine" of the communists. With "undivided attention," he would protect "American interests." He also advised company leaders to employ "an all-out barrage" to win support in the U.S. Senate. Gaddis Smith describes Patterson as a "hysterical, paranoic anti-Communist." Guatemalan officials regarded his undiplomatic behavior in their country as a form of intervention. In response, Patterson quit his job in the spring of 1950, claiming that communists planned to kill him.

Relations deteriorated further after Árbenz's inauguration in March 1951. The U.S. government expressed displeasure by means of economic pressure, cuts in foreign aid, and attempts to block the Guatemalan purchase of European military and industrial goods. The United Fruit Company encouraged direct action. In February 1952, company officials characterized "communist infiltration in Guatemala" as "a modern day violation of the Monroe Doctrine." Guatemalans, however, professed bewilderment. As foreign minister Guillermo Toriello told secretary of state Dean Acheson in the fall of 1952, his government merely wanted "to remove the evils" that had allowed communist sympathies to develop in the first place.

Covert military action was one way of dealing with Árbenz. The Truman administration considered it but held back. According to Gaddis Smith, Truman and Acheson adhered somewhat more literally than their successors to the nonintervention principle as "one of the very keystones of the Inter-American system."[49] Such inhibitions counted for less in the Eisenhower administration. As Supreme Allied Commander in Europe during the Second World War, Ike had become enamored of clandestine operations, particularly the exploits of "Wild Bill" Donovan and the Office of Strategic Services (OSS). Moreover, his administration could point to an actual success. In 1953 the CIA carried out a covert action in Iran: It ousted Mohammed Mossadegh's nationalist government for expropriating the holdings of U.S. and British oil companies and returned to power a more pliable figure, the Shah Reza Pahlavi.[50]

The Iranian venture reinforced fundamental assumptions within the administration. In the Guatemalan case, Ike and Dulles invested more faith in the workability of the Kennan corollary than in the principle of nonintervention. Republican leaders also regarded the Democratic version of the containment policy as too passive. During the 1952 campaign the Republicans supported a "New Look" in foreign affairs, advocating a more active approach. By seizing the initiative, they would roll back the communist tide and win victories in the Cold War. Otherwise, Dulles feared, "we might well wake up ten years from now to find that our friends in Latin America had become our enemies."

Covert action in this instance brought about the overthrow of the Árbenz regime and the establishment of the kind of government anticipated by Kennan: harsh, repressive, and undemocratic. As Gaddis Smith explains, this undertaking, "one of the most minutely studied in the history of U.S.-Latin American relations," followed three tracks: economic pressure, collective action through the Organization of American States, and a clandestine operation using anti-Árbenz rebels organized by the CIA in Honduras. Historians' interpretations have established different points of emphasis: a determination to defend U.S. corporate interests, the influence of anticommunism, the role of misperception, and the presumed necessity of standing strong in the Cold War struggle. But all agree on the effects. The Guatemalan intervention in 1954 closed down Franklin Roosevelt's Good Neighbor policy for keeps.[51]

At the Tenth Inter-American Conference at Caracas, Venezuela, in March 1954, Dulles hoped to obtain multilateral support for measures against Guatemala but failed to get it. Latin Americans again differed with the United

States over priorities and preferences. They wanted open discussions of economic issues focused on trade, aid, and the like, whereas the U.S. delegates insisted on the primacy of security matters and pushed for an anticommunist resolution. It declared that "the domination or control of the political institutions of any American state by the international communist movement . . . would constitute a threat" to regional security, therefore necessitating "appropriate action in accordance with existing treaties." This statement, a reference to the Rio Pact of 1947, specifically article 6, had procedural implications. It meant that a two-thirds majority among the OAS members would have to agree to take action against "an aggression which was not an armed attack," either by means of economic sanctions or a joint intervention. In conformance with the Kennan corollary, Dulles really wanted to extend "the Monroe Doctrine to include the concept of outlawing foreign ideologies in the American Republics."

The leaders in the Eisenhower administration wanted a demonstration for Latin Americans to illustrate the incompatibility of communism with nationalism. In the U.S. view, no conceivable mix was possible; therefore, communism in Guatemala constituted subversion, not reform. To counter it, the leaders contemplated drastic measures. A State Department memorandum circulating among U.S. diplomats in Latin America suggested the feasibility of a unilateral intervention. If Latin Americans refused to accept their responsibility to police the Western Hemisphere against communist incursions, so the reasoning went, then the United States would have no choice except to reassess "the soundness of the OAS relationship," perhaps by taking action alone.

At Caracas, Dulles pressed the anticommunist case during two weeks of debate. In the course of it, he urged immediate action and fought off fifty amendments proposed by Latin Americans. In the end, he got a resolution but not the one he wanted. Passed by a vote of 17 to 1 (Guatemala opposed), with Mexico and Argentina abstaining, the measure in Dulles's view lacked "vitality." Instead of calling for immediate action against the communist threat in Guatemala, the OAS advised in favor of future deliberations to consider the means of upholding treaty obligations. As Rabe notes, by employing the ancient tactics of procrastination and delay, "the Latin Americans rejected the administration's contention that communism in Latin America constituted external aggression."[52] At no point during the ensuing Guatemalan intervention could the United States count unambiguously on Latin American support.

Nevertheless, the plan for covert action got under way. In the middle of May a Swedish vessel, the *Alfhem*, arrived in Guatemala with a cargo of arms from communist Czechoslovakia. Presented as proof of communist complicity with Guatemalan officials, this event enabled Secretary Dulles to issue another indictment of "Communist penetration" of the Western Hemisphere.

Soon thereafter a clandestine operation supported by the United States successfully eliminated the offending Árbenz regime from power. A small rebel army of two hundred began the invasion of Guatemala on June 18, 1954, by moving across the Honduran border. Recruited and trained by the CIA, this force, commanded by lieutenant colonel Carlos Castillo Armas, was incapable of waging war against the much larger Guatemalan army; instead, it utilized indirect methods. As Allen Dulles reported to President Eisenhower, the success of the venture depended more on "psychological impact" than on "actual military strength." Nevertheless, Dulles wanted to create "the *impression* of very substantial military strength" through the use of deception and disinformation. Fake radio reports of large-scale fighting instilled panic and demoralization, and a real but small-scale bombing raid against Guatemala City produced hysteria.

The effects unhinged President Árbenz. Unsure of the reliability of his own army, he feared the possibility of U.S. military action. Reportedly influenced by strong drink, he resigned on June 27 and fled into exile, leaving the government to a military junta. For a week, army officers jockeyed for position. Then on July 2, under U.S. pressure, they settled on Colonel Castillo Armas, also the CIA's favorite choice. As head of state, Castillo Armas instituted a series of anticommunist measures, nullified Árbenz's reforms, and restored the old regime. The consequences were political polarization and civil war. During the next four decades, more than 250,000 Guatemalans died in the ongoing violence. Carlos Castillo Armas was one of them; assassins gunned him down in 1957. Throughout Latin America, the reactions were mixed. In the countries where dictators had control, official responses suggested at least a readiness to acquiesce in the U.S. intervention. But critics and protesters in Argentina, Bolivia, Chile, Cuba, Ecuador, Mexico, and Uruguay condemned the United States for what they called aggression against Guatemala, indicating at the very least their displeasure with the application of the Kennan corollary in their part of the world. [53] The supposed geopolitical imperatives of the Cold War held less importance for them than questions of economic growth and modernization.

As Stephen G. Rabe shows, Latin American leaders in the 1950s typically looked upon the inter-American system less as an anticommunist alliance than as "a mechanism for economic cooperation." [54] They wanted programs of economic assistance from the United States and ultimately compelled the Eisenhower administration to grapple with tough questions of trade or aid. During Ike's first term, U.S. officials expressed preferences for trade over aid as the primary engine of economic progress but shifted ground grudgingly during his second term, thereby allowing for a possibility of discussing both.

Ike's economic views conformed with convention by regarding free trade and private investment as the main requisites for peace and prosperity. Eisenhower regarded mass poverty, hunger, and insecurity as threats, that is, as incitements to the spread of communism. He believed that free enterprise could best advance the collective well-being: It would "allow backward people to make a decent living—even if only a minimum one measured by American standards," and the United States would also benefit. In his diary, he underscored the importance of ready access to raw materials—tin, cobalt, uranium, manganese, crude oil—and noted that "unless the areas in which these materials are found are under the control of people who are friendly to us and who want to trade with us, then . . . we are bound in the long run to suffer the most disastrous and doleful consequences."

As a self-styled fiscal conservative, Eisenhower fretted over the excesses of government spending, yet between 1953 and 1961 his administration granted or lent nearly $50 billion in military and economic aid to other countries. But for him, such programs had limited applicability; as he told his brother Milton, they pertained only to those regions directly imperiled by "the Communist menace." Consequently, Latin America ranked low in priority. On March 18, 1953, the National Security Council in NSC-144/1 confirmed this view with a statement of expectations. Latin American governments would have to learn that if private enterprise could best supply "the capital required for their economic development," then "their own self-interest requires the creation of a climate which will attract private investment." The same admonitions appeared in November 1953 in Milton Eisenhower's report of his fact-finding tour to South America. Subsequently regarded as orthodox and unimaginative even by the author, it expressed views that unsurprisingly favored fiscal responsibility, "honest money," and balanced budgets over other approaches featuring economic nationalism, "industrialization for its own sake," and "creeping expropriation." For their own good, Milton Eisenhower exhorted Latin Americans to uphold the principle of free trade and the sanctity of foreign investments and to understand that private monies "must be *attracted* by the nation desiring the capital." Such banalities amused Brazilian diplomats, who wondered why Milton Eisenhower had to make a trip to Latin American to arrive at these conclusions.

In the State Department, assistant secretary John Moors Cabot developed doubts about them. He had accompanied Milton Eisenhower on the tour and drew some bleaker inferences. In much of Latin America, he reported, per capita income was about one-eighth that of the United States. In the poorest countries—Bolivia, Ecuador, and Haiti—the situation was even worse. Yet the United States sent only about 1 percent of its economic development assistance to Latin America, and Cabot warned, "We cannot indefinitely continue the present discrimination against our sister republics in this hemisphere without gravely prejudicing our relations with them." Moreover, he placed scant faith in the capacity of private investment to solve the problem. In his view, a variety of impediments obstructed economic advancement, including inadequate transportation and communication systems, multitudes of impoverished people who lacked educational and technical skills, and vast disparities of wealth and power with the upper classes exercising "an almost feudal control." For all these reasons, he concluded, "trickle-down" economics would neither produce great bursts of economic growth nor nullify communist appeals.

As a place to begin, Cabot suggested modest increases in developmental loans, relying primarily on the Export-Import Bank to support the improvement of infrastructure. In response, secretary of the treasury George Humphrey, an ideologue, took offense at the heresy. Devoutly combative in his fiscal conservatism, Humphrey demanded that Latin Americans conform with history and tradition by adhering to the developmental model of the United States. For him, this approach meant reliance on private foreign capital. Secretary of State Dulles supported Cabot's ideas but not Cabot. Convinced that boom-and-bust cycles increased Latin American vulnerability to communist insinuation, Dulles secured the president's consent for the use of the Export-Import Bank in support of "sound development projects." He also agreed to take part in a long-deferred Latin American economic conference. Nevertheless, he punished Cabot for pushing too hard. The assistant secretary lost his job and went off to Stockholm as the ambassador to Sweden.

More bureaucratic wrangling occurred as plans developed for the economic conference, scheduled to begin in Rio de Janeiro late in November 1954. As head of the U.S. delegation, secretary of the treasury George Humphrey predictably favored trade, not aid, but on this occasion the president differed with him. Ike, as it turned out, had agreed to expand the operations of the Export-Import Bank in Latin America and to increase its overall lending capacity by $500 million. This move ranked as "the only significant initiative" by the United States at the conference. It also conformed with the administration's understanding of Cold War imperatives. As Ike explained to Humphrey, U.S. policy in Latin America was "chiefly designed to play a part in the cold war against our enemies." Extraordinary measures had become necessary because the "United States was not merely doing 'business' in Latin America, but was fighting a war there against Communism."

Latin Americans had hoped for more. According to the Brazilian ambassador, João Carlos Muniz, government leaders had believed ever since the Second World War that "the vast resources of the United States were going to be brought to bear on wide and rapid economic change in Latin America." But delay and inaction has caused "an intense process of disillusionment." Brazilians could not understand why the United States used large-scale programs of economic aid and assistance in the fight against communism in Asia and Europe but depended upon "politico-police" methods in the Western Hemisphere.[55] Evolving Latin American economic theories dissented from the established orthodoxies in the United States. Latin Americans depicted free markets and private investments as failures in their part of the

Western Hemisphere. Such practices simply had not worked. Instead of diffusing growth, progress, and modernization throughout the region, free trade and private investment had locked Latin America into conditions of economic dependency and underdevelopment. In other words, they perpetuated an inequitable economic system based on neocolonial relationships.

For Latin Americans, integration into the world capitalist system meant dependence on market fluctuations in Europe and the United States, entailing extreme vulnerability in times of economic downswing. Their experience during the two world wars and the Great Depression appeared as cases in point. Moreover, Latin Americans operated at a disadvantage because of the terms of exchange. As producers of primary commodities, they provided the industrialized world with low-cost agricultural products and mineral resources and purchased in return high-cost manufactured goods. The very structure of the transaction placed them at a disadvantage and enabled foreign interests to exercise control over their economic destinies. Indeed, as described by the Argentine economist Raúl Prebisch, the situation was getting worse. The cost of manufactured products had increased steadily in comparison with the prices obtained for raw materials and agricultural goods. For a decade after 1952 the combined price index of commodities sold by Latin Americans—coffee, wheat, corn, tin, cotton, sisal, lead, zinc, nitrates, sugar—declined in every year except one. [56]

For many Latin Americans, the impact of traditional trade and investment practices helped account for the poor performance of their economies. The statistics were disheartening. In the early 1950s, annual per capita income in Latin America amounted to $250; life expectancy was forty-three years; and an expanding population eroded whatever gains might come about in productivity. Structural considerations contributing to the difficulties included unresponsive and unstable political systems, a maldistribution of wealth and land, insufficient economic infrastructure, inadequate educational systems, and indifference among the ruling elites.

The dimensions of the problem became clearer in a series of studies by the Economic Commission for Latin America (ECLA), a UN agency headed by Prebisch. These reports described shortages of investment capital for economic development as the chief deficiency and accounted for them by tracking the flow of money in and out of Latin America. According to Prebisch, the economic outlays in Latin America—that is, interest payments and profit remittances on public loans and private investments—exceeded the inputs. In other words, the advanced countries took more money out than they put in. As a consequence, economic growth was calculated at 1 percent a year. To enhance it, ECLA economists estimated that Latin America needed $1 billion a year for ten years, most of which would have to come from international lending institutions and the United States.

U.S. traders and investors already played an enormous role in Latin American economies. By the early 1950s, their investments in Latin America ran to $6 billion, about 40 percent of direct U.S. investments in the world. Most of the money went into extractive industries such as Chilean copper and Venezuelan oil. Annual trade between the United States and Latin America amounted to $7 billion, the overall balance slightly favoring the United States. Latin America accounted for 25 percent of U.S. international trade.

In these circumstances, Latin Americans still looked to the United States for assistance. In anticipation of the Rio economic conference from November 22 to December 2, 1954, Ambassador Muniz expressed his hope for "great things." Specifically, he wanted an Eisenhower Plan for Latin America, presumably something like the Marshall Plan for Western Europe. But his hopes failed to materialize. U.S. leaders rejected any such approach as inconsistent with established policies, priorities, and preferences; they favored free trade and private investment. During the conference the U.S. delegation made a small concession by agreeing to expand the lending authority of the Export-Import Bank but otherwise provided no satisfaction for Latin Americans. As Rabe remarks, "By intervening in Guatemala and by ignoring Latin America's economic needs," the Eisenhower administration appeared to endorse the "attitudes and practices" of an earlier time.[57]

After the Korean armistice on July 27, 1953, the United States enjoyed a period of peace and prosperity. Eisenhower won reelection in 1956, following a campaign in which Latin America figured hardly at all. The main policy tenets—anticommunism, free trade, and private investment—persisted into the second term, as did the practice of supporting military dictators. Though privately a bit ambivalent about the matter, Eisenhower usually evaded questions concerned with civil liberties and human rights. In all likelihood the president would have preferred the existence of more democratic regimes and on occasion may have maneuvered behind the scenes to curb abuses. When Juan Perón fell from power in 1955, Ike expressed his approval. At the same time, he embraced military strongmen as necessary allies in the anticommunist struggle. By the mid-1950s, military aid in Latin America was one of the costliest budget items in the region. Ike understood that Latin American forces possessed scant fighting ability. Yet he wanted not only "to preserve . . . the good will of the Latin American Republics" but also "to assure their internal security, without which their good will would be useless to us." As Rabe concludes, "The transfer of arms and the training of Latin American officers and soldiers continued, because the administration wanted powerful, anti-Communist friends in Latin America."

Also in the mid-1950s, changes in the Soviet Union caused mounting concern. Following Stalin's death in March 1953 the aspiring heirs engaged in a complex power struggle in which foreign policy played a role. An early claimant to Stalin's position, Nikolai Bulganin, offered in January 1956 to expand diplomatic, economic, and cultural relations with Latin America, especially through trade and technical assistance. As part of a larger Soviet effort in the Third World, Bulganin's initiatives anticipated more effective forms of peaceful competition. But in Latin America, they accomplished almost nothing. As consumers, Latin Americans regarded Soviet merchandise as shoddy and unattractive. Moreover, they disliked the brutal Soviet suppression of the Hungarian uprising during the fall of 1956. Consequently, Secretary Dulles arrived at the comforting conclusion in 1957 that "we see no likelihood at the present time of communism getting into control of the political institutions of any of the American Republics."

Anticommunist apprehensions escalated in 1958 following vice president Richard M. Nixon's disastrous visit to South America, which produced protests, riots, and a life-threatening mob scene. First conceived by Roy Richard Rubottom, then serving as the assistant secretary of state for Latin American affairs, the plan envisioned the trip as a goodwill gesture, conveying to Latin Americans some new readiness to address economic issues. Rubottom had worried late in 1957 that "the economic situation in the whole area has deteriorated" and that communists would take advantage. He suggested that Dulles lead the delegation, but the secretary begged off, claiming other responsibilities. Eisenhower then sent Nixon.

Unenthusiastic about his assignment, Nixon went to Latin America grudgingly late in April 1958. The schedule called for a stop in Argentina to attend the inauguration of president Arturo Frondizi and for others in Uruguay, Peru, and Venezuela. In Montevideo and Lima, Nixon encountered hecklers, and in Caracas, even worse. Earlier that year, Venezuelans had ousted Marcos Pérez Jiménez, a dictator formerly cultivated by the United States. Now they vented their anger against Nixon with menacing demonstrations. As he moved through the streets, they even threatened his life directly by attacking his car before the driver sped away to safety. Nixon later described this event as one of the six crises shaping his political character.

These incidents elicited a new round of debate among Eisenhower officials. Nixon blamed communist agitators, but others had different views. CIA director Allen Dulles found no evidence of linkages with Moscow and reasoned "there would be trouble in Latin America [even] if there were no Communists."[58] Nevertheless, both houses of the U.S. Congress launched inquiries, and Eisenhower sent his brother Milton on a second fact-finding tour, this time to Central America. Such concerns, as Rabe explains, "merged into a wider debate in 1958 about the United States' position in the world and the quality of President Eisenhower's leadership." One source of high anxiety was the Russian *Sputnik,* a satellite placed in orbit around the earth late in 1957, which immediately took on military and strategic implications. A Soviet missile capable of such a feat also presumably could hit targets in the United States. Other Cold War crises in Lebanon, in Berlin, and in Asia (over the islands of Quemoy and Matsu) kept tensions high. Finally, a crowning blow, the U.S. economy went into recession. Unemployment rose, production fell, and so did Eisenhower's popularity. Later, Ike described the year 1958 as one of the worst of his life.[59]

These events produced modest changes in Latin American policy. Notably, while retaining the emphasis on military assistance, the administration displayed somewhat more readiness to support political democracy and human rights. To an extent, this shift made a virtue of necessity. Between 1956 and 1960, ten military dictatorships in Latin America tumbled from power. Corrupt and incompetent, they had provided neither political stability nor economic growth. Tad Szulc, a journalist, referred to the process as "the twilight of the tyrants." Eisenhower leaders, although they responded with more enthusiastic defenses of representative government, still regarded military establishments as valuable anticommunist allies. In 1959–1960, assistance programs in Latin America expanded, providing more than $160 million in military aid.[60]

The administration also accepted modest changes in economic policy. In part because of Nixon's misadventure, in-house critics became more persuasive, especially those who feared that collapsing dictatorships might precipitate revolutions. Such critics included the president's brother Milton and State Department officials Rubottom, Thomas Mann, and C. Douglas Dillon. Among the Latin American leaders, Juscelino Kubitschek, a former state governor of Minas Gerais and president of Brazil from 1956 until 1961, pressed especially hard. Embracing the slogan "Fifty years of progress in five" and seeking dramatic results, he intended to stimulate economic growth by the unorthodox means of government action based on deficit spending. He also instituted a national development program for building infrastructure, roads and railroads, and created new state enterprises such as an automobile industry. Most spectacularly, he built a new capital city, opening up the interior and symbolizing the advance of progress. Brasília, a showplace, attracted world attention because of its advanced architectural conceptions. But the high costs of such endeavors also had negative consequences, notably, high levels of debilitating inflation.

Two weeks after the anti-Nixon riot in Caracas, Kubitschek called for a "thorough revision" of U.S. programs. Cleverly linking economic development with presumed Cold War imperatives, Kubitschek wanted a solution to "the problem of underdevelopment" so that Latin American nations could "more effectively resist subversion and serve the Western cause." Specifically, he suggested a pledge of $40 billion from the United States to aid Latin America during the next twenty years. Called Operation Pan America, Kubitschek's plan, if accepted, would have established an equivalent of the Marshall Plan.

U.S. officials withheld endorsement from anything so grandiose, but they did display new readiness to take part in commodity agreements to stop falling prices for coffee and other such goods. In addition, in August 1958 they announced U.S. support for a regional development bank in Latin America, resulting in the creation of the Inter-American Development Bank in October 1960. These modifications implied "a moderate shift in the administration's philosophical approach toward Latin America." But many traditional commitments remained firm; as indicated by NSC-5902/1 in February 1959, the administration still sought the expansion of trade and investment, the promotion of capitalism, and the exclusion of economic nationalism. At the same time, the leaders embraced a new objective, endorsing the view that "Latin America is and must be dealt with primarily as an underdeveloped area." To accommodate rising levels of expectation, the United States must encourage free enterprise but with recognition of a need to adapt "to local conditions." Such shifts implied hardly any fundamental change. Administration leaders anticipated only modest expenditures in Latin America through the Inter-American Development Bank. They still believed that progress in Latin America depended upon private enterprise.[61]

There remained deep divisions over basic issues. For U.S. leaders the inter-American system served national security interests as an anticommunist alliance in defense of order, stability, and the Monroe Doctrine. For the Latin Americans the main rationale took other forms. They wanted regional devices to contain U.S. intervention and to facilitate economic aid and assistance. The absence of a Marshall Plan for the Western Hemisphere disenchanted Latin American leaders, widened the political fissures, and undermined the security apparatus. The shifts that developed during Ike's last two years never had much impact and, in the U.S. view, the circumstances worsened significantly when Fidel Castro took over in Cuba. This event marked the most significant change in the Americas since the Mexican Revolution and established the foremost issues of the next thirty years.

NOTES

1. Irwin F. Gellman, *Good Neighbor Diplomacy: United States Policies in Latin America, 1933–1945* (Baltimore: Johns Hopkins University Press, 1979), 179; Gellman, *Secret Affairs: Franklin Roosevelt, Cordell Hull, and Sumner Welles* (Baltimore: Johns Hopkins University Press, 1995), chaps. 13–14.

2. Enthusiasts include J. Lloyd Mecham, *The United States and Inter-American Security, 1889–1960* (Austin: University of Texas Press, 1961), chaps. 9–10; Gordon Connell-Smith, *The Inter-American System* (New York: Oxford University Press, 1966), chaps. 6–7; and Robert Freeman Smith, "U.S. Policy-Making for Latin America Under Truman," *Continuity: A Journal of History* 16 (Fall 1992): 87–111. Critics include Lloyd C. Gardner, *Economic Aspects of New Deal Diplomacy* (Madison: University of Wisconsin Press, 1964), chap. 10; and David Green, *The Containment of Latin America: A History of the Myths and Realities of the Good Neighbor Policy* (Chicago: Quadrangle Books, 1971), chaps. 7–9.